CREATING A PSYCHO

Bringing a fresh contemporary Freudian view to a number of current issues in psychoanalysis, this book is about a psychoanalytic method that has been evolved by Fred Busch over the past 40 years called *Creating a Psychoanalytic Mind*. It is based on the essential curative process basic to most psychoanalytic theories – the need for a shift in the patient's relationship with their own mind. Busch shows that with the development of a psychoanalytic mind the patient can acquire the capacity to shift the inevitability of action to the possibility of reflection. *Creating a Psychoanalytic Mind* is derived from an increasing clarification of how the mind works that has led to certain paradigm changes in the psychoanalytic method. While the methods of understanding the human condition have evolved since Freud, the means of bringing this understanding to patients in a way that is meaningful have not always followed. Throughout, Fred Busch illustrates that while the analyst's expertise is crucial to the process, the analyst's stance, rather than mainly being an expert in the content of the patient's mind, is primarily one of helping the patient to find his own mind.

Creating a Psychoanalytic Mind will appeal to psychoanalysts and psychotherapists interested in learning a theory and technique where psychoanalytic meaning and meaningfulness are integrated. It will enable professionals to work differently and more successfully with their patients.

Fred Busch is a Training and Supervising Analyst at the PINE Psychoanalytic Center, a Geographical Supervising Analyst of the Minnesota Psychoanalytic Institute, a member of the Faculty of the Boston Psychoanalytical Institute and the Massachusetts Institute of Psychoanalysis, and a member of IPTAR. He has published over sixty psychoanalytic articles, two books, and his work has been translated into several languages.

CREATING A PSYCHOANALYTIC MIND

A psychoanalytic method and theory

Fred Busch

Routledge
Taylor & Francis Group

LONDON AND NEW YORK

First published 2014
by Routledge
27 Church Road, Hove, East Sussex BN3 2FA

and by Routledge
711 Third Avenue, New York, NY 10017

Routledge is an imprint of the Taylor & Francis Group, an informa business

© 2014 Fred Busch

The right of Fred Busch to be identified as author of this work has been asserted by him in accordance with sections 77 and 78 of the Copyright, Designs and Patents Act 1988.

British Library Cataloguing in Publication Data
A catalogue record for this book is available from the British Library

Library of Congress Cataloging in Publication Data
Busch, Fred, 1939–
Creating a psychoanalytic mind : a psychoanalytic method and theory / Fred Busch.
     pages cm
   Includes bibliographical references.
   ISBN 978-0-415-62904-1 (hbk.) — ISBN 978-0-415-62905-8 (pbk.) — ISBN 978-1-315-88852-1 (ebk.)   1. Psychoanalysis.   I. Title.
   RC504.B87 2014
   616.89'17—dc23

                                                              2013010752

ISBN: 978-0-415-62904-1 (hbk)
ISBN: 978-0-415-62905-8 (pbk)
ISBN: 978-1-315-88852-1 (ebk)

Typeset in Times New Roman
by RefineCatch Limited, Bungay, Suffolk

MIX
Paper from
responsible sources
FSC
www.fsc.org   FSC® C013056

Printed and bound in Great Britain by
TJ International Ltd, Padstow, Cornwall

For my first reader – CSH

It is told that Isaac Asimov once said, "The most exciting phrase to hear in science, the one that heralds new discoveries, is not 'Eureka!' (I found it), but 'Hmm, that's funny . . .'"

CONTENTS

CONTENTS

FOREWORD

In a 1963 interview with B. Swerdloff, Heinz Hartmann mused on his Vienna analytic days. He commented how he and Ernst Kris "were greatly impressed with Freud, but never thought that it was the end of psychology. We always felt that one had the right to go ahead and develop his legacy." Fred Busch's lifelong work on psychoanalytic technique is an excellent example of development of Freud's legacy.

Busch is an original master in contemporary ego psychology. He is certainly the most prolific modern author of resistance analysis. Since the 1980s, he has published extensively on theory of technique in the best psychoanalytic journals. The present book is Busch's third and, avowedly, the one he took most pains to write. I would add that it is the most revealing of his evolution as thinker and clinician. The book has two main sections: *Paradigm shifts* and *Clinical methods*, illustrated with ample and detailed clinical vignettes. I hope that adherents to a technique grounded on Freudian structural theory, will find the conclusions of Busch's intellectual and empirical journey as stimulating and persuasive as I have.

Busch shows a familiarity with European authors that can be considered quite unusual for an American analyst, finding common ground between his method of resistance analysis and the techniques of Betty Joseph's London Kleinians, and some French authors, particularly André Green. He is also well acquainted with authors like Bion, Hinshelwood, Fonagy, Ferro, Bolognini, and the Barangers in their attempts at finding reliable accessibility to the analysand's unconscious mind.

From old, the experience accumulated by many analysts taught us the practical lesson that the lifting of neurosogenic repressions was insufficient for the resolution of conflicts, as these continued exerting their primary influence on the formation of character. In *Analysis Terminable and Interminable*, Freud had metaphorically remarked that the simple removal by a fire brigade of the oil lamp responsible for a blaze was not enough to carry out a good enough job. Busch comments that the technical shift from the "there and then" method to the "here and now" approach, necessary for effective character analysis, gained momentum thanks to the support received from analysts of divergent schools of thought.

The theoretical imperatives for working in the "here and now" (or *hic et nunc*, as we say in Southern Europe) can be found in three principles: the existence of an unconscious ego; the importance of "thinking about thinking" (a counterpart to Faimberg's (1996) "listening to listening"); and the unconscious thinking as pre-conceptual (Busch was a Piagetian scholar). The pre-operational lack of reflection about one's own thinking implies an infantile fixation. In order to foster the analysand's conceptual examination of primitive fantasies, Busch decidedly defends a "here and now" approach to material, as it is "before the eye reality": it is what is happening, and not a speculation about something that, purportedly, happened at some other time and place.

Busch's text deals convincingly with what Paul Gray famously described as the "developmental gap" in the evolution of technique, reminding us that, although the ways to analytic understanding of intrapsychic conflict have evolved since Freud's time, the methods for bringing this understanding meaningfully to patients have not followed along. To exemplify this, Busch uses pertinent close-process material. In his exposition he seems most successful when showing how to bring our conceptualizations of the patient's problems to his/her awareness in ways that are "digestible."

One can remember here Busch's 1993 article on "Aspects of a Good Interpretation," in which he expressed his opinion that many interventions were based less on what the patient was capable of hearing than on what the analyst was, supposedly, capable of understanding. I said "supposedly" because one of our inveterate myths is that analysts are capable of reading the unconscious, and need only to make sure that their interpretations of the material are not inappropriately "deep" (a dictum frequently honored in the breach). I am reminded at this point of Fabio Herrmann's (2001) sensible question, "Why do analysts like to say that the unconscious is what is unknown, surprising or new, when in reality they act as if it were an old acquaintance?"

In this book, Busch expanded the thesis presented in his 2000 article "What is a deep interpretation?" He underscores the importance of addressing what is present in the associations, rather than what is absent or missing. Busch emphasizes the need to work closely on what is most accessible to the analysand, rather than what is most repressed – again, assuming that the analyst had privileged knowledge of non-manifested contents. This approach is opposite to the traditional Kleinian method of interpreting unconscious material at the "urgency point" of the patient's maximal anxiety. Replicating Edward Glover's 1940 findings in his questionnaire research on technique at the British Society, Busch concluded that there were two paradigms of interpretation: one that maintained that making direct contact with the unconscious was the chief analytic endeavor; and another that favored interpreting in the preconscious "neighborhood" as the most efficacious method. Needless to say that Busch, as champion of contemporary modern ego psychology, defends the latter.

Busch advocates for the development of a psychoanalytic mind, based not only on "content knowledge," but on "process knowledge." In his proposed technique, what is essential is the facilitation of the patient's capacity to contemplate his/ her own thoughts as "mental events." Busch tries to embark patients onto the epistemological enterprise of learning how they know what they think they know, dispelling intellectualized insights (often acquired in previous treatments). I was reminded of Fenichel's (1941) simple interpretive solution to the association of a patient who "knew" from a former analysis that his driving inhibition was based on his sadism, because "unconsciously" he wanted to run over everybody. Fenichel wrote, "such an interpretation we should certainly not accept gratefully as insight into his unconscious, but we should ask: 'How do you know that?'"

The results of an analysis, Busch underscores, are based on the practitioner's efforts to transform the under-represented into something potentially representable, replacing the inevitability of action for the possibility of reflection. Cannily, Busch remarks that going slower usually implies going authentically deeper. The analytic interventions that allow symbolization of that which is inchoate in the patient's mind require steady, day-to-day work, and not the idealized flashes of intuitive insight frequently found in our early literature.

Busch stresses the fact that a human's earliest development is encoded in action terms. This conditions patients – or should I say human beings? – to use "language action" through which their unconscious speaks, inducing analysts to experience anger, seduction, boredom, and the rest. Faced with this universal transference phenomenon, Busch states, our discipline has undergone a "paradigm shift" *from unearthing buried memories to transforming what is pre-operational*. Practitioners adhering to a contemporary Freudian technique are therefore advised to help patients convert those reactions that are close to a stimulus–response model into self-observation and inquiry.

Using the alliance of our observing ego with the patient's preconscious as the "beacon light in the darkness of depth psychology," to use Freud's 1923a words (p.18), has been considered often a mere intellectual exercise. This implies a serious misunderstanding. Busch shows how, on the contrary, the "deep diving" interpretations and emoting defensiveness of yore lead to unnecessary intellectualization and doctrinal compliance, whereas disciplined defense analysis, i.e., the exploration of what keeps unconscious resistances in place, represents a more naturalistic avenue to the understanding of anachronistic dangers and the reasons for the strangulation of their associated affects.

In my experience, Busch's approach tends to get interpreted often as spelling coldness and detachment from the patient's feelings, when the opposite is true. I think that the clinical examples expounded herein eloquently demonstrate how the detection of the analysand's readiness to meaningfully integrate the analyst's interpretations requires great synchronization with his/her "vantage point" (Schwaber, 1992), as well as profound empathy.

In this book, Busch stresses also the practical importance of coining questions to the analysand in an "unsaturated" (Ferro, 2002a) fashion, in order to interfere as little as possible with the free display of his/her associations. By "questioning" Busch refers mostly to observations that can be shared and refined, or elaborated upon, by the patient. "Questioning" here is not supposed to rely on psychological-mindedness or sophistication, but on the analyst's tactful assessment of the patient's disposition to explore certain issues.

In this book an important emphasis is laid on the analysis of transference, denouncing the "difficult to resist" quality of transference interpretations. This pull can be traced to James Strachey's 1934 work on "mutative" interventions which so influenced Kleinian analysts and practitioners from other theoretical traditions who feel neglectful for not addressing transference in almost every session. Busch sides with Freud's 1913 classical advice to make interpretations of transference when it is being used as resistance. Implicit in Busch's approach is the distinction between *transferential* and *intraclinical* phenomena. Not everything preconsciously available in a session is necessarily transferential. This view may seem "superficial" to some colleagues, when in reality it represents a more reliable base for access to deeper strata with a minimum of iatrogenic contamination.

In agreement with Gray's (1987) emphasis on the analysis of the "transference of authority," Busch comments on how Freud, after his 1926 epiphany of considering the ego as both the seat of anxiety and defense against it, couldn't see a way of analyzing resistances other than wrestling them down through the utilization of the analysand's positive transference. This was more pronounced in Wilhelm Reich's (1933) understanding of resistance as the response of a menaced ego, on one hand, and, on the other, his recommending a frontal attack on the characterological armor. Busch has illustrated how the tradition of overcoming (instead of analyzing) resistances was kept alive in very eminent representatives of American ego psychology, from Greenson to Brenner and Arlow. Many analysts in the United States – let alone other parts of the world – did not quite differentiate analysis of the fantasies and feelings from analysis of the defenses used by patients to protect themselves from the primitive fears that kept resistances in place.

For his technique Busch favors Richard Sterba's 1934 concept of *therapeutic ego split* and the development of "an island of intellectual (not intellectualized) contemplation" in analytic work. Central in Busch's methodology is the dedication throughout the treatment to obtaining a division between the *experiencing* and the *observing* ego in the patient's mind. Inevitably, we are reminded here of Freud's 1933 revolutionary technical positioning in his *New Introductory Lectures* (no. XXII):

> We wish to make the ego the matter of our enquiry, our very own ego. But is that possible? After all, the ego is in its very essence a subject; how can it be made into an object? Well, there is no doubt that it can be. The ego can take itself as an object, can treat itself like other objects, can observe itself, criticize itself, and do Heaven knows what with itself.
>
> (2001, pp. 15–34; italics added)

Let me remark here that Freud published these words *after* the presentation by Sterba of his "therapeutic split" ideas to the Viennese Psychoanalytic Society.

Concerning countertransference, Busch recognizes its extraordinary importance as means through which the analyst can clarify, first for himself, how the analysand is communicating via unconscious "language action." The technical "trick" here is how to assist patients to objectify the analyst's subjective perceptions. Rightfully, he stresses that feelings and reveries implanted by the analysand below the analyst's radar screen make the latter particularly vulnerable to enactments. However, Busch expresses disagreement with the old Kleinian method of automatically interpreting countertransference as the patient's projected unconscious fantasies. This technical strategy is described as "I feel, therefore you are" (wittily named by the author "a Descartian somersault").

Busch wonders why the psychoanalytic method has evolved in ways tilted toward the topographic rather than the structural model long after Freud's introduction of the latter. It may seem puzzling that the extant tradition in many institutes of teaching techniques is based on the formulation of interpretations that circumvent the analysand's preconscious awareness. Busch describes this proclivity as an "urge," a "visceral pull," attributing this magnetic tendency mostly to uncontained countertransferences. These would revolve around feelings of threat, or "analytic deadness" in cases of sluggish clinical progress. These negative feelings would then get flung onto the patient as interpretations. Busch makes the remark that, in earlier times, in the United States these countertransferential reactions were usually dealt with through withdrawal into silence, whereas current trends abet moving into action.

Busch describes three phases in the treatment. The first one is characterized by the patient's familiarization with the inhibitions that have restricted him or her from living his/her own stories. Busch states that until analysands become aware of the chronic interruptions of their wondering, wondering is not possible. The harbinger of the middle phase is the creation of a psychoanalytic mind, i.e. the development of an effective self-observation in the sequence of free associations. After competently equipping the patient to evaluate the multidetermination of mental productions comes the termination period. In this last phase, the patient learns how to interpret more veraciously his/her own associations, reflecting on them. Although not devoid of the traps of discovering deeper meanings of previously understood issues, the termination phase is supposed to leave the analysand with sufficient capacity for self-analysis.

This book represents a definite step toward bridging the existing developmental gap between the old classical technique and modern approaches based on Freudian structural theory. In an interview Freud had in 1930 with G. S. Viereck, he stated,

> Life changes, and psychoanalysis also changes. We are in the beginning
> of a new science [. . .]. I am only an initiator. I had some success bringing
> to surface monuments buried in the mind's substrate. However, where
> I found a few temples, others may discover a continent.

I think that contemporary technical "discoveries," such as the ones elaborated throughout Busch's work, would have stirred the utmost interest in the father of psychoanalysis.

Cecilio Paniagua, M.D.
Madrid

INTRODUCTION

This is a book about a psychoanalytic method that evolved for me over the last 40 years, which I call *Creating a Psychoanalytic Mind*. It is based on what I consider to be the essential curative process that has been basic to most psychoanalytic theories, i.e., *a shift in a patient's relationship to his own mind*. As we know, without psychoanalysis an individual is inevitably drawn to continuously enact unconscious fantasies designed to satisfy wishes, protect against fears, and heal fragmented self-states and/or object relations. With the development of a psychoanalytic mind the patient acquires the capacity to shift the *inevitability of action to the possibility of reflection*. It is an enormous psychic achievement to view one's mind as a playground for motivations rather than only a representation of reality, and most importantly potentially frees one from the slavery of the repetition compulsion.

The method presented here is based upon increasing clarification of how the mind works that has led to the possibility of refining the psychoanalytic method. While our methods of understanding the human condition have evolved since Freud, our methods of bringing this understanding to our patients in a way that is *meaningful* have not always followed along. Over time I have tried in various ways to understand why this was, and how we might rectify it. This work is my latest attempt to present a theory and technique where *psychoanalytic meaning and meaningfulness are integrated*. While the analyst's expertise is crucial to the process, the analyst's stance is primarily one of helping the patient *find his own mind*, rather than mainly being an expert in the content of the patient's mind.

My method focuses on the patient's development of a *psychoanalytic mind* as a key to the curative process in psychoanalysis. In a highly condensed explanation this involves the patient's capacity to grasp that the way towards a deeper understanding of himself is through his own mind, and that this is the essence of what psychoanalysis has to offer. While this seems like what we have always strived for, I will present a specific method that hopefully gives *greater clarification on how this happens and the methods to bring this about*.

In broad-brush strokes, the basic paradigm shift in the psychoanalytic method revolves around *thinking about thinking*. It has allowed us to better understand unique ways patients communicate or attempt to not communicate. We've also come to know more about patients' *states of readiness* for interpretive success, and the ways we may help or hinder this process. We've also come to realize that *how we help a patient know his own mind is as important as what he comes to know.*

Further, I have learned from and found similarities with the work of others, often viewed as having a very different perspective. As I've said previously, "the analyst of today might best be known as the contemporary Freudian, countertransferentially aware, self psychological, relationally interested, Kleinian-inspired, ego psychologist" (Busch, 2005, p. 43). This broad tent of inclusion revolves primarily around how we understand our patients. *My tent narrows in how I see the best way to bring this understanding to the analysand.* Throughout the book I will attempt to show a *surprising common ground* between my method of analyzing and other theories often considered disparate, especially the Betty Joseph inspired London Kleinians, and some French psychoanalysts.

I agree with Bolognini (2010) that we have to come out of our own "shadow zone," where we hold on to excessive simplification of the theoretical field. "The symptom of this shadow zone is precisely the incapacity for an interchange with the 'non-self,' which is unconsciously feared as dangerous and too disturbing" (p. 11). For too long, each "school" has tended to guard the purity and effectiveness of its own position.

The book is divided into two parts: "Paradigm shifts" and "Clinical methods." It is a somewhat artificial division in that while the first part highlights what I propose as theoretical changes that provide an altered way of thinking of the psychoanalytic method and its goals, there are numerous clinical examples that demonstrate the how and why of these changes. The second part describes specific clinical aspects of the basic psychoanalytic method. The clinical examples will present little or nothing about the patient's history or the course of treatment. This reflects my view that the main ways we help our analysands develop a psychoanalytic mind is by focusing on what is occurring within the immediacy of the analytic session. While understanding the past in the present is a significant part of building a psychoanalytic mind, it becomes meaningful primarily through what is occurring in the present.

In 2001 Martin Bergmann wrote,

> Because psychoanalysis aims at more than restoration, the issue of its goals is both interesting and controversial. In the present climate of opinion, psychoanalysis is pressed to demonstrate its cost effectiveness against other therapies. The outcome of that controversy is still in doubt, *but what remains certain is that if the value of "know thyself," first articulated in the city of Delphi in Ancient Greece, is still important, psychoanalysis has no rival among other forms of psychotherapy.*
>
> (2001, pp. 15–34; italics added)

It is in this spirit of "know thyself," and what this means psychoanalytically, that I present these ideas. In this spirit I have focused in this book primarily on the psychoanalytic theories of treatment where "know thyself" is seen as the primary goal of treatment. This is in contrast to those theories where the analyst's *way of being* is emphasized as curative. As you will see, my view is that the nature of the analyst's way of being is an important component of the treatment. It is a *necessary* but not *sufficient* explanation for creating a psychoanalytic mind.

In an attempt to write this book in an uncluttered fashion I have not presented a review of the vast literature on each area I discuss. However, there should be enough to help the reader's understanding of the influences on my thinking. I unashamedly quote myself liberally, and the reader can consult these papers for further references.

Finally, I am sorry that I cannot individually thank all who inspired, helped, and encouraged me. There have been too many, both as teachers, colleagues, students, and patients.

Chestnut Hill, MA
Fall, 2012

1

A PERSONAL JOURNEY

I feel fortunate that throughout my professional life I always felt the need to write. Yet this in itself was perplexing since I never planned to be a writer. Finally I came to understand that I write to try to comprehend something that's puzzling me, and psychoanalysis is a fertile ground for many puzzling questions, if one allows it. This current volume is a reflection on my most recent puzzles, and how I've understood them. However, before launching into these issues I want to share some of how I came to this point.

I never planned to be a psychoanalyst. In fact, in my era "therapy" was something children were threatened with for misbehavior. Further, almost everyone in my extended family owned a business, so that after realizing my wish to be a major league baseball player was never to be realized, I thought of becoming a corporate lawyer. However, in the third year of college I took my first psychology class, and was so smitten that I changed my major, stayed an extra year in college to fulfill graduation requirements in psychology, and went to graduate school in psychology. It was at a time when Freud was still read a bit in graduate school, and it was his theories of the mind that made the most sense to me. Reading the *Interpretation of Dreams* I felt like the great explorers of the fifteenth and sixteenth centuries, discovering new worlds.

After graduate school I was able to find my way to training settings with forward thinking psychoanalysts. At the time there were only a handful of psychologists in the American Psychoanalytic Association. In my internship at the University of Colorado Medical Center, two psychologists were being trained at the Chicago Psychoanalytic Institute. In my post-doctoral training there were a number of psychologists trained as child analysts at the Hampstead Clinic (now the Anna Freud Centre). At the Michigan Psychoanalytic Institute, where I received my psychoanalytic training in the 1970s, in my class of seven there were three psychologists and one professor of philosophy. At a later time, when I had the chance to play a role in the opening up of opportunities for psychologists in the American Psychoanalytic Association, I did so.[1]

In one way, this book is about a single theme, meaning. That is, how do we bring our understanding to analysands in a way that is most meaningful to them? It was only in writing this book I realized I started to write it over 40 years ago.

As a psychologist and psychoanalyst, I've been thinking about the role of how to find meaning in a way that is meaningful for over four decades. One of my first publications, *Basals Are Not For Reading* (Busch, 1970), explored the way the content of books used to teach children to read had little to do with what children were developmentally interested in. Using developmental data and research on reading, I made the argument that reading success would be greater with content more meaningful to the beginning reader. Compare this with a quote from one of my first papers on clinical technique (Busch, 1993):

> Listening to discussions of the clinical process, one is impressed with how many interpretations seem based less on what the patient is capable of hearing, and more on what the analyst is capable of understanding. We too often confuse our ability to read the unconscious and the patient's ability to understand it. We are frequently not clear enough on the distinction between an unconscious communication and our ability to communicate with the patient's unconscious. What the patient can hear, understand, and effectively utilize – let alone the benefits of considering such an approach – are rarely in the foreground of our clinical discussions
>
> (p. 153)

So while I've been thinking and writing about a psychoanalytic method for the last twenty-five years, I've been thinking about the role of meaning in learning and understanding for a lot longer.

A search for answers

My psychoanalytic training was fairly typical for institutes of the American Psychoanalytic Association at the time. It gave me a deep appreciation for the power of the mind, along with the importance of having a model of the mind. While the theoretical bent of my Institute was Arlow and Brenner's view of the Structural Model, we studied the works of different authors (e.g., Gill, Kohut, Sandler). As my pre-analytic training was in child therapy and child observation, I came into psychoanalytic training with an appreciation of the significance of early object relations in pathology, along with the importance of a developmental model.

However, throughout my psychoanalytic training there was a feeling that the psychoanalytic method was still evolving, and needed further elaboration in defining the method that was compatible with a workable theory of mind. In clinical seminars we spent our time attempting to glean the deepest unconscious fantasies of the patient, with fewer attempts to consider how this understanding could be translated into a useful interpretation for the patient.[2] As I came to understand it, we were being taught the necessity to follow the Structural Model in our theory courses, but analytic technique was taught according to the topographic model and Freud's first theory of anxiety, where uncovering the deep, unconscious fantasy leading to symptoms was the curative factor. Historically this was the model that prevailed at the time, although it was said to be otherwise, especially in the United States (Busch, 1992, 1993; Gray 1982, 1994; Paniagua, 2001), and it's my impression it remains a favored model in many places in the world. In an interesting twist, what was characterized as the dominance of ego psychology in American psychoanalysis (Wallerstein, 1988) often seemed interpretively close to the deep interpretations of the Kleinians and French, albeit from a different understanding of dynamics.

It was in my pre-psychoanalytic training that I learned to appreciate the significance of the ego in degrees of pathology, and *accessibility to change*. Trained as a psychologist, I did a lot of psychological testing from a Rapaportian–Schafer perspective. Over time it became clear that the ego's flexibility, rigidity, or porousness, was the main determinant of the level of disturbance. In my post-doctoral training in child therapy, my supervisors were trained at the Anna Freud Centre, where the accessibility to treatment was based on the ego strengths of the child. At the same time I was fortunate to be in a seminar where we spent 2 years reading and discussing, line by line, Anna Freud's (1965) *Normality and Pathology in Childhood*, which gave me further understanding of pathology based upon her view of the ego within the Structural Model. Finally, beginning in my post-doctoral and continuing through much of my analytic training, I did a lot of observational research with nursery school children, which confirmed Erikson's (1950) picture of drive dominated play, but also highlighted the role of the ego and object relations in the creativity or rigidity of the play (Heinicke et al., 1973a, 1973b).

Two psychoanalysts, Paul Gray and Anton Kris, published works in the early 1980s that crystallized my understanding of the significance of the ego in understanding what seemed to be one of the most critical, yet overlooked factors in analytic success, i.e., *interferences in an analysand's capacity to think freely*. Further, their views of the psychoanalytic method were integrated within a consistent psychoanalytic view of the mind, which I felt was missing in my clinical reading, and the clinical technique I had been taught. In many ways psycho-analytic technique was in danger of turning into folklore, passed down verbally from generation to generation. Close examination of these ideas often showed their inconsistencies, and idiosyncrasies. One analyst's mantra was high on another's "not to do" list. In many ways we still struggle with the same issues today (Busch, 1994, 1999a).

Anton Kris's (1982) book on free association placed this method at the center of psychoanalysis in a unique fashion. As stated by Kris (1982), "The basic aim of psychoanalytic treatment, viewed from the perspective of free association, is to enhance the patient's freedom of association" (p. 408). I will not go into this in depth here, in that the reader will soon discover how much my view of psychoanalysis is based upon the method of free association. In essence, I believe with Kris that almost everything we need to know to help our patients comes from their use of the method of free association, if we define it as all the patient's use of words as communications and words as actions, and we focus on "the clinical concepts of psychoanalysis, for example, resistance, transference, conflicts of defense and ambivalence, and narcissistic phenomena . . ." (Kris, p. 408).

A chance encounter over 20 years ago at the meetings of the International Psychoanalytic Association in Rome solidified my psychoanalytic interests in the direction they took for the next decade. A dashing analyst from Spain[3] spoke in a discussion group, and his thoughts seemed to speak to the many ideas that had not been fully formed in my mind. When I spoke to him briefly after the meeting, he suggested I read the work of Paul Gray. When I went back to read Gray's work, I was surprised that I had read one of his papers many years before (Gray, 1982), and had written numerous notes in the margins that showed how stimulated I was by the article. I had recently graduated from my Institute, and I think I needed a long period of time to work on my own and see the problems I encountered in doing psychoanalytic work before I could fully appreciate the value of his work. Gray's (1982, 1994) work on the technique of resistance analysis brought clarity to the significance of the unconscious and preconscious ego, long misunderstood and misrepresented. His work helped me crystallize many ideas, and influenced my work for the next decade. During this time Paul Gray was a gracious mentor. My impression from the hundreds of clinical discussions I've participated in is that, worldwide, Gray's work is still not fully integrated into our clinical thinking.

The reader will find ample demonstration of Kris' and Gray's influence on my work in this book, but ultimately my theory and method of working is my own. Approximately 10 years ago I began to seriously study some of the writings of the European analysts, which has broadened my view of the psychoanalytic method. I have been influenced by the use of countertransference and descriptions of the total transference in the work of Betty Joseph and Michael Feldman. Gray felt the analyst's countertransference was neurotic, and his focus was primarily on verbally expressed material. My own explorations led me to understand the significance of what I call language action,[4] which is language unconsciously designed to "do" something in the analysis or to the analyst (i.e., the meta-communication in the communication). The work of André Green, especially his emphasis on preconscious thinking and representations, also influenced my thinking. However, what allowed me to consider the thinking of European analysts were my discussions with and reading the work of my colleague and wife, Cordelia Schmidt-Hellerau, whose understanding of aggression and the preservative drive were inspiring to me.

As fortunate as I've been as a psychoanalytic clinician and writer, I've also been a teacher for over 40 years, twenty-five of those in psychoanalytic institutes. My students have borne the burden and pleasure of helping me understand my ideas, and have been invaluable in modifying and elaborating them. For many years as a teacher and supervisor in psychology and psychiatry at the University of Michigan, I had the opportunity to share my enthusiasm for psychoanalytic ideas, and many of my supervisees from that time have gone on to psychoanalytic training. It is immensely gratifying to see how many have established distinguished careers, and have become psychoanalytic writers themselves.

Finally, in the last 20 years I've written a great deal. Colleagues often say, "I'm envious as writing seems so easy for you." However, this is hardly the case. I find writing a great pleasure mixed with agony. This last part is especially true as I approach new concepts, and this book is my attempt to integrate what I've been learning over the last decade with my earlier understanding of the psychoanalytic method. This may be incorrect, but I think I found my two previous books much easier to write than this one. There are many chapters in this book where I started out with one idea, but ended up with a different perspective than the original one. Sometimes I have written a chapter four or five times before I feel like I have a "good enough" version. This is the "agony" of stumbling around in the dark for long periods of time, thinking you finally understand something, and then coming back to it again to find a lot more needs to be understood or explained. The pleasure is in finally feeling I've understood something new, and in writing about it in a way that doesn't cheat the concept or the reader. I've found that one of the greatest dangers in my own writing is in "hoping" I've explained something, rather than working to make sure it's understandable, and in this way giving the reader more of the pleasure, and less of the agony.

At the end of writing this book I was left with many questions I want to think about. I can't think of a better place to be.

Notes

1 I've never written about my experiences of being one of a handful of psychologists in APsaA, and maybe one day I shall. In my own Institute I rarely felt any negative reactions because of my degree. Once I became involved in APsaA I felt welcomed as an individual, but the reluctance to deal with the issue of training for psychologists was palpable. In Europe it was quite different. Even after the lawsuit against the Americans to allow training for psychologists (Wallerstein, 1998), there was opposition amongst some to treat psychologists equally. When I was a member of the APsaA Executive Council, each year the chair of the Fellowship Committee would come before the Council and describe the stellar residents who were given fellowships. Each time I would get up, and suggest that the fellowship be opened to psychologists. The chair of the Committee said his committee would take this under advisement, and the next year we would go through the same process. Finally, I was able to obtain 300 signatures on a petition to have the fellowship opened to psychologists. I alerted the chair of the Fellowship Committee that I would be bringing this petition to Council, and a short time later he wrote that the Committee had voted to do the same. It was in these small ways that I tried to open involvement in APsaA for psychologists and later social workers. It was always this type of negotiation at first, or gentle reminders. When on committees, members would talk of trying to recruit residents to psychoanalytic training, and I would remind them that psychologists would also make excellent recruits.

2 I have been in clinical conferences throughout the world, and the discussions usually follow this same pattern. We hear the clinical material and the discussion revolves around finding the deepest possible meaning. Paniagua (2001, 2008) has consistently

pointed to this phenomenon, and the problems it raises. I think I've finally understood why this might be, and approach this topic in the last chapter.

3 This young analyst, Cecilio Paniagua, became my dear friend, and generously gave my work careful readings. Only later did I learn he received his psychoanalytic training at the Baltimore–Washington Psychoanalytic Institute, where Paul Gray supervised him. He now lives in Madrid and has published widely on the method of close process monitoring advocated by Gray.

4 In previous publications I have labeled this type of thinking as action language. However, in spite of numerous attempts to explain the differences, some continued to confuse this phrase with a Schafer's (1968) theory of action language. It seemed prudent to change the term rather than continue to risk confusion.

Part I

PARADIGM SHIFTS

2

PSYCHOANALYTIC KNOWLEDGE
AS A PROCESS AND A STATE

Two types of psychoanalytic knowing

It useful to distinguish between *two types of psychoanalytic knowing* in order to better understand the effectiveness of psychoanalysis in creating a psychoanalytic mind. The first, and the one we are most familiar with, is what we might call *state knowledge*. In this kind of knowledge we are in a *state of knowing*, i.e., something that was unknown is now known, for example, what was previously unconscious is now conscious. Over time we have come to some new understanding why this is helpful, and some methods that might make it more helpful.[1] The other type of *knowing* one can gain from psychoanalysis, and the one that has been less familiar to us, is what I call *process knowledge*. This is where the analysand gains knowledge of the *process by which he can understand his mind*, and its affect upon him. *Together, state knowledge and process knowledge are at the core of a psychoanalytic cure, and play the major role in the development of the capacity for a psychoanalytic mind.* I will explore the concept of process knowledge first.

Process knowledge

A hyper-masculine but inhibited 32-year-old man began an analytic session by wondering if I noticed that he was walking with a limp. He went on to explain he sprained his ankle playing soccer, and then associated to what he didn't have. He didn't have any dreams, and had no further thoughts about the previous session. He went on to elaborate how he'd been hurt in the soccer game by diving for balls he couldn't possibly get. He found himself wondering about why he did that, and then realized that while he was talking to me, he wondered "if what he was talking about was important or nothing."

F.B.:   Diving for something or nothing?

This led the patient to think of a time when he was about 10, lying in his bed at night, feeling like the room was getting smaller and yet taller, like a rubber band that stretches when the rubber band gets longer and the sides come closer together.

He then said, "It was scary. [Pause] Now I'm not sure if I was experiencing it. Did I even think it?"

F.B.:   Was it something or nothing . . . It's hard to know if the pursuit could leave you injured.

I would like to suggest that my interventions in this brief vignette raise an important clinical question regarding how we think of the curative process in psychoanalysis. Let me describe what I find significant in this vignette.

The analysand begins the session making sure I notice he is damaged. His mind then goes to not having thoughts. So we now have these *no thought thoughts*. Are thoughts hurtful? In soccer he was hurt by diving for something that wasn't there, the "no ball–ball." He then muses on whether what he said is something or nothing. In another form we are back to these *no thought thoughts*. My intervention attempts to capture this *process*, which I believe contains an unrepresented question . . . i.e., Can these dangerous "not there" thoughts be thought?

The patient remembers a time, never previously reported, that seems to have obvious symbolic significance. However, it immediately becomes part of this *no thought thoughts* mental space. My intervention is an attempt to again represent this dynamic where, in response to some danger, *thoughts become non-thoughts*. This is in contrast to interpreting what seemed like the underlying fears of castration.[2] This choice-point (i.e., When do we focus on the process and when do we focus on the content?) occurs throughout all analyses;[3] the rest of this chapter will attempt to explore this issue.

A new view on an old question

What do we hope our patients have developed at the end of a "good enough" psychoanalysis? The way most of us have been taught to practice in the international community is that knowledge of the unconscious is what patients most urgently need to know. Our basic theory suggests that the more of these unconscious elements we can bring into awareness, the less likely the pull of their manifestations in action will occur. There is, of course, a great deal of merit in this perspective. However, there is another perspective to be considered, which is *the process of knowing is as important as what is known*. It is my underlying thesis in *creating a psychoanalytic mind* that what is accomplished in a relatively successful psychoanalysis is *a way of knowing*, and not simply knowing. My experience in doing second analyses is that patients often come in knowing a lot, but they *don't know how to know*. They are stuck in knowing what they learned from their analyst in a previous treatment, and can't continue to grow and develop when the exigencies of life arouse variations of previous anxieties. It can lead to a belief in a kind of knowing we might call *formulaic intuition*. Its expression can be seen in patients who, when hearing a surprising association, say something like, "Oh, that must be my critical father (mother, sister, brother, etc.) emerging," or "That must be my fractured self," or "my homosexual side." These are "insights" that stop thinking rather than stimulate it. They can become part of a self-deceptive personal narrative to protect from unconscious fears and/or enact wishes.

Basic to my premise is that psychoanalytic knowing comes, in part, from analyzing the process of knowing. It requires a different form of attention that focuses on analyzing the patient's way of analyzing, the resistances to analyzing, and the analyst's way of bringing what he knows. It leads a patient into a different psychological state that I would call a *psychoanalytic mind*. This is where the analysand has a different relationship to his thoughts and feelings than previously, seeing them as psychological events that can be observed, thought about, and played with.[4]

State knowledge

Broadly speaking, then, there are two kinds of knowledge patients gain from psychoanalysis. Each works differently, are used differently, and are central to analytic success. The one we are most familiar with is *knowledge as a state*, as in a state of knowing. Such knowledge leads to increased structure (Freud, 1895). With this knowledge, the whole process of reacting to internal and external stressors gets slowed down. The general dictum of making the unconscious conscious is geared toward this type of knowledge. What wasn't known is now known. By slowly moving what was unthinkable into ideas and feelings that are representable (i.e., what was unconscious into preconscious thinking), we change psychic structures from something simple to something more complex, and the *inevitability of action into the possibility of reflection.*[5]

Thinking of *state knowledge*, consider the following. When Max started his analysis, every time the analyst moved in his chair, Max had a startle response. His whole body tensed, his heart began racing, and he clenched his fists. Four years later, Max no longer consciously hears the sounds behind him. What has happened? Starting with a memory of how, when his mother started drinking in the afternoon, she would suddenly start berating him for some imagined slight, we gradually built a complex representation (including his projected rage and other factors) of why he was always ready for an attack. To think of it pictorially I would suggest that when entering analysis, key conflicts and unconscious fantasies are like walking into a room with two doors, the purpose of which is to go in one door and out the other. With no obstacles the path from one door to another is swift and direct. Now imagine that there have been a number of obstacles set inside the room, so it is like entering a maze. Getting from one door to another now takes a longer time, and one might not even get to the other door. While in this maze you might have the time to wonder why you're even in this room, or whether it's worth the effort to try and find the other door. In thinking about Max we can see how his initial readiness to fight off an attack has gone from a simple stimulus–response mode to a more complex structure so that an immediate reaction is forestalled.

Process knowledge

Process knowing is dissimilar, leading to a difference in *how one thinks rather than what one thinks*. Patients' thinking in the beginning of an analysis is concrete.[6] They think, but they cannot think about their thinking. In the midst of conflict patients often think of their thoughts primarily as realities. At these times, a man describing an argument with his wife is not wondering why these thoughts may be on his mind. He can't observe his thoughts as thoughts, let alone reflect or play with them. Over time, certain methods of working, along with a focus on the process, lead to a change in the analysand's capacity to become the kind of thinker capable of a self-analytic capacity. It is this method that more often leads to self-analysis rather than identification with the analyst's functioning, which has been the primary way the development of self-analysis has been hypothesized. To summarize, process knowledge works differently than state knowledge. Process knowledge leads to an appreciation of the methods necessary to obtain state knowledge. Process knowledge is not silent. It is the result of active, but not directed mental activity. It often has the quality of a daydream, but unlike a daydream where the dreamer luxuriates in his thoughts, process thinking includes the capacity for an observing ego and the ability to play with thoughts for self-knowledge.

In short, at the heart of process knowledge is *the capacity to think of one's thoughts as mental events*. This seemingly simple capacity is a hard won accomplishment for all patients in analysis. However, the benefits are enormous, as it potentially allows the patient to step back and reflect rather than act. Let me present a typical example.

Eric

Eric, a patient near the end of his analysis, began a session in a convoluted manner. References to people and places were absent, associations appeared to spin off in many directions, prepositions were left out, and sentences weren't finished. After a while, Eric was able to observe that his way of talking was reminiscent of the beginning of treatment.

At that time, we understood Eric's manner of talking as a wish to have me clean up his messes, with the meaning of this symptom revolving around narcissistic gratification and hostility.[7]

After Eric is able to step back and observe what he's been talking about (a major analytic achievement), his associations went to the previous day at work. Upon returning from getting a cup of coffee, Eric noticed the spilled unused content from his previous cup of coffee along a trail leading from his desk to the coffee machine. He briefly wondered about leaving the mess for the cleaning woman, but, as the telltale signs immediately identified him as the perpetrator, he decided to clean it up himself. He felt irritated at having to clean up the mess, but while doing so he became amused at "this long trail of brown mess tracing my movements." Eric found himself thinking of his mood before departing on his coffee sojourn, and realized he had been irritated. He wondered why and laughed when the thought came to him, "I've spent the last hour cleaning up other people's messes." His mood brightened after this. His thoughts then turned toward an interpretation I made the previous day. He thought about it a lot, but couldn't quite get it.

F.B.:   It felt like you had to clean up my messy interpretation.

Eric went on to say he hadn't realized till now how irritated he was at my comment, which he felt was "convoluted."

While there is much that could be explored in this rich analytic interaction, what I would like to highlight is Eric's capacity to view his way of talking as a mental event. Once he does this, he has access to an abundance of memories, feelings, and thoughts, while his whole mood changes. His associations lead us to see how the initial transference in the session ("I want you to clean up my messes") was stimulated by his reaction to my interpretation the previous day, which he felt was a real mess that he had to clean up. Another patient, without this capacity, may have spent the session irritated by how much he has to do for others. I see this as a typical example of a patient once he has developed the capacity for self-observation via his appreciation for process knowing. It is not the core unconscious fantasies of the patient that change. These remain intact ready to be stimulated (although less highly cathected). What does change is the patient's capacity to consider his thoughts and feelings as mental events. In this way, he can gain access to his thoughts as unconsciously motivated. In this way state knowledge and process knowledge work together. Further, we see Eric's ability to reflect on his thoughts, and chuckle over a feeling that earlier in the analysis might have seemed frightening. This is another important analytic achievement.[8]

Others have captured the idea of *process knowledge* in a variety of ways. We see it in Green's (2005) statement, "the aim of an interpretation is not to produce insight directly but to facilitate the psychic functioning that is likely to help insight" (p. 5). Sugarman (2003), writing from the perspective of child analysis, and later considering adult analysis (2006), highlights what he calls "insightfulness." This concept focuses on how we help our analysands develop a theory of mind. Fonagy and Target's work (Fonagy and Target, 1996, 2000; Target and Fonagy, 1996) on mentallization and mindfulness touch similar concerns, although the definition of these terms and the methods used to arrive at these states are different. Gray's work (1982, 1990, 1994) on freeing the mind to do the work of analysis stimulated many articles on the attention to the process, although he focused more narrowly on the role of the unconscious resistances. Paniagua (2001, 2008) has focused on how our technique has mostly emphasized state knowledge based upon the topographic model.

The techniques of analyzing the process[9]

This technique focuses on the importance of using certain methods of analysis to analyze. We try to show that by listening to what is on the patient's mind we learn everything we need to know. In general this means working in an unsaturated fashion (Ferro, 1996), while analyzing resistances to help free the analysand's mind, and aiming our interventions to what is preconsciously available. Using these methods leads to a focus on the analysand's mind as the source of insight, rather than the analyst's. While the analyst's understanding and empathy are crucial to the effective use of this method, it is the persistent focus on the psychoanalytic information provided by the patient via free association, or the resistances to the process, that is central to this way of analyzing. Below are some working principles:

Unsaturated preconsciously directed interpretations

I often begin an interpretation by saying: "I *wonder* if you noticed . . ." and then recounting a series of associations, or a change in affect; or "From what you are saying I *wonder* if you're suggesting . . ." and synthesizing the theme in the associations. In essence, what I am continually highlighting is the view, that if we follow the process via listening carefully to what is going on in the analysand's mind, we can learn what is causing their difficulties. While this sounds like what we as analysts are always doing, there are a number of differences. First, what is more typical in the way we work is to listen to the patient's associations, and say something like, "You feel lost when I don't speak." Here it is the analyst who synthesizes what the patient is saying, and *tells him what is on his mind*, rather than helping him see *what is on his mind* in his associations.

What I'm describing is a way of working where interventions are less *saturated* so that the patient is freer to choose which path he is ready to follow. I also try to *wonder* with the patient, indicating that listening to oneself is about *imagining, and not defined realities*. *The plasticity of unconscious thinking* makes definitive, highly saturated interpretations more likely to close off thinking. Further, most of the way we have been taught to listen is symbolically, while the way I'm describing is listening to more of the narrative of the patient's mind. Often we listen first for what is *missing* from the patient's associations rather than what is there in the patient's associations. Using the patient's narrative as the starting point for analytic investigation takes into account the concreteness of analysand's minds in the midst of conflict. Others have pointed to this same necessity with the same rationale.[10]

Clinical vignette

In his first analytic session, a patient began by starting to say something, and then stopping. After a lengthy pause he started complaining that he was having difficulty seeing how he could juggle the demands of work and home with a five times per week analysis. He went on to describe a recent vacation he had just returned from where, in incident after incident, his wife complained about his behavior. When he tried to be sensitive to her needs, she got mad that he never had his own ideas. When he tried to take charge, she felt her needs were not being taken into consideration. His attitude seemed to be that no matter what he did, he was unable to please her. The analyst then said to the patient, "These feelings must have to do with how you feel about beginning analysis."

In general, I support the analyst's attempt to bring something important to the surface. The patient has these two associations. The first is the feeling that getting to the analysis will be difficult, a beginning resistance that might derail the treatment, immediately followed by a second association of not being able to do anything to please his wife. The preconscious nature of the associations (Busch, 2006a) makes it possible that the patient is close enough to an understanding of this to make, with help, the connection conscious. That is, he is aware of and able to bring up these two ideas, but not able to connect them at this early stage. However, the manner in which it was interpreted during the first analytic hour would make it difficult for this connection to become conscious. "What did I say," the analysand might rightfully ask, "that led the analyst to assume I was talking about beginning the analysis?"

By connecting what is present, rather than what is absent, we give the patient a far better chance to see the connection, while also helping to *establish the process*. Rather than the analyst conveying the idea that "I will give you interpretations that only I can know where they come from," the analyst can convey, "If we listen carefully to what is on your mind . . ." Here are two interventions I might make. When the patient begins the session by starting and stopping, I would note this by saying, "There seems to be something that's making it difficult to keep talking." While in one way acknowledging the obvious, I would be conveying that I am listening to what he's saying (or having difficulty in saying in this case), and acknowledging a beginning resistance, without suggesting what it is (unsaturated). In this way *we begin the analysis by analyzing the process*, giving the patient the freedom to talk about the difficulty in starting to talk, or the content of what he's holding back, or anything else he does or doesn't want to talk about. Once his associations began I would say, "I'm trying to understand what's changed since we agreed to meet five times per week. After bringing this up your thoughts go to someone you can't please. I wonder if there is a concern that this might happen here?" In doing this we rely on what the patient has a better chance of understanding: the *specific content and connections of his associations*. For long periods of analysis this is the data of analysis. Second, we begin to make the connection between what is presently on the patient's mind and the method of analysis, rather than insights primarily from the analyst's mind. This doesn't mean that the analyst's creative understanding from multiple sources is absent from what is occurring. Rather, it is just this understanding that allows the analyst to see the connections in the patient's associations, leading him to connect the dots for the patient, or not. For those who worry this is more like educating the patient, I can assure you this method is only gradually used by patients, and then sporadically, in the middle phase of analysis, after the many resistances to it have been cleared away.

Further, when the analyst says that the patient's associations *must* have to do with the beginning of analysis it suggests analysis is about looking for *definite answers*, which is what patients do to interrupt creative musings, and often stops thinking. I think we would hope to convey that psychoanalysis is about *wondering*, *reflecting*, and not coming up with *answers*.

Attention to surfaces (a metaphor for preconscious knowing)

Paniagua's (1991) notion of three surfaces captures a way of working psychoanalytically that *focuses on the patient's preconscious use of the process*. Paniagua stresses that any one time there are three surfaces operating in the clinical moment. First there is the patient and what he thinks he's talking about, then there is the analyst and what he's thinking about the patient's material, and then there is the *workable* surface, that space between the patient's and analyst's thoughts that can lead to a meaningful intervention that, as Fenichel (1941) put it, "is not too superficial and not too deep." To put it another way, we try to say something meaningful that furthers the analytic process without arousing too much anxiety.

By working in this way we introduce a synergy between the patient's inner thoughts and feeling, and the analyst's interventions. Again we are emphasizing the importance of the analyst listening to the patient's preconscious associations. Rather than conveying the message that insight is based on the analyst's magical ability to glean deep meanings, we convey that insight comes from considering what is on the analysand's mind, emerging as a mental process, *metabolized, translated and recorded by an empathic listener*. The analyst who is brilliant in reading the unconscious may be at a disadvantage with this technique, in that translating his insights into what can be synthesized through the patient's preconscious may not be so easy.

The essence of the complexity of what it means to find the workable surface can be found in the following:

Immediately before an extended vacation break in the treatment, a patient is talking about being emotionally abandoned by a friend. The patient surface is that he is upset because his friend has left him. The analyst may be thinking that this is about the upcoming vacation. That is the analyst's surface. The workable surface is whatever part of the two surfaces in interaction may be usable by the patient. What leads to a judgment regarding the workable surface at any moment is an integration of a complex set of variables. In the example above it might include the following considerations: (1) the patient may be narcissistically vulnerable, and this is one in a series of slights that have been expressed in the analysis; (2) this is an unusual foray into feelings by the patient; (3) the story is told in a bored, detached manner, or with icy hatred; (4) the analyst may be moved, infuriated, or detached while the patient is talking. In evaluating the patient surface, one might note the patient using the story as the beginning of an associative process that includes some self-reflection – e.g., "I wonder why this is coming to mind today." This may be said in an inquisitive manner, or as part of a reflexively masochistic pattern of self-recrimination. Though the patient's story may not appear to be a direct expression of psychological-mindedness, it may be brought up during a period of openness to psychological understanding in general, or of a growing appreciation of the ubiquitousness of the transference. Alternatively, the patient may describe the abandonment as a purely external event, with no seeming interest in why the topic has come up. This disinterest may be feigned, sadistic, or masochistic. In short, the variables playing a role in determining the workable surface are part of a complex grid. All of them enter the analyst's judgment regarding the workable surface, and are part of an ongoing evaluation of the structural components operating within a dynamic framework at any given moment.

As one can see, interpreting at the workable surface requires an assessment of multiple factors and, finally, a judgment of the ego's capacity to meaningfully integrate an intervention. Faced with an analysand talking about abandonment before a break in the treatment, we are now forced from the comfortable position that we understand as transference to what is occurring, to wondering about the relevance to the patient of this understanding (even if correct) when the current state of the patient's mental structures is considered.

Enactments, projective identification, and countertransference

Unconscious communications via patients' enactments and uses of projective identifications stir up the analyst's countertransference, as they are first registered in the analyst's unconscious. This makes it more complicated to empathize with the patient's use of the process, as understanding comes first from the analyst's mind, which synthesizes feelings, fragments of ideas, bodily sensations, etc. However, once the analyst recognizes these countertransference reactions, and reflects upon them, they have begun to be processed, i.e., represented within the mind of the analyst. From here the analyst attempts to formulate into words the specific nature of how the patient is trying to bring about the analyst's countertransference reaction. That is, we try to understand what a patient is *doing with us or to us* in their words, tone, phrasing of sentences, and ideas expressed. "Good morning," said cheerily to the analyst, can be uplifting, depressing, distancing, discouraging, and a multitude of other meanings, depending on subtleties in tone, phrasing, intonation, and its context within the transference, all occurring outside of awareness. It is the collaboration with the patient of how this doing takes place that begins the analysis of the process.

Our primary focus at these times is the process by which the projective identifications and enactments are delivered, beyond the meaning of individual words. If we focus on the process the content of a dream becomes, for a while, secondary to such things as the way the dream is told, whether there are associations to the dream, or not, how dreams are used in the analysis, etc. We hear one patient tell a dream at the beginning of each session, and we see it as a sign of a new-found capacity for regression as a result of the analytic work. We hear another patient do the same thing and we inwardly groan as we anticipate the patient dutifully telling a dream that will last several sessions with an absent narrator. With the first dreamer we are more likely to pay attention to the content, and with the second the process. With the first dreamer the process emphasizes the content, while with the second the process contradicts the content; the process then tells a different story than the content.

A seeming conundrum

Many years ago I was in a group of analysts discussing clinical material over several days. Near the end of our time together someone raised the question, "What do we remember from our analysis?" As we went around the room, what immediately came to everyone's mind were times when the analyst was especially humane or unempathic. A moment of kindness or a period of oafishness dominated our memories of analysis. The consistency of this phenomenon surprised most of us, and led to a discussion of the role of interpretation in psychoanalysis. In fact, no interpretation or line of interpretation was as immediately memorable as the affective coloring of the analysis, always captured microscopically in a single event, even though most felt their increased understanding of themselves was important in their professional and personal life. What seemed like an inescapable conclusion at the time, generally agreed upon by the members of the group, was the significance of the atmosphere in the analytic setting in comparison to insight.

From time to time over the ensuing years I have wondered about this discussion. In thinking about my analyses, my work as an analyst and those I supervised, I believe I have seen the profound effect of steady interpretive work albeit in a general atmosphere of safety and humaneness. Many have written why interpretation works, and interpretation has been the basis of psychoanalytic treatment since its inception, in contrast to talking to a good friend.[11] How, then, do we explain the absence of any memories of interpretations in a group of experienced analysts? From my perspective, in most "good enough" analyses we wouldn't expect the analysand to remember a single interpretation or even a theme except in the broadest of terms. First of all, state knowledge leads to increased structure, which works silently. Second, we don't only help our patient just know, but rather we also help our patient *know how to know*. I wouldn't expect these two types of knowledge to lead to memories of significant moments in the analysis. The results of analysis are based on the steady, day-to-day work of analysis, not the idealized flash of insight sometimes to be found in our early literature. It is my impression that what was remembered in our group was the atmosphere which allowed analysis to take place or not, and the transferences that remain, sometimes defensively.

Notes

1 I will touch on this here, but return to it in more depth in Chapter 5.
2 These fears appear to drive his entrance into the session as damaged, and make his childhood fantasy of an erection so frightening. The question of whether something is there or not there also embodies the castration fear.
3 I am presenting this as a dichotomy for expository purposes when, indeed, for most analysands, it is more a matter of degrees along a continuum.
4 It is my impression that across a certain theoretical spectrum there seems to be an acceptance on the necessity of focusing on process knowledge, although not acknowledged as such. This will be covered in more depth in the later chapters, but includes those normally not seen as related, such as Betty Joseph, André Green, and contemporary ego psychologists.
5 In a highly simplified version of the findings from the neurosciences, we can say that information processing occurs along neural networks that are activated together. Knowledge occurs in connections between nodes in a network. By changing simple networks into more complex ones, information processing slows down, so that reflection is possible (see Westen and Gabbard, 2002). The mind works in thousandths of a second, so we are not thinking of an obsessional process here.
6 Understanding and working with a patient's concrete thinking will be specifically discussed in Chapter 4, and will also come up in many places in the book.
7 When describing clinical material in this book, I will put my reflections, private musings, and any historical background in *italics*.
8 Elaborated in the chapters on the middle phase and termination.
9 The techniques I'll be describing are applicable to my general view of how psychoanalysis works that will be covered in more depth in later chapters. In this section I'll only be describing their application to furthering process knowledge.
10 There are, of course, times when it is desirable to interpret more elliptically or metaphorically, using symbolic content. What I'm describing in this section is a way of working that furthers process thinking when it is needed.
11 The emotional atmosphere in which any intervention is given is, of course, crucial. However, this not only refers to the relationship of the analytic pair, but also the analyst's use of psychoanalytic technique that leads interventions to be generally correct enough without arousing intolerable anxiety.

3

SPEAKING TO THE PRECONSCIOUS

Its importance in the analysand's understanding[1]

One of the most important changes in technique that evolved over the last 35 years revolves around working more closely with what is most accessible to the analysand in the clinical moment rather than what is least accessible. We've learned, belatedly and not always consistently, *that one cannot interpret what is unconscious without preparation for making it accessible to preconscious thinking. Working in the preconscious cuts across theoretical lines, and is the basis for one element in a new common ground. Further, it is a crucial ingredient in creating a psychoanalytic mind. If the analysand cannot grasp how understanding comes from his own mind, it is difficult to see how he can use his mind to analyze the struggles the mind creates.*

In 1993 I introduced the term *in the neighborhood*, which came from Freud's (1910) paper, "'Wild' Psycho-Analysis." It was an attempt to capture a way of working analytically that was closer to what was available to a patient in a way that was deeper than what was conscious, but wouldn't arouse undue anxiety. It seemed to me that this was the most advantageous way of helping patients move slowly into the realm of the unconscious. When I wrote the paper my interest was primarily in understanding the role of the ego in this process, but over time it became clear to me that I was also suggesting interpreting to what was *preconscious* (Busch, 2006a). More on this later.

Let me go back briefly to describe how Freud came to the term *in the neighborhood*. In his paper Freud tells of a woman consulting him after having gone to a young physician for problems with anxiety after a recent divorce. The physician diagnosed the women's problems as due to lack of sexual satisfaction and suggested various sexual activities as a remedy. Freud chided the physician for assuming that the woman's primary problem was a lack of information, and providing this would result in cure. He presented the difficulty with this approach using captivating metaphors:

> If knowledge about the unconscious were as important for the patient as people inexperienced in psycho-analysis imagine, listening to lectures or reading books would be enough to cure him. Such measures,

however, have as much influence on the symptoms of nervous illness as a distribution of menu-cards in a time of famine has upon hunger . . . Since, however, psycho-analysis cannot dispense with giving this information, it lays down that this shall not be done before two conditions have been fulfilled. First, the patient must, through preparation, himself have *reached the neighborhood of what he has repressed*, and secondly, he must have formed a sufficient attachment (transference) to the physician for his emotional relationship to him to make a fresh flight impossible.

(1910, pp. 225–226; italics added)

By introducing the concept of the analysand needing to be "in the neighborhood" Freud is noting the centrality, among the principles of clinical technique, of the preconscious. The patient must be able to make some connection between what he is aware of thinking and saying, and the analyst's intervention. No matter how brilliant the analyst's reading of the unconscious, it is not useful data until it can be connected to something the patient can be preconsciously aware of. From this perspective the young physician Freud described did not consider what his patient might understand, let alone if she might find his intervention objectionable. The potential difficulties with this approach are succinctly captured by Freud (1910) in the following:

Attempts to "rush" him at first consultation, by brusquely telling him the secrets, which have been discovered by the physician, are technically objectionable. And they mostly bring their own punishment by inspiring a hearty enmity towards the physician on the patient's part and cutting him off from having any further influence.

(p. 226)

Freud (1914) elaborated this changing view of the psychoanalytic method when he stated,

Finally, there was evolved the consistent technique used today, in which the analyst gives up the attempt to bring a particular moment or problem into focus. He contents himself with studying whatever is present for the time being *on the surface of the patient's mind.*

(p. 147, italics added)[2]

However, Freud remained ambivalent towards this perspective in future writings (Busch, 1993), and it remains more honored in the breach. Indeed, for much of our history an analysand's associations were used as sparks for the analyst's attempt to make unconscious contact with the unconscious derivatives in the surface material, and interpretations were expected to deeply penetrate into the unconscious.[3]

Freud's espousal of two different principles for bringing what was unconscious into consciousness (i.e., first and second theory of anxiety) remained as the basis for two different paradigms for interpretation. These are:

(a) Making direct contact with the unconscious.
(b) Interpreting to what is in the preconscious neighborhood.

The validity of each approach was captured in two papers published simultaneously by Sterba (1934) and Strachey (1934), which will be discussed in more detail in in the final chapter.

Preconscious thinking

Buried in Freud's (1915) paper on the unconscious he briefly conceives of *complex preconscious thinking with infusions of unconscious elements*. In a few sentences, Freud, still in his topographical model, presents a view of *preconscious thinking that goes from a permeable border of the system Ucs to the permeable border of the system Cs*. However, Freud remained ambivalent about this idea, and in his last published paper Freud (1940) returns again to define the concepts of conscious, preconscious, and unconscious, by stating that everything that isn't conscious, in the everyday use of this term, is (descriptively) unconscious. Preconscious thoughts become, again, as thoughts that are capable of becoming conscious. The preconscious remained in this murky territory until rescued by French psychoanalysts. In a key paragraph, Green (1974) captured two elements of the significance of preconscious thinking for the psychoanalytic method . . . i.e., the psychic levels at which we listen and respond to our patients.

> The analysis of the preconscious and in particular the use of the patient's analytical material (in his own language) has been neglected since Freud. The reason for this appears to be straightforward in that, since the preconscious can be reached by the conscious, the importance of the preconscious is negligible and language is superficial. To me, however, this viewpoint is superficial itself. The preconscious, as we have seen, is a privileged space where both the analyst and the patient can meet to share part of the transference and go forward together. *There is no point in the analyst running like a hare if the patient moves like a tortoise.*
>
> (1974, p. 421, italics added)

In this paragraph Green highlights the significance of the preconscious in two ways: (1) the importance of a patient's preconsciously driven verbalized associations; and (2) the analyst's interpretation taking into account what is preconsciously available for the patient to hear. In general, working with the preconscious in mind leads to:

1   Listening for what derivatives are available to the patient in her associations as a guide to the patient's capacity to understand and utilize an intervention in an emotionally and cognitively meaningful manner, and the ways the analyst functions that may foster or hinder this process.
2   Listening to patient material and thinking about the interpretive process differently than we did earlier in our history, where interpretations seemed based less on what patients could hear, and more on what the analyst could understand at a deep level.

We can see the essence of these views articulated by analysts of very different theoretical persuasions.

•   The interpretation arises at the moment when the analyst considers that he has understood the point of urgency *and worked out how to make it accessible, at least in part, to the patient's understanding* (Baranger, 1993, p. 23).
•   No interpretation can be seen as a pure interpretation or explanation but *must resonate in the patient in a way that is specific to him and his way of functioning* (Joseph, 1985, p. 447).
•   *I do believe, however, that it is essential to respect the patient's threshold for tolerating interpretations, and to recognize that a feeling of persecution in the session is a glaring sign of excessive insistence* (Ferro, 2003, pp. 189–190).

How does all of this look in the clinical moment? Here is an example from a supervisee.

The patient, a 30-year-old man, came to analysis because of his never having had a long-term relationship with a woman, often feeling inadequate, and unable to even approach a woman he was interested in. His analyst is a woman. Around the sixth month of treatment, after another failed attempt to make an impression on a woman, the patient remembered a time when he was about 5.

Patient: I was in the schoolyard, playing baseball, and I wanted to hit the ball very hard to show how big and strong I was. I wanted to show off. I hit the ball and it dribbled off my bat. When I ran to first base I fell down. I hit my head on the concrete and started to cry. The girls who were watching found it very funny, and started to laugh. I felt like an idiot.

Analyst: I wonder if you feel I don't appreciate your strength.

We can all understand how the analyst might come to this interpretation. However, *it's about what's not there in the patient's thoughts, what's hidden, what's absent, rather than what is there that might be preconsciously available.* I would think about saying:

"At one time you wanted to show off for a girl how strong you were, but you associate it with being made to feel like an idiot. It seems to be linked to why it's difficult for you to approach a woman. In your mind, to try is to fail."

In this I would be trying to stay closer to what is available to the patient. After this unsuccessful evening with a woman he has a memory of feeling like an idiot when he tries to show off his 5-year-old maleness. He is able to make this association, and therefore it is possible to link them together. The patient isn't showing any resistance to the analysis at this moment, or holding back thoughts, so why bring in the transference? We tend to bring in what's least available, while avoiding what's still new and available. Further, the analyst is not helping the patient see how his mind works. He might rightfully wonder why the analyst thought this had to do with her. It can lead to a routinized search for transference, rather than a dynamic living out that gives transference interpretations credence for the analysand.

Going deeper by determining preconscious availability

There is no easy answer to how we determine the availability of material to the analysand's preconscious. Descriptively, the music of the words tells us a lot about the patient's state of mind. Further, it is only over time we learn whether we learn such things as whether telling a dream is part of a newly found ability to represent unconscious derivatives, or the beginning of an obsessive monologue. *In general, the availability to preconscious awareness is based upon a combination of the state of the ego, along with the drive to enact.*

Thus, one of the first considerations is the degree of anxiety or threat (to the ego), as seen in the strength of the resistances. When resistances are lowered, the analysand is often able to have narrative associations that open up new meanings. However, as almost anything can be used as a resistance, when the patient is in a more resistant mode it can sometimes be difficult to determine. Any outward sign of a productive analysis can be its opposite. Free association, reporting dreams, agreeing with an interpretation, etc. . . . all can be potential resistances. Over time the analyst can better understand these activities, and their potential readiness for preconscious accessibility, by their role in the progression or regression of the analysand.

It is my impression that we have the greatest difficulty in considering the degree of resistance *when interpreting transferences.* Often we confuse our ability to see transference implications with the patient's readiness to preconsciously understand them. Here is an example, which demonstrates our readiness to interpret transferences when the patient is resisting such an interpretation.

In the first year of his analysis, a young man comes into a session angrily denouncing a professor who lectures, "without thinking of whether the students can follow." As he continues in this vein, he slips and says that he hates "to have him treat – I mean, teach me." He then challenges the analyst with the comment, "I suppose you will make something of that." When the patient continues to complain about the professor, then the analyst tells him, "Aren't you trying to run away from your anger toward me?"

As we can see, from the beginning of this vignette the analyst seems not to be taking into account what may be preconsciously available to the patient. As with the analysand's complaint about his professor, he does not consider "whether the students can follow." The patient challenges the slip, which indicates the patient has already made the unconscious connection between his feelings about the analyst and the professor. It is clear the patient is in a feisty mood, and connections between the analyst and the professor will not be welcome. However, the analyst ignores this, and goes ahead and makes the transference connection anyway. What he did not pursue was the patient's reluctance to make a connection between the analyst and the professor (i.e., the most observable component of the resistance at that time).[4]

Interpreting split-off enactments

One of the most difficult times to determine preconscious availability is when the patient is driven to enact something, while it is simultaneously split off from the ego. The analyst is in the position of observing a crucial dynamic, while the analysand is desperately protecting herself from awareness of that same dynamic. In general it is most helpful to approach this issue from the protective side. That is, the patient isn't aware of the panic that drives the split-off nature of her behavior, and the analyst's appreciation of this side of the dynamic helps the patient approach what is driving the enactment. In general, understanding in terms of *self-preservation and/or object preservation*[5] is most readily available to the patient. The idea that the patient is *protecting* him or herself, or another (whether from the past or present), is usually accurate and less anxiety provoking than whatever else may be going on. However, with the narcissistic/borderline character, it may even be difficult to do this at times, as the analyst assuming he knows anything about the patient, or the idea that the patient has a problem, can feel denigrating to him. A typical example is the following.

A businessman in his fifties, with narcissistic rage barely covered by reaction formations, and a sexual perversion, spoke in a manner I would call tightly controlled associations. That is, his thinking had the appearance of freely associating, but it rarely led to any deeper understanding, and was often confusing. His sudden bursts of crying were mystifying, and seemed like a parody of a patient in analysis. The analysand later was able to talk about how he planned out everything he was going to say in the sessions, and that while his crying was genuine, it was what he felt he should do whenever he recalled a painful memory after reading a novel where the primary character did this in his analysis. After several months of interpreting the content with little change occurring, the analyst said that *it seemed like the patient was having difficulty freely saying what was on his mind, but instead kept returning to specific traumatic events in his life to re-live them.* After a long silence, the patient said, "It felt like you just threw cold water on me." In subsequent sessions the patient transferred ownership of this comment to the analyst, and continued his idealization of the analyst while subtly returning to his particular use of free association.

In this example when the patient's control of the method of free association (i.e., emoting as a defense) is questioned, we can see how his anger is projected, split off, and continued at the same time. Careful attention to these defenses, *the catastrophic fears that motivated them*, and the continued appreciation of the way the patient needed to keep in control of what was coming to mind to ward off narcissistic humiliation, eventually proved fruitful. The patient who continues to feel outraged, while blaming the analyst for his feelings, is one of the knottiest problems for psychoanalysts. One of the major challenges for the analyst at these times is to contain one's countertransference reaction, while paying attention to what it may tell us about the myriad possibilities of what is being enacted with us. However, it isn't easy to appreciate the patient's narcissistic vulnerability when our incompetence is constantly pointed out in an arrogant fashion, leading to our own narcissistic imbalance.

Going deeper by going slower – an extended clinical example

In the example to follow, gauging the availability of the analysand's preconscious via careful attention to the fluctuating state of his defenses, leads the patient to deeper material. Though I may be thinking about deeper unconscious meanings while listening to my patient, it is my ongoing evaluation of the many factors that determine preconscious availability that leads me to intervene as I do.

The patient, Michael,[6] a man in his mid-thirties, had been unable to practice his profession, despite a brilliant academic record. When he came to analysis he was unclear about what had led him to leave his most recent position. He could cite only vague feelings of anxiety and irritation. Similar problems had occurred through undergraduate and graduate school, but with supportive therapy over many years he finally completed his studies. He came to analysis after having left several positions. His relations with both men and women were superficially pleasant but devoid of any sustained involvement or emotional depth. Recently, hints of homosexual anxiety came to the foreground. The patient's early history was dominated by the early divorce of his parents, in conjunction with his mother's mercurial temperament and his father's self-absorption. Yet there was a basic structural integrity to the family, with both parents continuing to offer a presence, despite their emotional absence.

Michael is in the fifth year of his analysis. After a rocky start, including frequent absences and moving between the chair and the couch, the analysis has seemed to move productively. His increasing freedom with a range of feelings and thoughts has been accompanied by a sustained, if tumultuous, relationship with a woman in which marriage has been proposed, and steps toward a professional position commensurate with his interests and skills.

Michael's girlfriend was at his place for the entire weekend, which seemed another symbolic step in cementing their relationship. He came in describing how upset he had been most of the weekend. His speech was pressured, with a panicky tone to it. This was unusual at this time in the treatment. The primary conscious focus of his upset was a sore on the side of his mouth that had seemed to get worse over the weekend. He struggled with a tendency toward feeling convinced this was a spreading cancer, the result of an AIDS virus, and noted that there was significant swelling in a lymph node on his neck. Although he "knew" this was a premature diagnosis, his mind kept going back to the most frightening possible causes of the sore with a sense of certainty that led to a feeling of terror and doom. This alternation between worrying over a potentially fatal illness and assuring himself it wasn't so was repeated in the session. For example, after stating how absurd his concern was at this point, he would go to thoughts that clearly indicated that he needed further reassurance; for example, one thought he used to reassure himself was that he remembered giving blood just last month and had been screened for the AIDS virus. He had fooled around with a woman from work a few weeks ago, but neither of them had taken their clothes off. Yet all weekend he had kept looking in the mirror, convinced the area was rapidly spreading. His girlfriend's assurances were only temporarily comforting.

Noteworthy during this part of the session was the fluid state of Michael's ego, with a tendency toward more regressed functioning. He was in the grip of a powerful unconscious force. In spite of his brief preconscious "awareness" that it was premature to panic, he kept being drawn to do so. The regression was notable in that it harkened back to earlier times in the analysis, when he could easily feel panicky. We see the theme that he is being punished for his sexual activity; however, given Michael's ego regression at the moment, it would be difficult to interpret in a way that could be meaningfully integrated by him. Michael is not sure at this moment whether his panicky feeling is based on a realistic possibility or is all in his mind. (The diagnosis, made later in the week, was that he had a cold sore.) An interpretation might alleviate some of his anxiety via acceptance of my perspective on the basis of authority. However, given Michael's general psychological resilience at this point in the analysis, and his growing capacity for and interest in self-exploration, it seemed in his best interest to see what he could do with these feelings on his own – a decision based also on the principle that the analytic process should be viewed as a growing partnership (Busch, 1995a; Gray, 1994). With a patient who was less resilient, if I felt sure of my judgment, I might intervene more quickly as a way of helping him understand that this feeling he was having was potentially understandable. However, I think it is imperative that we not move too quickly to interpret Michael's experience. It is Michael's fear, and we should treat it respectfully and seriously. It should be interpreted when he is ready to have it interpreted, or we run the risk of dismissing the authenticity of his experience.[7] While the work of analysis necessarily includes

27

investigating the analysand's views based on unconscious fantasies and relational models, this is far subtler than I believe we have considered. Every interpretation can be viewed as an attempt to balance the questioning of perceived meaning in a way that does not iatrogenically undermine the analysand's appreciation of his thoughts. We want patients to end up with curiosity about their thoughts, and this goal is compromised by our seeing those thoughts primarily as raw material for content interpretations, and by our not taking their experience into account in considering what is closest to preconscious availability. While at a given moment it may be necessary to privilege the analyst's perspective, as an unquestioned, constant therapeutic attitude the approach has drawbacks.

Michael's thoughts then went to the past weekend, and how he had kept vacillating between thinking he would marry his girlfriend or break off the relationship. Something similar had happened earlier with regard to taking a high-powered position he'd been offered. At times he was convinced he would take it; at others he thought of leaving his profession completely. He then described how, in the midst of sex with his girlfriend over the weekend, he had lost his erection. He then went into familiar obsessional detail about whether, or to what degree, he finds her sexually attractive. He focused on the smallness of her breasts. He then noted, with some irony, that on occasion during the weekend he had found himself thinking longingly about a woman who lives in his neighborhood, and whom he frequently sees jogging in the morning. He was struck by the fact that, when he thought about it, she was built remarkably like his girlfriend, with smallish breasts.

Here in the session we see a beginning shift in ego functioning, whereby Michael can begin to observe his thoughts. He recognizes that the jogger he is attracted to has the same characteristics as his girlfriend, who he feels is not sexually attractive enough. The panic is now gone from his voice, and his whole manner is shifting to a more reflective mode. Given that this shift is taking place, I find it prudent to see what develops next. Such a shift in the ego's relation to its own thoughts often heralds an elaboration of what has just occurred. While at this point we don't know what has caused the shift, and though an explanation would certainly be of interest, I have opted for privileging whatever area Michael is ready to explore. If one believes that Michael's attempt to use the method of free association involves an unconscious scanning by the ego to determine where it is safest to go in the context of a wish to understand oneself, then analytic listening is best conducted by privileging his use of free association. While the analyst may have many questions or observations, these should take a back seat to Michael's associations. Most often, patients will tell us, if we allow them to, which area they are ready to explore. Thus the link I had considered making earlier in the session between his anxiety and sexuality has now been raised by him, and seems more preconsciously available. After he talks about his panic, his associations eventually turn toward what occurred sexually over the weekend. In the context of the change in ego functioning we have just observed, why not follow Michael's thoughts to see what he can elaborate?

28

Michael's thoughts then turned to a time when he was driving with his girlfriend to her mother's home. They had a number of things to do before leaving, and realized they would be a few minutes late. He found himself getting very upset. In retrospect, he wondered why. *(Again we see a greater ability to think about his thinking.)* On the ride there his girlfriend indicated, in what he felt was a snide fashion, that she didn't like the radio station he had on. He slammed off the radio, and she got mad at him, which infuriated him even further. Yet he wonders why he turned the radio off the way he did. He must have been feeling angrier than he thought, and sensed he was being provocative. He must have felt criticized by her statement about the radio station, yet he wasn't sure that's what she meant.

F.B.:   It seems to be a continuation of what you describe feeling all weekend – that is, someone or something is doing something to you that is threatening or dangerous. This feeling seemed to reach its height in your conviction that you had a fatal illness caused by sex, although you had some inkling this was a premature diagnosis.

Of all the possible interventions, why would I choose this one? There are two components to my answer. The first is that this issue is one Michael was struggling with all weekend, and it was therefore emotionally alive for him. Second, his thoughts keep returning to this theme, with an increasing capacity to observe them, suggesting a greater preconscious readiness to think about the events leading to the panic. My intervention is an attempt to work with what is most meaningful to Michael, both emotionally and in terms of his preconscious readiness to accept the ideas. At this point in the session Michael senses he is reacting to something. What I judge to be preconsciously available in my intervention is based on Michael's readiness to think of himself as playing a role in his reactions, rather than primarily reacting as if something bad were happening to him, whether a fatal illness or his girlfriend's scolding him. In each individual moment he was aware, to varying degrees, that his reaction might possibly be off-base. He was unaware, however, of the consistency, throughout the weekend, of this feeling of being threatened. The linking of the various events is what gives them their power. To this point in the session, Michael is unaware of the connections between his reactions over the weekend. There seems to be no point in suggesting possible causative factors until I can see Michael's reaction to the linked power of these multiple reactions. Will he need to deny the connection? Will it become part of what he experiences as a series of snipes at him? Or will his associations lead us to a deeper understanding of the link between his sexual thoughts and the punishment he has been waiting to befall him?

After some reflective moments, Michael stated that it felt like he's been waiting his whole life for some calamity to happen. (I had never heard him say anything like this before.) He reminded me of various times through college and graduate school when he ended up in the emergency room, convinced he had a fatal illness. The strange thing, he now realized, was that he always felt calmest when there was something actually wrong with him. He found himself thinking about a time, after his first year of graduate school, when he was being considered for a prestigious fellowship. He was a basket case until he came down with mono-nucleosis that summer, and all his anxiety seemed to flow away.

His thoughts then turned to his other preoccupation that weekend – what to do regarding his profession. He found himself "disgusted" by all his prospects. He was surprised that he used that word. He realized it wasn't how he was actually thinking about things, and it seemed to be a word that he has more often thought of in relation to sex. As always, he said laughingly, "the plot thickens."

F.B.:   There being something terribly wrong about sex seemed prevalent in your feelings over the weekend, especially in your conviction that you were dying from a sexually transmitted disease. You seem to feel you are doing something disgusting, and are expecting to be punished for it.

Michael: I'm always waiting for something bad to happen to me after sex.

After my earlier intervention, Michael's associations led to confirmation of the interpretation, with the recognition of a lifelong unconscious expectation of being punished, along with a beginning elaboration of a feeling (i.e., disgust) that seems part of what triggers the expectation. Michael now feels free to explore his thoughts. My intervention here is intended to synthesize the disparate elements that individually are capable of coming into consciousness, but that remain at the level of individual observation. In the midst of his increasing emotional openness, within the context of an affectively alive conflict, an interpretation is given that offers a set of constructs to organize his thinking while lending further structural clarity to the problem. The intervention tries to respect the structural elements operative at the time, while attempting to build structure. It offers Michael a new way of conceptualizing what happens when he is in a particular difficulty.

Over time we understood this material as based on homosexual anxiety stirred by the weekend separation that led to a fantasy of taking in the analyst's breast/phallus. This stimulated both his feeling of panic over the conviction that he had AIDS, and the loss of his erection during intercourse. In speaking about the latter, Michael focused on his girlfriend's small breasts – more like a man's – while he noted feeling turned on by a woman with a similar breast size. While elaboration of this fantasy over time proved important in Michael's understanding, I considered it a significant piece of analytic work first to identify the underlying feeling during the weekend that dominated Michael's associations (e.g., imminent danger) but that was experienced by him as discrete incidents. It is this step of clarifying what we can see in a patient's associations (e.g., feelings of pleasure followed by depression, successes undermined by self-sabotage) that are too often bypassed as we look for what is hidden by the associations.

I can imagine some readers wondering why I didn't interpret the homosexual transference. I will give my answer to this question in greater detail in Chapter 10 on 'Working within the transference." For now, let me mention two factors.

1   *I didn't see his homosexual anxiety in the transference as being "in the neighborhood." Michael's neighborhood in this session was his anticipation of a catastrophic disease after sex with his girlfriend. Given his regression over the weekend and in the beginning of the session, I felt it prudent to see if he could re-find a reflective stance. For the sake of helping him towards finding his psychoanalytic mind, it wouldn't have been useful to rush in and "explain" what was going on. Of course, if he remained in a regressive stance I would try to help him find his mind. However, it would have been in trying to help him see how psychologically endangered he felt, rather than focusing on the unconscious danger. Once he could re-find his mind on his own, I tried to stay with what I saw as most preconsciously available rather than what was unconscious. Over time it led to exploration of his homosexual anxiety, but in a way that was emotionally understandable for Michael. An interpretation of his homosexual anxiety in this session would have led Michael towards intellectualization. I could observe the process working as Michael went from regressive thinking to the capacity to reflect and associate to the material as the session progressed, even producing a "slip" indicating his fears were connected with a feeling of disgust.*

2   *Many may wonder why I didn't at least raise the issue that his fear was of a disease often associated with sex between men, thus confronting his homosexual anxiety in displacement. This brings us to a basic question about how we best bring what is unconscious to consciousness so that what was unthinkable will be thinkable. Many analysts believe that it is only by bringing unconscious derivatives into awareness that begins this process. Some, like Green, add the proviso that the derivatives are close to preconscious awareness. Not said, but implied, is that the analyst can do this due to his position as a benign ego or super-ego, which moderates the patient's anxiety about being judged. My own view is that by slowly expanding what is available to the ego via respecting the dangers that lead to unconscious resistances, understanding them, and not causing undue anxiety with our interpretations, the patient will gradually find the freedom to approach what has been so frightening.*

The power of unconscious fantasy comes alive in the context of patients' first seeing how irrational thoughts and destructive behavior impact on their lives via a close following of their associations. By staying with what is preconsciously available we help the patient move in gradual steps to what is deeper. To quote again from Green, "There is no point in the analyst running like a hare if the patient moves like a tortoise" (1974, p. 421). Michael was able to grasp how his weekend was ruined by a persistent feeling of danger, while also discovering an unconscious feeling (i.e., disgust) that was linked to his thoughts and difficulties over the weekend. Such a process, by providing a powerful demonstration of unconscious forces at work, brings the analysis alive for the patient in a way that more abstract interpretations of unconscious fantasy cannot.

In thinking about this session with Michael we can see how at the beginning, whatever preconscious awareness he had was drowned out by feelings of panic that his fantasy of having AIDS was real. With another patient I might have pointed out this process (i.e., how in spite of his thoughts that these concerns couldn't be real, he kept being drawn back to the feeling they were real). That is, I would try to highlight what was preconsciously available, to see if I could help him gain the necessary distance to explore what was going on. Michael had reached the point in treatment where I thought he would be able to see this for himself. This was borne out, and as he continued to associate I could stay with what was potentially preconsciously available to deepen the process.

In summary, while there have been major changes in how closely analysts work "in the neighborhood," I still find many analysts tend toward deeper interpretations than I think are preconsciously available. In this chapter I've considered some of the factors involved in what it means to work preconsciously, and its importance to the patient's capacity to develop a psychoanalytic mind.

Notes

1 The reader will find some overlap between this chapter and the previous one. This is because, in part, there are certain ways of working that are at the core of what I'm describing. However, in this chapter I will explain the importance for working in this way for *understanding*, while previously I elaborated this perspective as a method for *appreciating psychoanalytic knowledge as a process*.

2 The theoretical basis for Freud's clinical observation wasn't articulated until his appreciation for the power of unconscious resistances, which was one important part of the move to the Structural Theory, and the articulation of the second theory of anxiety. In his first theory of anxiety Freud saw anxiety as due to dammed up libido, and the psychoanalytic method was based upon freeing the unconscious wishes leading to deep interpretations. In his second theory of anxiety, Freud (1926) saw it as due to the unconscious ego anticipating a danger, leading to the importance of analyzing the unconscious resistances, which hasn't been fully integrated into our psychoanalytic method. This will be explored later in Chapter 9 on resistance analysis and working through.

3 As Freud (1912b) put it,

> To put it in a formula: he must turn his own unconscious like a receptive organ towards the transmitting unconscious of the patient. He must adjust himself to the patient as a telephone receiver is adjusted to the transmitting microphone. Just as the receiver converts back into sound waves the electric oscillations in the telephone line which were set up by sound waves, so the doctor's unconscious is able, from the derivatives of the unconscious which are communicated to him, to reconstruct that unconscious, which has determined the patient's free associations.
>
> (pp. 115–117)

4 The example is from Greenson (1967). It is especially interesting that Greenson was presenting it as a way of working with resistances, while from my perspective it was antithetical to this approach (see Busch, 1992, 1993).

5 Schmidt-Hellerau (2006) has pointed out that what many consider as the aggressive drive might more usefully be considered as the intensification of the preservative or sexual drives. It is enormously helpful in understanding a patient's aggression not primarily as a bedrock feeling, but as a reflection of an attempt to protect the self and/or reach the object.

6 Explored earlier in Busch (2000).

7 In general, we underestimate the fear factor in the formation of the psyche.

4

THE TRANSFORMATIVE FUNCTION OF THE ANALYST'S WORDS

To paraphrase Flaubert from *Madame Bovary*:

> While few of us can ever speak exactly of our wishes, longings,
> or sorrows, and language is a cracked kettle on which we beat out
> tunes for bears to dance to, while all the time we long to move the stars
> to pity.

And yet we still have a kettle, cracked though it may be, and we still long to move someone, and maybe one day someone will hear our longing, name it, help us understand it, transform it, and we may find that the longing for pity is to ward off our excitement over dancing, and in this way, maybe, we begin to joyfully play music and dance with whoever we want, or not. As I understand it, this is fundamental to the analytic task.

Flaubert's quote captures one of the many dilemmas posed for psycho-analysts regarding the complex meaning of words and language, especially the analyst's attempt to translate the polyphonic music from the cracked kettle into something meaningful and analytically useful for the patient. It has led some analysts to eschew the significance of words in analytic work,[1] while others continue to make discoveries about the use of language within the psycho-analytic situation (e.g., Green, 2000a; Rizutto, 2002, 2003, 2004), rethink why certain words appear in the way they do (e.g., words as actions), reconsider the purpose of the analyst's words (e.g., Lecours, 2007), and investigate the underlying structure of language.[2] The analyst's appreciation for the transfor-mative effect of words is the *sine qua non* for helping patients to develop a psychoanalytic mind.

As analysts we have had to find a way of navigating between the post-modern view of language that a signifier may mean whatever the interpreter wants it to mean, and the view expressed by Green (2000a):

> By constructing an analytic space in which free association and psycho-
> analytic listening are possible, the analyst can *voice and link* previously
> catastrophic *ideas*, quite unknown to the patient's consciousness, to help

the patient to create meaning and obtain relief from previously dominant but unknown terrors.

(p. 429, italics added)

Can we appreciate both positions?

Freud (1915) embraced both positions when he described the move from unconscious into conscious via linking "thing *presentations*" with "word *presentations*." In his use of the term "presentations" Freud indicated it was not a thing in itself he was referring to, whether as a *thing* or a *word*.[3] As clarified by Laplanche and Pontalis (1973), "The thing presentation is not to be understood as a mental correlate of the thing in its entirety" (p. 448). Although not stated as such, we can assume the *word presentation* is also not "a mental correlate of the thing in its entirety" (ibid). In short, Freud recognized the highly saturated nature of words (and things) for the individual. This post-modern view, in itself, doesn't negate the importance of words in lifting "thing presentations" from the maelstrom of primary process thinking, it just highlights the complexity of the task. Freud (1914) was clear in his belief that what could not be remembered in words, would be expressed in action.

Another complication for analysts today, is the observation regarding the *possibility* of the analyst's words representing actions. It is my impression this insight into the way we may, *at times*, communicate, has led some to a position where they no longer see it as useful to consider a distinction between the analyst's words and action. As stated by Stern (2002),

> Contemporary clinicians also take it for granted that *every time* they speak, they are taking some kind of action with and toward the patient. The effect of the analyst's language, like that of the patient's, is hardly limited to its truth value.
>
> (p. 230, italics added)

Greenberg (1996) believes, "Freud's starting point, the fundamental assumption that the word and the act are dichotomously alternative modes of expression, is flawed. We know that words do not restrain or substitute for action; they *are* actions" (p. 201). In fact, some contemporary American analysts seem to believe, as Vivona (2003) suggested, in the futility of trying to distinguish between *words as communications* and *words as actions*.

In contrast, throughout a large part of the psychoanalytic world,[4] there have been certain paradigm shifts based upon an increased understanding of the analyst's words as central to the curative process. Basic to this shift is the increasing understanding of the significance of *transforming* the under-represented into something potentially *representable*,[5] or *represented in a more complex form*. In this process one can imagine the *inevitability of action being replaced by the possibility of reflection*. This is why I see the discounting of the power of the analyst's words, as in an extreme post-modern view, as leading us away from some significant developments in psychoanalytic thinking, and potentially interesting psychoanalytic questions.

In psychoanalysis the increased understanding of words and language has come from various sources. We've come to realize that unconscious mentation is "presymbolic" (Basch, 1981), "pre-conceptual" (Frosch, 1995), "concrete" (Bass, 1997; Busch, 1995b, 2009; Frosch, 2012) and "preoperational" (Busch, 1995b, 2009). What these labels attempt to capture is that the patient's thinking, at these times, is without *sufficient symbolic representations*. Thus, before any meaning can be interpreted, the psychic mechanism (i.e., conflict, defense, self-reparation, internalized objects, etc.), and content, will *need to be represented verbally in a way that leads to symbolization*. Words and thoughts serve as efficient, and structuring signs for what is signified.

For over 60 years French psychoanalysts have highlighted the importance of building *representations* to the curative process. Aisenstein and Smadja (2010) captured this perspective from one of the founders of the French psychosomatic school, Pierre Marty (1952), when they pointed out the significant step Marty took in understanding psychosomatic patients: "it was not a question of looking for the *content* to give sense to the somatic symptoms but rather of observing the *inhibition or failures of psychic elaboration that preceed or accompany them*" (2010, p. 343, italics added). In short, Marty saw the symptoms of psychosomatic patients as a result of a particular type of problem in thinking, or nonthinking, i.e., *the failure of representation*, rather than primarily the result of a physical enactment of an unconscious fantasy or conflict. The concept of representation, or lack thereof, has been central in French psychoanalysis. Green, in fact, sees the essential paradigm of psychoanalysis, on the side of representation.[6] We see in Bion's (1970) concept of *thoughts without a thinker* (p. 563), and the idea of changing beta elements into alpha elements, notions very close to the French representational concept. Ferro (in Brown, 2009), writing from a Bionian perspective, highlights that "there is not an unconscious to be revealed but a capacity for thinking to be developed, and that the development of the capacity for thinking allows closer and closer contact with the previous non-negotiable areas" (p. 102).

In fact, there has been a paradigm shift *across psychoanalytic cultures*, captured by Lecours (2007) as the movement from *lifting* repression to a paradigm of *transformation*. That is, rather than *primarily* searching for buried memories, we attempt to transform the under-represented into ideas that are representable. For example, we attempt to build representations as a way of helping the patient *contain* previously threatening thoughts and feelings so that he can move toward deeper levels of meanings. As noted by Lecours (2007), what is represented can continue to build structure and enhance the ability to contain. This leads to what Green (1975) called "binding the inchoate" (p. 9) and containing it, thus giving a container to the patient's content and "content to his container" (p. 7).

What are representations? What is transformed?

Any time we name something that was unnamed we attempt to represent it. Any time we give greater *meaning* to something that previously had no meaning, or capture meaning in something that seemed meaningful (to the listener) but without meaning (to the speaker), we are building a representation. A representation can be as concrete as a word, or as abstract as a metaphor. It can be a sound with a meaning, like "Ugh," or a symbol. Whether it becomes something that is representable for the analysand, depends on many factors, *including how close it comes to what is tolerable at that exact clinical moment.*

In areas of conflict, a patient's mind coming into analysis is filled with simple, but highly saturated representations. For the patient they are one-dimensional realities. For example, a patient with a brilliant graduate career but continual difficulty in the work place comes into analysis with the simple representation: Boss = Despot = Anger = Fear. The patient is working on something close to a stimulus–response model. *Through analysis this representation becomes more complex* so that: Boss = Father = Arrogant Authority = Domineering = Disciplinarian = Feeling Abandoned = Feeling Unloved = Oedipal Rival = Love Object = Homosexual Anxiety = Analyst . . . and to each there is a story along with the myriad feelings that go with these stories.

In essence, this is how simple representations become more complex, leading to the capacity to contain what previously led to immediate action. What has been *transformed* is a simple, saturated *representation* into a more nuanced complex *representation* capable of further elaboration. We do this by increasing the associative links.

Psychoanalytic and research data indicate that the earlier the experience, the more likely it is to be closer to an action. I would *suggest also that the deeper the repression, the weaker the representation and the closer it becomes to action.* In considering the work with more disturbed patients with early trauma, an added difficulty is their tendency to deal with anxiety via action.

In summary, I would suggest that the question of how something unconscious appears in psychoanalysis depends upon the depth to which it has been repressed, and the level of representation at which it was experienced. *The earlier the experience, or the deeper the repressed material, the more likely it will appear in action form.*[7]

Building representations

As I've tried to indicate it is not that *representations are there or not there, but are there in a variety of forms. In broad-brush strokes, then, when we talk about building representations in psychoanalysis we are talking about two separate but related issues. The first is building more nuanced, complex representation from a highly saturated, simple representation. The second is building a beginning representation from what is expressed in language action.*

One can think of representations as having multiple dimensions, for example: from deeply unconscious to within the range of the preconscious (Busch, 2006a); simple to complex; or degrees of saturation. In this model, building represent-ations means attempting to make them more complex, closer to consciousness, and less saturated (or more nuanced). For example, we try to just build a represent-ation from one that is conceptually primitive (e.g., somatic representations). With a highly saturated, simple representation that is close to consciousness, we would attempt to make the representation more complex and less saturated. With a more complex representation that is unconscious, we would attempt to bring the repre-sentation to increasingly higher levels of preconsciousness. To complicate matters, as I will show in Chapter 5, the closer we get to what is unconscious the more likely we find thoughts expressed in the language of action. This is what Freud (1914) understood when declaring that what couldn't be remembered in words would be remembered in action. Further, as Piaget's studies showed, *early thought is in action terms*, and this continues in degrees through the age of 6. In short, our earliest history is encoded in action terms, and the same is true for the working out of conflicts. As Loewald (1971, 1975) noted, the deeper one goes in psycho-analysis the greater is the likelihood the patient will express him or herself in the language of action.[8]

Broadly speaking, then, there are ranges of representations we attempt to build. At a more primitive level, we attempt to build a simple representation from what is poorly represented and often expressed in the language of action (Busch, 2009; Loewald, 1975; Rizutto, 2002); for example, helping a patient see he or she is *doing* something. At a more neurotic level, we help to build more complex repre-sentations by understanding the *meaning* in preconsciously formed associative links. In the first situation we are we are more like ethnographic researchers trans-lating cave paintings into a written language, while in the second we are like a sophisticated translator who understands the music that goes with the words. In the first situation we are building a representation where previously there was primarily action. In the second we are building simple representations into some-thing more complex by adding links of meaning.

A clinical example of building complex representations via associations

In this example from a patient in the termination phase, analyzing the meaning of a resistance leads to a series of preconscious associations. At these times the analyst's interpretations focus on building preconscious *meanings from the associations*, rather than assuming the preconscious meanings were inherent in the associations.

Claude, a 42-year-old businessman, was well into his analysis. While Claude benefited greatly from analysis, a particular transference remained whereby Claude both eagerly looked forward to, but could not hold on to the analyst's words.[9] This had been understood in a variety of ways, but remained a particularly notable part of the transference.

In this session Claude was talking of his reaction to two colleagues. One was the CEO (Charles) of the company he worked for, who was presented as a bully who Claude professed hatred for, and the other was the head of his division (Nick), who was a "nice guy." As the CEO was retiring soon, and this "nice guy" was likely to be the new CEO, Claude surprised himself by wondering if Nick would be able to get him to work as hard as the current CEO. As much as he disliked being pushed by someone, he realized that he always did best when there was someone pushing him. His thoughts then drifted to a meeting on a new computer system the company was investing in, and he worried about his capacity to "*take in*" information. Immediately after Claude used this phrase "take in," he tried to find another phrase. He stumbled around for a while, and then in further associations, whenever he came to the part of the sentence where the phrase *take in* might be used, he stumbled some more.

F.B.:   You seemed to notice this phrase "take in" troubled you, but were reluctant to linger on this.

Claude is able to represent[10] a problem he's had with authority figures in a new way, i.e., his ambivalence about being pushed. There is then something about this phrase "taking in" that makes Claude so anxious that he is forced to try and cover up his palpable discomfort. My comment is meant to represent the resistance to representing the resistance, i.e., the attempts to find alternate ways to express "taking in" rather than being able to think about the difficulty with this phrase.

Claude: I sort of noticed it and put it out of my mind. [Pause]. Now that I can think about it, I imagine taking in a penis. [Pause] I'm surprised at what comes to mind now. I was thinking about my colleagues at work, and how we don't socialize. I find them too caught up in the academic world, and I can't imagine watching a football game with them. Yet with the people in our neighborhood who watch football, I feel they're not intellectual enough.

Claude is able to represent his ambivalence over feeling connected to others (e.g., like in the analysis), and associatively links it with this taking in of a penis.

Claude: [continues] I got up at 3 a.m. last night and couldn't go back to sleep. I kept thinking about this remodeling project we're doing. I got an offer from one company, and it seemed pretty good, but during the night I kept worrying that *I was getting screwed*. Should I have checked with a few other companies, and gotten more bids? The other thing I was worried about was a seal around a crawl space we have in our basement. For some reason there is a danger of radon leaking from this space, so it had to be sealed up. Yesterday I noticed that the seal was broken, and last night I kept thinking about these dangerous gasses escaping from this hole.

F.B.: If we put these two worries together, we might say that feeling screwed is a way of plugging up this hole where these dangerous gases come from.

Claude's associative chain of representations deepen, so that his ambivalence over "taking in" can be seen as the fantasy of needing to be penetrated to plug up these dangerous gases, while arousing intense homosexual anxiety.

Claude: I just remembered this dream from last night. In this dream I was supposed to make a presentation to Charles and other colleagues. When I went into the room it was so bright, there was no way I could show the slides. I was thinking Charles was a real asshole for picking this room. He had put these shades on the windows that were ineffective. The room was connected to a library, and when I tried to turn the lights off to make the room dimmer, the people in the library were yelling at me. They kept yelling "bum." I was trying to get to the other room to tell this one person who kept yelling that I was a "bum" something, but it was up a steep vertical ramp and I couldn't make it there.

When I thought of how bright the room was I was thinking how bright it was in here, but then I thought "you don't have shades on the window." When I'm reading to Alice [his daughter] at night, after I turn off the light she often keeps repeating some word I said. The library reminds me of the library at Penn, which for some reason I'm thinking was brown, although it wasn't, and all the hours I spent there trying to learn stuff and how difficult it was to let it sink in.

F.B.: So unlike Alice, who wants to hold on to her Daddy's words, words are associated for you with this dangerous brown place, and these lethal gases that need to be plugged up.

Claude: Like the feeling that I'm not sure I can hold on to what we talk about. I wonder now about it being so bright in the room, like it certainly wasn't brown. I'm thinking now about the difficulty I had learning certain subjects, like French history [his mother was French]. I guess it makes sense. I wonder if it had to do with all the bullshit I had to put up with growing up.

I see this example as fairly typical of work with a patient who has reached an advanced capacity for representational complexity. Preconsciously organized associative chains, *not fully represented as meaning,*[11] are presented in a way that deepens our understanding so that further elaboration takes place. A highly defended phrase, "taking in," is identified, which leads to an elaboration of an anxiety-producing fantasy in the night, which leads to a dream. Each component deepens the associative links that play a role in Claude's conflicted feelings about taking in and holding on to the analyst's words. In this context it is the *representation of the meaning of the associations that contribute to the complexity of the representation*, rather than beginning to make simple representations out of what was unthinkable, or trying to make simple saturated representations less saturated.

From language action to representation

The analytic task when the patient is communicating via language action is different. At these times the analyst attempts to build a *beginning representation* where there was an attempt to discharge or evacuate thoughts and/or feelings via language action. The associative process only begins after the representation has taken hold.

Although graduating from a good university with honors, Richard, in his late thirties, had drifted unsuccessfully from one job to another, and was "sent" to treatment by his wife's therapist. Unlike many patients who are sent to treatment by a spouse or spouse's therapist, Richard, after some brief protestations, was eager to begin psychoanalysis. It became evident he wanted treatment for some time, but like with his jobs, he couldn't take sufficient initiative to get himself to do it.

Within the first 6 months of treatment, Richard seemed to be working well in the treatment. His associations had a narrative sense, and a mixture of current conflicts and memories from the past enlivened the sessions. Correspondingly his life outside analysis seemed to improve dramatically. Around this time I began to realize that while there were many associations Richard had in the sessions, they didn't seem to deepen. In one form or another the same stories were repeated. My interpretations were greeted with interest, but the same memories kept coming to mind. We were stuck in what I would call the "history as destiny explanation." Any potential new direction was deadened by phrases like "this must be because my mother (father, sister) . . ." etc. Like with his failed job opportunities, and his inability to get himself to treatment, his analytic ambition had been compromised. *There seemed to be a profound fear of any new representation.*

I began to feel increasingly as if my mind was deadened in our sessions. As I began to be aware of these associative patterns, and my own reactions, I realized that there was another sub-text to Richard's associations. Often times, when he would tell me about some incident where he felt he made progress he would say, "So that was a good thing." It was clear he was pulling for a mirroring response. Given Richard's history I initially felt there was some necessity to gratify this need. However, as the analysis went on, when he kept repeating this phrase I found myself thinking of retorts like, "Who knows?" or "It's not so easy to tell." Noticing the tenor of these remarks that came to mind, I realized I was feeling like I needed to assert my independence from how he wanted *us* to think.

At this point, I began to listen more closely to what Richard might be enacting in language action. Over time I began to see how everything he said was trying to lead us to *one* conclusion.

As I began to try and show him how this was happening in the sessions, he would link it to how his mother could only see him in a particular manner (not a new idea). I would point out how this was a repetition of this same process as now we could only think this was the "cause" of what was happening.

This went on for several months, and gradually new ideas emerged (*the beginning of new representations*), captured in the following. Richard, like his father, was interested in military history. With intense effort over many months, Richard had recreated a panorama of a crucial Civil War battle, complete with soldiers he had painstakingly painted over several months. One day he came home and his mother casually told him she had to move the panorama to a different part of the basement. When he rushed downstairs to see where she put it, it was a shambles. He was enraged, and had the thought that he wished she were dead. Previously, he'd accepted her empathic inattentiveness and casual disregard for his interest with clinging behavior. Richard was sure when his father came home he would be furious with her, but all the father could do was to say "We'll rebuild it." They never did.

Captured in this archetypal memory was the beginning understanding of the fear of *new representations*, i.e., the *fear of building anything new with the analyst/ father because it would only be destroyed. In his mind, I could not protect him from the destruction of what we may build, and he could not represent himself as someone whose products were safe and respected.* At the same time, Richard thwarted attempts to build new representations with him in an identification with the aggressor. Over time, other memories of attempts to build something followed by destruction came to the fore. Most poignantly, there was a time when Richard was a budding soccer star. His mother was driving him to buy new soccer cleats, when her carelessness led to an accident, and Richard ended up with his leg in a cast, causing him to miss the soccer season.

After explication of these fears, a new pattern of language action emerged. As Richard would be talking about a situation where it would be natural for someone to express anger, he would apologize for the behavior of the other. When I would bring up this sequence, Richard would agree and then go on as if I hadn't said anything. After following his associations, and not being able to glean a pattern related to what just happened, I would attempt to bring to Richard's awareness what just happened. At first Richard was confused. He couldn't remember my saying anything. After several repetitions of the same event, and as I brought what was occurring closer to the action, Richard was able to register what just happened, but at first without further thoughts. Eventually he became intrigued. At first he was only able to capture the experience, where it felt to him like my voice was coming from a distance. Then new memories began to emerge (these were not forgotten memories, but ones that hadn't come into the analysis yet). There was a series of memories where he was alone in some part of the family's spacious home, and he had no idea what to do. There was no place for a child to play in the house, except the basement, which was cold and dreary. In high school, where he's been accepted at one of the city's most prestigious programs, which was some distance from his home, he had to make his own way there and back via train and several buses. His mother, who had nothing else to do during the day, never offered to help.

Sensing this also as a metaphor for the analytic journey, I wondered if there was a way he felt I wasn't available to help with his current journey (dealing with Richard's narcissistic vulnerability before the possible identification with the aggressor, i.e., the unavailable one who couldn't hear the other). After some tepid denials, Richard remembered a time when an interpretation I made sounded like it came from an analytic textbook.

I remembered the interpretation, and felt at the time that it, indeed, sounded like it came from a textbook. I recounted this with Richard, and suggested that at that time he might have felt like I wasn't able to help him get to a better place.

Richard was surprised I would acknowledge being a less than perfect analyst, and then elaborated something mentioned earlier, only in passing. His mother was an alcoholic, and at times would fly into uncontrolled rages when inebriated. She would throw things, break dishes, and one time threw a knife at his father, which barely missed him. In the early evening when she began drinking, he would watch to see if she had an extra Martini, or maybe a few more glasses of wine with dinner. His response was to get back out of the situation as quickly as possible, and flee to his room where her yelling was only a distant voice.

I reminded him of how this was the way he heard *my voice* during these times we'd been talking about. It was only over a longer period of time that Richard became aware of his own narcissistic rages when not listened to, and the fears of killing me or being killed.

The fear that his irritation with something I said would lead to uncontained, chaotic rage, led Richard to flee to a protected part of the analytic space, where my voice was coming from a far away place. New representations couldn't be formed because they became potential sparks for rage that could only be fled from for self-protection.

In summary, Richard was only able to express his resistance to and enactment of the transference in language action. Thus, his fear of new representations or his hearing me from a great distance needed to be represented in language before a beginning understanding and further representation could take place via the emergence of painful memories of narcissistic derailments. It is the translation of language action into words that begins the process of representation for patients like Richard with severe narcissistic difficulties.

The power of words and thoughts

The study of language's effect on thinking is as old as Socrates, and *supports the psychoanalytic discoveries of the importance of words and language in shaping thinking.* At the beginning of the third century we find Tertullian (a prominent theologian) writing about the inseparability of thought and language, who came to the conclusion that *in uttering speech you generate thought* (in Holmes, 1870).

43

W. Chomsky (1957), summing up 2,000 years of thinking about these issues, states:

> Language is not merely a means of expression and communication; it is an instrument of experiencing, thinking, and feeling . . . We think in words, by means of words. Language and experience are inextricably interwoven, and the awareness of one awakens the other. Words and idioms are as indispensible to our thoughts and experiences as are colors and tints to a painting.
>
> (p. 3)[12]

The legitimate questions raised by those who see in post-modern theory the difficulty in ever knowing what a word means to the listener, or those who see words themselves as action, have led some to diminish the significance of words in a psychoanalytic cure. However, in my own experience analysands hear words in a variety of ways, and it is this very fact that helps us understand our patients in a deeper way. This is captured in Faimberg's (1996) concept of *listening to listening*. Further, we have all moved from the view that we are just objective observers of the patient's psyche, and we've learned that how the patient hears our words can sometimes give us important insight into our countertransference reactions. However, I find that in psychoanalysis we have a tendency to take new insights in the field as refutation of older ideas, rather than as a window into greater complexity. As noted by Anna Freud (Sandler and Freud, 1982), *"It is very interesting to look at the losses in psychoanalytic theory that occur under the name of progress. It is important to see that with every step forward we lose some very useful things"* (p. 10).

From this perspective I find it apt to end with a quote from approximately 500 BC:

> All that we are is the result of what we have thought;
> it is founded on our thoughts;
> it is made up of our thoughts.
>
> (Buddha)

Notes

1 See Vivona (2003) and Katz (1998) for summaries of this position.
2 See Litowitz (1975) and Shapiro (1988, 2004).
3 Freud used the German word *Vorstellung*, which is closer to "imagination" than "presentation," but Strachey's choice of "presentation," once elaborated, seems apt.
4 The French, the Kleinians, most of Europe and Latin America, and those still working within a Freudian tradition in America, and its developments over time.
5 Stern's (2002) concept of "unformulated" experience captures descriptively what is meant by unrepresented thinking. There are two problems with his conception. The first is that he ignores an admittedly difficult issue, i.e., in what part of the mind are

these unformulated experiences? Second, he contrasts unformulated experiences with the unconscious, which he depicts as something already inside the individual's mind, "just waiting for him to acknowledge it" (p. 241), as if the Freudian unconscious was populated only by already formed representations rather than the formless and inchoate, and that which exists in the language of action (e.g., Widlocher, 1986).

6 Fonagy et al. (1993) think of mental representations as structures, similar to Freud's view in "The Project" (Freud, 1895). It is a position supported by others (Busch, 2006a; Westen and Gabbard, 2002; Schmidt-Hellerau, 2001).

7 I will only mention the difficulty here of trying to understand what happens to the very earliest representations of experience. Somatic representations may be one of the earliest forms of experience.

8 I think Loewald was describing what happens with patients who are more neurotically organized, because with more severe character disorders language action is prominent from the beginning. It is what makes the analyst's task more complicated in that we are bombarded with transference reactions in a language we most often understand via our countertransference that we pick up unconsciously, and thus react before we understand.

9 Throughout this book the reader will find many examples of where I pay close attention to what the patient does with the analyst's words, as I find it becomes a central manner in which the transference neurosis is expressed, and becomes clearer as the treatment progresses.

10 One colleague asked me, "Why don't you just *say you are putting a resistance into words?*" While this is what I am doing, it doesn't capture the theoretical construct for why we put things into words. If one were to say the above we would be working at a *clinical descriptive* level, while what I'm trying to describe is from the perspective of *clinical theory*, which attempts to *add to our understanding of the underlying psychic mechanism*.

11 I find it useful to distinguish between the representations of experiences and representations of meanings in psychoanalysis, the latter occurring with increased understanding.

12 However, from the late 1950s to the present, following the discoveries of Noam Chomsky, linguists turned toward the general theory of universal grammar. It ruled out any examination of the ways in which languages may affect thinking. However, even Pinker, one of the most prolific explorers and explainers of Chomsky's theories, has stated that "one's language does determine how one must conceptualize reality when one has to talk about it" (Pinker, 1989, p. 360).

5

HOW THE UNCONSCIOUS
SPEAKS TO US

Vision without action is a daydream, but action without a vision is a
nightmare.

(Old Japanese proverb)

A patient was recently talking about a conversation with his father. It was a
type of conversation he had told me about many times. As he was talking I
realized he wasn't *telling* me about the conversation, rather he was repeating
his part of the conversation. His words and tone were apologetic, as if he had
to explain why his very existence was a bother to him and those around him.
We had seen many times how his sad, repentant feelings were often nostalgi-
cally revived with a bittersweet longing. In this he was creating a mood with
his words, a mood of sadness, of regret, of self-abasement, a mood designed to
have me love him ... or hate him ... it was all the same to him. During the
analysis I often had one feeling or the other, without a deeper grasp on it at
the time.

Listening to the patient talk I had questions I've had many times before: Why
was this conversation being repeated in action? Why, at this moment, couldn't the
patient *tell* me about the conversation, and his multiple thoughts and feelings
about it? From what part of the mind was this current form of expression coming?
It seemed different than an understanding of feelings we learn about via the
patient's associations.

There has been a recent surge of interest in this type of thinking seen in some
patients most of the time, and all patients some of the time. In the past it was
simply called regressive thinking, but as a clinical phenomenon I prefer to use
Loewald's term, "language action." What this label attempts to capture is that
the patient's thinking, at these times, is without meaningful verbal representation
and closer to action. That is, where words become attempts to bore, seduce, anger,
etc. It is where words become more like concrete acts, evocatively captured by
McLaughlin (1991) when he stated words, "become acts, things – sticks and
stones, hugs and holdings" (p. 598). While it seems like the patient is describing
a dream, an upsetting event, or complaining about his wife, the analyst feels

mocked for his interest in dreams, blamed for the patient's bad luck, or faced with a demand for unconditional love.

It is different than when words are used to communicate internal states via free association. In what follows I will elaborate how this special language, *language action*, is the primary method the unconscious speaks to us in psychoanalytic treatment, and why this is. *Transformation of words as actions into symbolic, representational thinking is part of helping the analysand to develop a psychoanalytic mind as the capacity to play with thoughts is dependent on their being representable.*

Certainly the regressive nature of action has been well known by psychoanalysts for some time. Unfortunately its exploration as an important psychic phenomenon became bogged down by pejorative judgments of what was called "acting out." For many years there was a strong tendency to exclude action as worthy of study. Over the past two decades this critical stance has been corrected, as many explored the role of action in psychoanalysis, bringing new understanding to its highly complex role for both patient and analyst alike. However, it is my impression that our thinking of language action *specifically in relationship to unconscious phenomena*, as well as the clinical implications of this formulation, has not been fully considered. Further, as noted in the last Chapter there is a worrisome trend amongst contemporary theorists to critique the distinction between *words as communications* and *words as action*, leading to the blurring of methods of interpreting when specific approaches may be necessary for each. Distinct methods for listening to and interpreting preconscious and unconscious thinking are necessary.

Freud and the move from action to language action

When Freud (1914) introduced the repetition compulsion, he used the phrase "the compulsion to repeat *in action*." Why did he need this addition, "in action"? If he were primarily trying to describe how certain mental events recur, the "compulsion to repeat" would have been sufficient. Since Freud did not use words injudiciously, we have to assume this term "in action" had particular significance for him. As so often happened, Freud left it open to us to think about this repeating "in action." In his 1914 paper we see Freud explaining the *in action* part of the compulsion to repeat as: *a resistance to remembering, and the patient's only way of remembering*. Puzzling is that Freud doesn't elaborate this seeming paradox, which has been a source of confusion for analysts ever since. Whole schools of psychoanalytic thought have been built upon one side, while the other side has been conveniently ignored as memories

Freud described *actions* in the following manner.

> For instance, the patient does not say that he remembers that he used to be defiant and critical towards his parents' authority; instead, he behaves in that way to the doctor. He does not remember how he came to a

helpless and hopeless deadlock in his infantile sexual researches; but he produces a mass of confused dreams and associations, complains that he cannot succeed in anything and asserts that he is fated never to carry through what he undertakes.

(1914, p. 149)

As you see, this is a very modern description of what Loewald (1971, 1975) also labeled action in speech. He was one of the first in the modern era to suggest words have a special power primarily because of their roots in the sensory–motor elements in the development of speech. In addition we have learned, primarily from the Kleinians, of the times when the patient's verbalizations are meant to *do something or bring about something*, rather than communicate something. This occurs, and remains at an unconscious level (for the most part). *As we've gradually learned, the whole range of psychic states and dynamics can be expressed via language action.* Language action is used to ward off anxiety, to repair a self-state, to bring about a response from the analyst that is gratifying, traumatizing, or reinforces a resistance, and to express every other human emotion or fantasy. Loewald (1975) captured the ubiquitousness of language action in psychoanalytic treatment when he stated that, "we take the patient less and less as speaking merely about himself, about his experiences and memories, and more and more as symbolizing *action in speech*" (p. 294, italics added).

I don't think there would be much disagreement with the statement that, within the neurotic to severe character disorder range, the more regressed the patient the more likely he will communicate via language action. When this happens we can no longer listen to the words as associations. Instead, we turn our attention to a feeling state conveyed by the words, usually captured best via our counter-transference. The Kleinians, who see more regressed patients (Hinshelwood, personal communication), have been writing about this type of communication for years, focusing on projective identifications. Ferro (2006), writing from a Bionian perspective, describes disturbances in the "apparatus for thinking thoughts" (p. 97), which leads to thinking dominated by action. In this, and in subsequent citations, you will see how seemingly widely different schools of thought have come to similar conclusions regarding action-thoughts.

The development of language action

What does this tell us about language action? Why would it be that the closer one comes to expressions of the unconscious in psychoanalytic treatment, the more likely it is to occur as language action? As I have indicated elsewhere (Busch, 1989, 1995b), thought is under the domination of action for a much longer period of time than has generally been recognized in psychoanalysis. The reason for this "action" type of thinking has to do, in part, with the way thought processes develop. As Piaget has shown, one of the major characteristics of all intelligence is that it is a matter of action. Imaging is not the foundation for thought; action encoded in sensory–motor schema is that foundation. The main distinction between different stages of intellectual development is the degree to which actions become internalized and behavior is based upon representations rather than a motoric underpinning. It is important to note that the process of internalization is a very lengthy one. It is not until a child is around age 7 that one can talk of his having an integrated cognitive system with which he can organize the world relatively free from action referents. Before that time, the child's thinking is heavily influenced by its motoric underpinnings. For example, a 5-year-old can successfully walk to school and negotiate a number of school corridors to find his kindergarten class, but he is unable to reproduce this in representational form, as his thinking is of a "doing" type. The younger the child, the more his thinking will be dominated by action. For children capable of higher-level functioning, conflict and regression will heighten the tendency toward thinking based on action.

Thus, what has not been sufficiently emphasized is that actions become increasingly woven into the fabric of the psychoanalytic process, in part, because of the long period of time the child's thinking remains under the influence of action determinants. Central conflicts and the adaptations to them are first experienced, organized, and worked out at an *action* level. Whatever the danger, the original defensive adaptations and compromise formations were undertaken in action terms, and thus may remain unavailable to higher-level ego functioning or remain in waiting as regressive flash points. *Up until the Oedipal phase and its crucial importance in shaping psychic development, action-tendencies remain as a primary mode of the child's thought processes.*

So what is earliest and most primitive in the unconscious is stored in action thoughts. That is why so many characteristics Freud identified as "primary process" thinking are similar to the way Piaget described the action determinants of children's thoughts.[1] Thus, the *closer* we come to what is unconscious, the more likely patients will express themselves via action. The deeper we go *into* the unconscious, and it is useful to think of gradients in the unconscious, the more thought is equated with action. What is most unconscious is always enacted. Think of our most disturbed patients where, in areas of their disturbance, thoughts are closer to reflex actions. McDougall (1978) captured the importance of action as a symptom in psychoanalysis, with its purpose being an anti-communication. She gives a compelling description of what happens at these times.

> He is unable to allow sufficient psychic space or sufficient time for the unconscious remnants to become available to conscious processes. Once the nascent thought or feeling has been ejected, he will frequently plunge into action of some kind in an attempt to ward off the return of the unwelcome representation and mask the void left by the ejected material. Economically speaking such action assures a certain discharge of tension, and might thus be termed an "action-symptom." In this way talking itself may be a symptomatic *act* and therefore an "anti-communication." The analyst might thus capture in negative, what has been up till then an

inexpressible drama.[2] The lost material behind such action-symptoms will often reach symbolic expression, for example, in dreams but then fail to stimulate associations or mobilize affect.

(p. 178)

Implications for treatment

What does all this tell us about technique when analyzing the compulsion to repeat in action? How can we access this compulsion, and how do we introduce it to our patients in a therapeutically effective manner?

Three main issues will be elaborated on in this section.

1   The use of countertransference in understanding language action.
2   The importance of changing actions into representations.
3   The emphasis on the *process* rather than the *content*.

Language action stirs up the analyst's countertransference, eliciting a reaction like being taken aback, wanting to reach out, or turning away from the patient. Once we recognize this countertransference reaction, and reflect upon it, this action has already begun to be translated, i.e., represented within the mind of the analyst. From here the analyst can formulate the language action into words as a necessary step in helping patients find increasing degrees of freedom to think and feel. That is, we try to understand what a patient is *doing* with[3] us in their words, tone, phrasing of sentences, and ideas expressed. "Good morning," said cheerily to the analyst, can be uplifting, depressing, distancing, discouraging, and a multitude of other meanings, depending on subtleties in tone, phrasing, intonation, and its context within the transference, all occurring outside of awareness. It is the understanding with the patient of how this *doing* takes place that is the first important step in freeing the patients from these repetitions in action by making them representable. It takes a different form of attention than the "free floating attention," which has been the staple of psychoanalytic technique in the midst of preconscious verbal associations.

Put another way, our primary focus at these times changes from the *content* of the associations to the *process* by which they are delivered, and the transference/countertransference meta-communication beyond the meaning of individual words. Thus in a first step the content of a dream becomes secondary to such things as the form the dream is told, whether there are associations to the dream, or not, how dreams are used in the analysis, etc. We hear one patient tell a dream at the beginning of each session, and we see it as a sign of a new-found capacity for regression as a result of the analytic work. We hear another patient do the same thing and we inwardly groan as we anticipate the patient dutifully telling a dream that will last several sessions with an absent narrator. With the first dreamer we are more likely to pay attention to the *content*, and with the second the *process*. With the first dreamer the process emphasizes the content, while with the second the process contradicts the content; the process then tells a different story than the content.

When working with language action we first need to address the *doing* because of the analysand's pre-symbolic thinking, governed by the rules of preoperational thought. Thinking is dominated by a "before the eye" reality. Therefore we must start with what can concretely be brought to the patient's attention, i.e., what he is *doing*. We are attempting to help the patient move from *doing* into *thinking*. Working in this way there is a theoretical shift, as noted previously, from a paradigm of repression to a paradigm of *transformation*, i.e., transformation of the non-symbolic into the symbolic.

Ogden (2007) provides an excellent example of what I'm describing, although this is not his emphasis. A patient in her second year of analysis had lost all hope that her analyst could be of any help to her. Most of what Ogden describes then is the analytic *process* and what the patient is *doing*. "She spoke spasmodically, blurting out clumps of words, as if trying to get as many words as she could into each breath of air" (p. 578). "She barely paused after I spoke before continuing the line of thought that I had momentarily interrupted" (p. 578). The patient flooded "the sessions with clump after clump of words" (p. 578). Ogden's interpretation is of this *process not the content*. He next tells us that over several months the patient's speech became less pressured. I bring this as an example of how the intuitive clinician senses the need to work with the process without labeling it as such. Ogden's goal in working with the patient is to increase the mental space for what he calls "talking-as-dreaming" (p. 575), which I would see as akin to creating the capacity for free association, the bedrock for self-analysis.

Our treatment goal is to try to change the inevitability of action to the possibility of reflection via representing what was previously un-representable, and thus only expressed in language action. This is the basis for insightfulness. That is, increasing the freedom of mind is what leads to insight, and not pre-formulated knowledge gained from the analyst or a sudden burst of intuitive understanding. Our method relies on trying to engage the patient's higher-level ego functions to deal with the most regressive parts of the personality. Put another way, at these times of language action there is no *thinker thinking*, and we try to wake up the thinker. We do this by putting words to actions and building up representations. Until this basic step is accomplished it is difficult to see how analysis of language action can occur. We attempt to build representations, also, as a way of helping the patient contain previously threatening thoughts and feelings so that he can move toward deeper levels of meanings.

As a first step we need to identify the occurrence and nature of the language action and communicate this to the patient. This basic step is often bypassed in favor of deeper interpretations. *We too often assume agreed upon meanings before we interpret.* It is my experience that unless the patient is in some agreement on what is being talked about, interpretations become authoritative directives. We cannot meaningfully interpret the patient's provocative behavior, until he can get a glimpse of this behavior.

In one of his few clinical examples, Brenner (1976) reports the following vignette. A patient returns from holiday saying she found romance with an old lover, and waxes rhapsodically about the encounter. She goes on at length about this. The analyst feels pressure from the patient to agree with her view. This moment of felt pressure (i.e., the countertransference) is what might lead us to consider the emergence of language action, and to begin exploring how this pressure is being communicated. This is best explored via analytic observation, rather than asking the patient to explain our feelings. However, the analyst does what many of us do in such a situation, which is react against the countertransference via an interpretation. Thus, the analyst feels highly suspicious of this old lover and, detecting an edge in the patient's voice, says, "Aren't you really angry at him?" The patient gets furious with the analyst, which the analyst sees as confirmation of her anger.

The problem with this intervention, looked at from the perspective I'm presenting here, is that the analyst was pointing out exactly what the patient was defending against via her use of language action. Her resultant anger seemed to be the result of a threat to a bypassed defense. The main way I would see bringing the patient's attempt to have me side with her defense (the language action), would be to see if I could help her begin to explore the defensive nature of her commentary on the weekend, i.e., *her need to go over the same material with no room for thought.* I would begin the exploration of this dynamic with the observation/question, "Have you noticed that in describing the weekend you've frequently emphasized how great it was?"[4] If the patient can see this, we have a chance to explore the *pressure* to have us both agree to her view of the weekend. If the patient can't see this, we have to accept that the patient needs to hold on to her defense for the moment, and wait for another time.

Another way to understand our goal when the analysand communicates primarily in language action is that we attempt to translate this language into words (i.e., making observable, and thus accessible to the ego, what is unconsciously enacted), leading to the formation of *new preconscious structures of thoughts* (but not yet meaning).[5] This helps to contain and modulate the fears that may keep the patient communicating in language action. The first step is clarification. What is clarified is the language action as a way of helping patients associate at a preconscious level. For example, the analyst finds his mind drifting to mundane matters halfway through a session. We then look for what is specifically happening in the patient's manner of talking that leads us to this drifting away (e.g., a shift from lively to robotic talking), and try to characterize what just happened in the session to the patient in a concrete fashion that doesn't arouse undue anxiety.

The purpose of a clarification is to find words for actions, not causes. Meaning would be added by interpretation once there were words. It is the elaboration of a dynamic process viewed via the analysand's language action. This is not a cognitive process, for without the analyst's empathic involvement with the analysand's emotional shadings and the analyst's psychoanalytic understanding at multiple levels, any communication will detract from a deeper involvement between the analytic pair.

Clinical example

In order to exemplify what I'm concerned with here, I'll present a case that was dominated by the language of action through much of the early part of the treatment. I will primarily focus on how I approached the language action so that it could begin to be represented by the patient, which eventually led to greater understanding of its meaning.

Kevin

It was about a year into Kevin's analysis when I realized during many of his sessions I was confused . . . not just confused but confused and slightly agitated. It was like I couldn't bear to listen to him anymore. I wanted to tell him to "shut up," or "stop acting so crazy." Realizing that I was in the midst of an important countertransference reaction, I changed my focusing from primarily listening to the content of what Kevin was saying to listening for the way he used his words (i.e., language action). With difficulty I could see that while individual thoughts about his life, or observations about his psychic state made sense when he was saying them, and it seemed that way to Kevin, who had no doubt about the rationality of his thoughts, *I would be left bewildered by how he'd gotten from point A to B, let alone C and D.* For example, he would start off with an observation that seemed benign enough on the surface, told in an indifferent voice, and then he would say, "I'm so scared." Then with great emotion he would talk about his attraction to a younger woman, and how "bad" it was he had such feelings. Kevin, outside of the transference, was neither a prude nor overly moralistic, so his self-condemnation rang strangely false. I considered he was living out an Oedipal triangle in the transference, and then this emotional "bad" feeling was totally dropped as he described some pleasant interactions with friends and family. I was then startled by the loud sobs coming from the couch, which seemed to have no context. This was not an unusual sequence.

There were other aspects of working with Kevin that were notable. The rhythm of the sessions went something like this. Kevin would talk for most of the session, and then with a few minutes left he would ask me if I had something to say. If I didn't have something to say it irritated him. If I did have something to say it irritated him. This usually involved my having a different idea to how he himself was thinking about what he said. Thus, when I tried to clarify what confused me he recounted a story of how in a seminar on Kafka, he was the only one who understood the underlying meaning that ran through Kafka's work *The Trial.* The implication was clear, i.e., if I was as smart as him I wouldn't be so confused. If I tried to be more appreciative of his ideas in a mirroring fashion, he would mock me for sounding like a "rabbi."

I thought it was essential for Kevin to see how he was conveying something in language action, before any understanding of its meaning could be determined. I kept identifying why I was confused in the sessions. Two technical changes helped Kevin start to increasingly observe that, indeed, he could be confusing. At some point I realized that it helped both of us to think about the confusion Kevin was sowing by clarifying how he was being confusing at an earlier moment in a session. Otherwise, he would get caught up in his grandiose fantasies, and I would become more confused. Also I would try to phrase my observations so that I owned the confusion as mine, and not only something he was putting into me. I was aided in this by Steiner's (1994) concept of analyst-centered interpretations.

I often began an observation by saying to Kevin that I thought noticed something in the way he was talking that might shed some light on the confusion I felt sometimes when he talked. In this way I emphasized that what he said was the starting point for my understanding.

Over time the elucidation of how he was confusing in the sessions (i.e., the demonstration of the language action) led to a growing awareness on Kevin's part that secretaries at work often didn't follow what he was asking them to do, and that his family complained he often thought he told them one thing, when several confirmed he said something else. I want to emphasize again that it was the specific clarification of *how the language action was taking place* that allowed Kevin to comprehend what was taking place, and led him to eventually articulate associations that helped us understand its meaning.

After several months, the following session helped me understand a central part of the transference meaning that was being communicated in language action leading to, in part, my countertransference reaction.

Kevin started the session by telling me he went out to see a play the previous evening that was directed by a friend of his. The play was *Death of a Salesman*, and Kevin said he felt some deep connection between the play and some things we talked about, but he didn't specify and I couldn't immediately see any connection. He went on to other topics, of which I couldn't fathom the connections either.

There was what seemed like a thoughtful pause, and then Kevin returned to what happened the previous evening. He went upstairs to go to sleep and his wife was in bed with their two children. "There was no room for me," he said, and he "panicked." He didn't offer any thoughts about the "panic," and went to sleep in a spare bedroom where he had difficulty going to sleep because he was so agitated. He thought this was meaningful, but he couldn't elaborate.

As Kevin was talking I thought of this agitated feeling I sometimes had experienced during his sessions, but also realized that when Kevin talked in his confusing way, I felt left out of his thoughts. Further, in the midst of his being confusing, he couldn't tolerate my saying much of anything. It was his private language I was only supposed to accept, while feeling totally confused. Thinking about this led me to wonder if this enacted transference in language action was about who's in and who's out of the bedroom. "Who gets it and who doesn't," with all its potential symbolic meaning. In the countertransference I was the one outside listening to these things I couldn't understand. I remembered that Kevin slept in his parents' bedroom on and off until he was age 6. He remembered nothing except noises, and it later turned out he developed obsessional rituals before going to sleep to "make sure he was alive in the morning." As I was thinking about this, my mind became clearer. I wondered how I could begin to explore this, with Kevin, given his need for me to be the confused outsider.

I started by saying that after seeing this play about a family drama, he finds no room for him in the bedroom, which got him agitated. I wondered if when I felt confused, something similar was going on here, but now I was the left-out one, like he felt excluded from the bedroom. When he talked there was no room for me, and maybe that resulted in my becoming confused about what was going on.

Kevin's first reaction was to feel critical of my blaming him for what was my confusion. He was then able to step back and say, "I know we talked about this." A memory came to mind. Every Sunday the family would go to the movies and then to a restaurant. On the drive home Kevin would sit in the back seat, and his mother would start criticizing his father for something. He never understood what triggered it, and he wanted to yell at his mother to "Shut up."

I want to emphasize that this enacted primal scene in the language of action was understood first via my countertransference reaction. It was by translating my countertransference into understanding what Kevin was unconsciously doing when he spoke that led me to grasp what was happening. Kevin's ability to see *that something was being enacted in language action allowed for the elaboration of part of the experiences that formed the primal scene enactment.* It is my contention that in this way we transform language action into a representation that can contain the fearful feelings of the little, confused, left out one, and in this way allow for further psychic elaboration.

A final thought

Words are not just convenient labels for "things"; rather they are powerful mental tools, as are representations. Once there are symbolic entities, there are many things the mind can do that are not possible when actions remain unrepresented. Representations can be played with, observed, turned upside down, or back-wards, flipped into other representations, or build into a thought, a novel, or a psychoanalytic paper.

Notes

1 One puzzle in understanding primary process thinking is the use of symbols. Those who study cognitive development see symbolic thought developing as a result of advanced degrees of thinking, making it stand out as an anomaly in primary process thinking. Basch (1981) pointed out that what we call symbolic thought and believe to be primitive,

possibly even inherited, is an example of the highest form of complex thinking, a point made by the Kris Study group in 1961 (N. Segel, 1961).

2 For an extension of this idea see Green (1998) on "The Negative," and (2000a) the "Central Phobic Position."

3 I say *with* us, rather than *to* us, as the primary motivation may be self-protective.

4 In this I would be exploring, in a very concrete fashion, the patient's capacity to view the defense. Thus I start with what I think is most observable by the patient, i.e., something she's repeatedly done. Again, the patient's ability to think in the midst of conflict is dominated by concrete thought. Further, I put my observation in the form of an invitation to consider the question, rather than my view of what's happening. As the patient is pressing for her perspective, presenting an alternative view as a fact could easily be interpreted by the patient as a battle of wills.

5 Pally (2007) has shown how, as we move toward conscious awareness, thinking involves more fine-grained perceptual distinctions and choice, while unconscious thinking is automatic and imprecise. From this we can see the importance of preconscious thinking in understanding threats and meanings.

6

THE WORKABLE HERE AND NOW AND THE WHY OF THERE AND THEN

Essential to creating a psychoanalytic mind is the shift in *one* focus of psychoanalysis, and changes in the psychoanalytic method that flow from it. This shift has been characterized as the change from working in the *there and then* to working in the *here and now*. As indicated earlier, it is essential to *process knowledge*. Further, the shift to the here and now has gained momentum, in part, because of the support it received from analysts of divergent schools of thought. However, imbedded within this general support are important differences in understanding what *is* the here and now, the clinical approach that stems from these differences, and how the role of the there and then is understood. In this chapter I will focus on the major clinical and theoretical changes that are the bases for this paradigm shift, along with the reasons for why I see both perspectives (here and now, there and then) as necessary, *albeit for some different and some modified reasons than previously postulated by others*.

To briefly preview my perspective, let me first point to the fact that for many years our psychoanalytic methods of working were based exclusively on uncovering the repressed drive derivatives and unconscious fantasies from childhood. The patient's thoughts were scanned for evidence of this buried material, which was then brought to the surface in an attempt to connect fantasies from the past with present symptoms. Uncovering the repressed was thought to be *the* curative factor. This is what we ended up calling the "there and then" method of working. While I understand a *modified version* of this approach as central to an analytic cure, I don't think it is for the reasons originally presented, nor is it sufficient by itself for the curative process psychoanalysis has to offer.

Working in the here and now as a general rubric for the paradigm shift in clinical work is a useable phrase. However, as noted earlier (Chapter 4), I would see the shift more accurately depicted in conceptual terms as the move from an exclusive emphasis on *lifting repression* to an additional focus on *transformations*. What is transformed has been characterized in different ways, but every perspective conveys the same idea, i.e., the necessity to change something unconscious, *which is not sufficiently represented in any conceptual form*, into an idea, thought, or representation that can be thought about, reflected upon, played with and mused over. Most current authors agree that it is only in the here and now that we have the opportunity to grasp these pre-conceptual or unformulated thoughts and experiences, most often via our countertransference.

It has generally been recognized that because of certain qualities of the mind described earlier (Chapter 5), the patient can primarily grasp what needs to be transformed in the here and now. Further, it is these transformations that lead to more complex structures that is a central part of the *why* of there and then interpretations. *Finally, I would suggest that with each type of interpretation we are dealing with separate approaches to a curative process through psychoanalysis, with each type necessary but not sufficient unto itself. Each method is geared toward something different in the analytic task.*

A history of the issues

While some of Freud's statements are viewed as evidence for his support of a *here and now* position,[1] his last statement on the matter (Freud, 1937b) made it clear that he saw lifting repressions as the main curative factor in psychoanalysis. He viewed the goal of analysis as the patient being "brought to recollect *certain experiences and the affective impulses called up by them which he has for the time being forgotten*" (pp. 257–258, italics added). The analyst's "task is to make out what has been forgotten from the traces which it has left behind or, more correctly, to *construct* it" (pp. 258–259). In short, Freud's last word on the subject left no doubt it was to the there and then he felt interpretations should be directed.

In contrast, interpreting in the here and now has gained support from a significant number of contemporary analysts from a wide variety of psychoanalytic schools. It is my impression that as different as these perspectives can appear, there is a subtle relatedness between the authors. For example, while the work of Paul Gray and Betty Joseph would seem to have little in common, they both hold a radical here and now perspective (Busch, 2011a).

The workable here and now

I would suggest there is no one here and now, only a workable here and now. There is no one specific dynamic or content that should take preference over any other, only what is salient and workable at the clinical moment. There is no one royal road to a curative process in psychoanalysis. The workable here and now is multiple and shifting. Sometimes we focus on an unconscious fantasy or defense, a self or object state, a conflict, whether in the transference or not, etc. It depends on what is most salient in the clinical moment. What makes it workable fluctuates with the patient's capacity for preconscious awareness.

I am suggesting that the workable here and now is best conceptualized not only in terms of the content of the patient's communication, but also in terms *of what is knowable by the patient at any one moment, which is a reflection of the patient's relationship to his own mind.* As one can see, I'm shifting the focus from the *primacy of the content* to the *equal primacy of the patient's affective relationship to that content.* We have tended, to our disadvantage, to predominantly listen to the content of the patient's communication rather than in conjunction with the patient's relationship to the meaning of his communication. *We cannot usefully communicate meaning if the patient is afraid of meaning. We cannot communicate meaning if the patient denies meaning. It is difficult to effectively communicate meaning if the patient communicates there is only one meaning. It is difficult to effectively communicate unconscious meaning if the communication is unconscious.* In terms of clinical theory, we are always trying to speak to what may become preconsciously available and emotionally meaningful to the ego without arousing undue anxiety.

Yet we persist in our attempt to communicate meaning when the patient may not be ready. Sitting with a group of analysts listening to clinical material, one universally hears the analysts trying to understand the content. We are experts in this, and one is often dazzled by the capacity of colleagues to stitch together creative formulations. However, as Paniagua (2001, 2008) pointed out, these formulations are usually at the deepest unconscious level. There generally seems to be less interest in conceptualizing what the analysand will be able to hear in a meaningful way, and why this is.

Early transference interpretations, except when they threaten to disrupt the treatment, are a prime example of how we interpret meaning before the patient is ready to hear or understand meaning. It is my impression from hearing clinical case material from around the globe, that we interpret transferences far too early and too often, leading to a premature intellectual acceptance of transference meanings, while the depth of feeling associated with transference feelings remains split off. In my own work I find that it is many years into the analysis before transference interpretations ring true for patients.

There is one group of patients where the transference is usually the here and now from the beginning, and these are the more severe character disorders where from the moment the analyst says "hello" in the first appointment, we are caught in a maelstrom of projections and enactments. From this perspective more direct methods of working in the transference are more applicable. However, this needs to be modified to take into account that while the transference is most salient, the patient desperately wards off the sense that the feelings he has are within him. He is terrified, but not consciously. He is reacting to some great danger, without knowing of this danger. In such a situation we are continually trying to find some part of the ego that can step back for a moment to contemplate what is going on. We attempt to do this by staying very close to the surface of the material, and working *within* the transference and not talking *about* the transference for some time. That is, we try to show the patient something about his way of relating to the analyst as close as possible to the moment it is happening. It is only after the patient can grasp this that his greater freedom might help us understand something more about the meanings of his particular transference.

Why the here and now?

While working in the here and now seems to make intuitive sense to many psychoanalysts, as noted earlier it seems like we have no consistent theory as to why this is central to the curative process. *It is my position that the theoretical imperatives for working in the here and now can be found in three key clinical constructs: the nature of thinking about thinking; unconscious thinking as pre-conceptual; and the unconscious ego.*

A central principle of the analytic method uniting these constructs is the necessity for the analyst to *identify and clarify* the psychical phenomenon before interpreting it. Consider the following simile. Think of a patient coming to us for help who speaks Russian, who doesn't know he speaks Russian, and who doesn't understand Russian. We, on the other hand, have been trained to speak and understand "Russian." How would we begin to help this person? I think there would be general agreement that our first task would be to help them see they are speaking in a foreign language. This is our position as analysts. We first have to help the person see their conscious language is conveying the language of the preconscious and unconscious. Qualities of the mind, universal in all patients (e.g., concrete thinking in the face of conflict), make this possible only in the here and now.

Thinking about thinking

In the midst of conflict a patient's thinking is very concrete. He can only see and think about what is immediately before his eyes (or ears). For long periods of time the patient is incapable of keeping a sequence of thoughts in mind while talking. Clinically we see evidence of this in that it is often only in the middle of treatment that we can make a surprise interpretation, capturing in a short form the essence of a reverie, and have some hope the patient will understand it in a non-intellectual fashion. What is missing earlier in treatment is the patient's capacity to follow his own thoughts, and integrate them at a higher level of abstraction. Most analysts would agree that this is the level on which analysands are thinking through much of their analysis – they think, but do not think about their thinking. Piaget (1930) and Piaget and Inhelder (1959) described this type of thinking as pre-operational. Inserting the word "patient" for "child" we can see how accurately pre-operational thinking fits the thought processes of our patients throughout the analysis. As described by Flavell (1963), the patient

> feels neither the compunction to justify his reasoning to others nor to look for possible contradictions in his logic. He is, for example, unable to reconstruct a chain of reasoning which he has just passed through; he thinks but he cannot think about his thinking.
>
> (p. 156)

Flavell further describes thoughts that are considered "solely in terms of the phenomenal, before-the-eye reality" (Flavell, 1963, p. 203). This is why through much of an analysis we need to work in the here and now. The here and now is the "before the eye reality." It is concrete; it is what is happening, it is not a speculation about something else.[2] By working with what the patient is capable of thinking, we help him see how to think about thinking. *Premature use of metaphor or symbols in interpreting can lead to an iatrogenically induced intellectualization, confusion, and submission.*

Much of our work involves following a series of associations. Historically we have taken these associations, integrated them, and made an interpretation to the patient. A typical example is when a patient asks us about the dates of our upcoming vacation, and then starts to talk about a friend who was supposed to meet him for lunch but didn't show up. He goes on to say how angry he was at the friend. A likely interpretation would be that the patient is really angry with the analyst for his upcoming vacation. While certainly such an interpretation would have merit, the problem with it is the inability of the patient to keep in mind the sequence which led the analyst to his interpretation until later in the analysis. Another way of interpreting associative sequences that take into account the patient's thinking in a pre-operational phase is the following.

A talented patient who hides behind studied incompetence starts a session by talking about some success he's had at work. He then tells of how when he came home last night his wife asked him to look at a sink that was dripping. When he tried to replace the washer he made a total mess of it. They had to call the plumber this morning, and it was extravagantly expensive. Basing what I say on the patient's inability to follow a sequence, and the ability to see what is immediately before him, I might say, "If we follow what you said, after telling me of your success at work your thoughts went to what a failure you were at fixing the sink. As if you became uncomfortable with telling me about your success." In this I am recreating the sequence in simplified form so that first the patient's thinking can become, for him, a *before the eye reality*. Thereafter we can work at bringing in a possible meaning.

The pre-conceptual unconscious

As noted earlier (Chapter 5) the patient brings much of what is central in analysis via language action, i.e., words unconsciously designed to have us think of the patient as exceptional, talented, beautiful or limited, unattractive, an ingrate, etc., or where the aim is to have the analyst feel something. These are the enacted expression of unconscious compromise formation of drives, defenses, self and object states, etc., all felt as pressures to make something happen. The first step in analyzing these unconscious states is to give them a way of being represented in words and concepts, and this can only be done in the immediacy of the here and now. There is no way, other than the present, that we might help a patient catch a tone of defiance, abasement, seduction, or anger. How else to help a patient see the insistence of his views, leading the analyst to lose his own thoughts? How, but in the present, can we help a patient see that every time he successfully analyzes a series of thoughts, he disparages his conclusions? It is only as representations in preconscious thinking that the patient's unconscious fears, assumptions and urges, previously expressed in language action, can be *dreamt about, or appear in linked free associations.* In short, the nature of unconscious expressions lead to the necessity of working in the here and now. At these times we have the greatest chance of having the analysand hear us if what we bring before him is tangible and concrete. In this way we don't stretch his capacity for representation beyond the level at which he is capable of operating.

Unconscious ego resistances

This is one of our central analytic concepts, yet is most honored in its breach (see Chapter 9). What Schafer (1983) stated over 25 years ago remains true in many places: "Certain things about resisting which ought to be well known, and are said to be well known and sufficiently appreciated and applied, are in fact not known well enough and not consistently attended to in practice" (p. 66). Thus, while there is universal acknowledgement of the necessity to work through unconscious resistances, this is honored more in the breach, and there is little agreement on how this might best be done. Yet, working through resistances remains as one of the central components of the psychoanalytic curative process. This is because *the most important resistances are unconscious, and behind these resistances are the most frightening fears known to man (death, loss of those closest to us, disintegration of the self, castration, debilitating guilt, shame, etc.). I cannot think of a problem a patient comes in with that doesn't have, as a significant component, these unconscious fears.*

It is useful to think of unconscious resistances in this way. Most of us have seen movies where there are incredibly intricate patterns of invisible laser beams protecting a valuable diamond in a museum or private home. In the "resistance movie," a museum (the psyche) protects something valuable (a shameful wish or forbidden hope), with a laser pattern of defenses. To get to the diamond you have to shut down, one by one, each of the protective lasers. In this way, as each resistance appears we try to work through the fears until the protection is not so necessary. What was highly protected slowly becomes touchable and workable.

Once again, as the most profound resistances are unconscious, we have to start by helping patients see there is something going on outside their awareness. Take the following example. An inhibited patient is talking about how angry she is at her sister. After a period of time she stops talking, there is a pause, and then she says, "Well underneath it all she's a good person." It would seem something just happened at the pause that led the patient from acknowledging her hostile feelings toward her sister, to needing to undo these feelings. This is a key moment for helping a patient begin to observe a defense in action, and the beginning of analyzing it. It would not be unusual to hear an analyst say, "It sounds like you're protecting your sister against your anger," or "You're really angry at your sister." The first comment, while pointing out the defense, doesn't help the patient see the defense in action, possibly necessitating the patient taking in the comment from the analyst's position as an authority. In the second comment, the defense is bypassed. I might say, "You were talking about your anger at your sister, paused, and then described how she's really a good person. It was as if there was something about your angry feelings toward her which made you uncomfortable." In this way one takes into account the likely working of the patient's mind, i.e., the inability to follow a sequence, and the concrete nature of thought.

The significance of there and then interpretations[3]

While the significance of there and then interpretations has been a cornerstone of the psychoanalytic method, the reasons for their importance seem not to have been significantly updated since the cathartic method and Freud's first theory of anxiety. The revisions and explanations offered have been geared more toward clinical understanding than a theory of the mind. In some sense, we only have a clinical theory of reconstruction, i.e., how it helps the patient in psychoanalysis, but we have no meta-theory for what happens that makes this useful. Blum, who has written most convincingly on the importance of reconstruction, states the following,

> Without reconstruction, psychoanalysis tends to become a-historic, dissociated from the infantile unconscious, and the context and shaping of life experience. Reconstruction restores the continuity and cohesion of personal history, correcting personal myths while simultaneously fostering greater and more realistic self-awareness, knowledge, and insight. Spanning life experience, reconstruction integrates past and present, fantasy and reality, cause and effect.
>
> (Blum, 2005, p. 309)

While as a clinician all of the above makes sense, I think we also have to be clearer as to *why historical constructions lead to changes in the mind, and how this is beneficial to patients.* To do this let's first take a schematic look at what leads patients to our offices. As noted earlier, functioning dominated by the unconscious is a "doing" type of thinking, leading to the idea that the unconscious is made up of *action representations* that have a magnetic pull. Clinically we see this magnetic pull daily in our offices where for a patient every lover becomes the same unsatisfying loser, every authority figure is the same outrageous dictator, and in the patient's mind we become whoever the patient needs us to be.

Psychoanalytically we understand this magnetic pull as serving multiple functions for the individual's pleasure and survival. We also can understand this activation level as due to the experience of cumulative trauma leading to certain fantasies and defenses, resulting in constant vigilance throughout life for similar situations, along with the ongoing pressure from unconscious fantasy and gratification. The pleasure, pain, and/or guilt, and/or fear keeps these attractors out of consciousness, while they continue to maintain their strong pull on how the individual experiences psychological events.

In psychoanalysis every insight becomes the basis for a more complex structure. Thus rather than the immediate stimulus–response equation "male equals competitor," there are multiple links with males, previously unconscious, that have been represented throughout the course of an analysis. Over time, the representation "male" becomes more complex. It helps explain why single insights are never particularly helpful and why psychoanalysis takes a long time. We are constantly building up more complex systems until the patient reaches a critical point, where the *inevitability of action has been replaced by the possibility of reflection.*

Historical constructions are one important component of transforming simple structures into more complex ones. For example, as we help the patient to allow in more thoughts and feelings, the equation "authority figure equals mean father" becomes modified. As the patient can allow in thoughts on how mean he was to his younger brother, and elaborate on them, we can begin to see how his split-off identification with his father now projected on to other men plays an important role in seeing them as mean. Further, as we learn how silently rivalrous the patient is with the analyst, we can help construct how furious the patient must have been when his father came home from business trips and dominated the mother's time. Also, as the patient can expand, even in displacement, his love of the analyst, cherished times with the father are remembered as interrupted by his narcissistic mother. In this way, historical constructions change structures from hundreds of simplified stimulus–response enacted reactions, to more complex structures made up of mental representations leading to the capacity for myriad nuanced reactions. To say it once again: what has occurred is the *inevitability of action has been replaced by the possibility of reflection.* I believe this is what Freud (1933) was suggesting when he stated the goals of treatment as "Where id was, ego shall be," and what Bion (1962) captured in his conceptualization of changing *beta* elements into *alpha* elements.

Notes

1 As stated by Freud, "we must treat his illness not as an event of the past, but as a present-day force" (Freud, 1914, p. 151). Also, his much quoted view, "For when all is said and done, it is impossible to destroy anyone in 'absentia or in effigy'" (Freud, 1912a, p. 108).

2 Fonagy and Target's work (1996, 2000) on mentallization and mindfulness touches similar concerns.

3 I will not get into the interesting debate of whether we construct or reconstruct the past, or whether we are describing narrative or historical truth. I am more interested here with how interpretations of the past lead to significant changes in the mind as part of a psychoanalytic cure.

Part II

CLINICAL METHODS

7

FREE ASSOCIATION

The Little People came suddenly. I don't know who they are. I don't know
what it means. I was a prisoner of the story. I had no choice. They came,
and I described it. That is my work.
(Haruki Murakami, author. From an interview with Murakami in
"The Fierce Imagination of Haruki Murakami," by Sam Anderson,
New York Times Magazine, October 21, 2011)

Murakami's description of his thought process in writing *1Q84* describes well
what happens in the creative freedom of free associations. This capability
can develop over the course of analysis when certain conditions are present.
Not always, but often. As Donnet (2001) has put it, "Thus in accordance with
the project of an analytic cure, the method consists in carefully creating the
conditions in which free association proves to be practicable, interpretable and
beneficial" (p. 129). The freedom for free association is central to creating a
psychoanalytic mind.

My basic assumption in using the psychoanalytic method is that all we need to
know can be found in the patient's use of the method of free association. In the
patient's use of the method of free association we can see how unknown thoughts
guide her, inhibit her, and destroy her. We can also come to understand the process
by which patients guide, inhibit, and destroy their thoughts. Thus we can learn
how effective our methods are (or are not) in increasing the freedom of mind to
say or not to say thoughts that are coming to mind. Sometimes thoughts are told
in words, sometimes in the absence of words. Sometimes they are more like
actions, designed to have us love, hate, believe, or suspect the patient. All of this
comes in an order and sequence we cannot ask about because it follows the
individual fabric of the patient's preconscious or unconscious mind.

I would suggest then, *in one form or another*, everything that happens in an
analytic session is a free association. An evasion is never just an evasion, what
seems unrelated is never unrelated, what seems boring is never just boring. While
an obsessional patient may be droning on about a moment in his history that he's
gone over before, he is *communicating* something; for example, a resistance to

67

something in the present, an attempt to help us understand something in a different way, a transference reaction to some exciting thought, an attempt to make the analyst feel something, and so forth. In broad-brush strokes, the analysand is always *communicating* or *doing*[1] something. Free association is not something the patient is supposed to do, but *what they are doing*. Kris (1982) stated it most succinctly when he said: "Psychoanalysis does not create free association in the treatment setting. It merely provides an alteration in the condition of ordinary association. . . . It replaces silent soliloquy with spoken words" (p. 14).

To put it in another form, in free association we find:

1   The patient's preconscious communications of unconscious derivatives.
2   The patient's interruptions of preconscious communications as a sign of resistances.
3   The patient's use of words as actions, unconsciously designed to make something happen.

Associations as communications and actions

While I have given various examples of how I see the method of free association working within a psychoanalysis throughout the book, I will present a vignette that shows the shifting use of free association as a series *of preconscious associations and as an action (i.e., language action)*. While more severely disturbed patients or patients in a regressive phase communicate almost exclusively in language action, more neurotic patients reveal themselves in a mixture of associations as preconscious communications and action language.

Milton

Milton was at a phase in the analysis where, in his associations, he would express rivalry with me, while his feelings remained split off. His ability to express these thoughts was an important development in treatment, as previously Milton could only be aware of idealizing me in the abstract, while ignoring me in the present.

In the session to be explored, Milton began by saying that he frequently had a thought while coming into the driveway that I really had the perfect set-up here. He went on to say that there was room for patients to easily park, a separate entrance for patients, a waiting room, and an office. He also described how much he liked the modern architecture, and the interesting paintings on the wall. Milton's capacity to acknowledge *anything* having to do with me was a new development (e.g., vacations were treated as non-events). Milton continued by saying how "lucky" I was to have found this place, which was so perfect. His thoughts then went to various universities in the area, and how they provide housing for some faculty (my office is in a separate part of my home). He wondered if psychoanalytic institutes did the same thing, i.e., buy houses that would fit an analytic practice, and then rent them to their members. His thoughts then went to how "lucky" he was to have found an analyst who was so convenient to both his work and home.

While appreciating Milton's new-found capacity to "look" around, and say something about it,[2] I understood his associations in the following manner. His admiration for the surroundings was tempered by his presenting it as "lucky" that I was able to find such a place. I sensed there was a denigrating quality to my being "lucky," rather than skilled or determined to find a good place to live and work. Further, the idea that I might have changed anything to make it good was not part of his thinking. I saw Milton further retreat from the idea that I had anything to do with this ideal set-up, by thinking of it as an Institute-found and owned building. As Milton continued to associate it turned out that I wasn't even "lucky" to find this house-office, rather he was the "lucky" one to find it.

I see this sequence as typical of preconscious associations that, in spite of ongoing resistances, are meant as a communication to the analyst. These associations are like stories. Once one is attuned to the underlying message they have a logical flow. However, I had the sense that if I interpreted this sequence it would be "understood" by Milton, but not integrated in an emotionally meaningful way. That is, he had brought in similar associations previously, and even after many interpretations Milton seemed to not be able to stand aside and observe his own dismissive or competitive thoughts. While I could see this as a resistance that still needed working through, I had a sense (more than any concrete understanding) that there was more going on, so I waited.[3]

Milton's thoughts drifted to a situation where he was talking to a younger colleague about his work. He then mentioned that another colleague was sitting in and listening to this conversation.

This seemed unusual to me as the nature of what he and his younger colleague were discussing had some personal details involved. Thinking of myself as the onlooker while he talks of personal issues, I was reminded of Milton recently remembering a feeling of intense fear he had while walking past his parents' bedroom door. Was this what was being enacted in the session via language action, i.e., his thoughts were there for me to listen to and be curious about, while I remained an outsider watching something I shouldn't be watching?

He was about to tell me what he said to this younger colleague, and then said he was hesitant because he imagined I would criticize him for this remark, as he had imagined with the other colleague in the room. This was puzzling to him, as what he said was very mild. He went on to tell me what he said, which seemed quite neutral, and then continued with many other thoughts that had come to his mind during different parts of the day.

I found myself a bit overwhelmed by all these stories, and wondered if this was the point. I then said that I had the sense that this was one of these times where having me just listen to his thoughts was uppermost in his mind,[4] but after a while it seemed a bit much. In this, I was trying to clarify the language action via my countertransference reaction of the overwhelmed listener.

69

Milton affirmed that he noticed how many stories he was telling, but like so many times before he wanted to tell me all the thoughts he had first. He thought he would return to this moment, but history showed this was unlikely. Milton felt we were on to something, as he realized there was something uncomfortable about his colleague being in the room listening. He wanted it, but felt there was something not quite right about it. His thoughts then went to a conference he attended recently, where after listening to a paper by a graduate student he made ten points that she should consider. He felt all of them were important, but wondered whether it was too much for this graduate student to take in. She seemed overwhelmed after he finished talking. He was reminded of an earlier time when another graduate student complained to him about how she saw his remarks as overly detailed.

After clarification of what I thought he was "doing" with his use of language action, Milton returned to a series of preconscious associations that confirmed the clarification. This led me to be able to interpret a bit deeper what was occurring in his use of language action.

F.B.:   I think the same thing may be happening today when you continue with story after story, eventually blurring why it was important to continue your stories.

It was the end of the session, but Milton mentioned before he left that he realized he was having a hard time listening to me.

I see this session as typical of the work with neurotic patients in a fully engaged treatment. Milton's associations range between preconscious communications and action language. As he begins to be able to "look" around he finds it difficult to imagine my "ideal" situation is anything but temporary (i.e., renting from the Institute). For him, what is ideal is who's in the parental bedroom and who's outside. This latter part can only be expressed in language action. As Freud (1914) noted, at these times the patient cannot remember, but can only act it out. So like Milton's colleague, I am on the outside listening to these private and confusing sounds from the parental bedroom. Once I can begin to represent what is enacted, Milton can return to verbal associations as preconscious communications, which confirm and give depth to the interpretations. We then see the projection at the end of the session where Milton has difficulty listening to me.

An interim summary

In short, I take the position that everything we need to help our patients can be learned by listening to what is coming to the patient's mind in its polyphonic complexity. In the analysand's preconscious associations, resistances to associations, dreams or lack thereof, the words meant to protect the patient, or make us feel what the patient can't, in our countertransference reactions to all of the above, etc., we learn why our patients came to us, why they do and don't want to change, why they want to stop or never end analysis. As in the case of Milton, it isn't only the words that we hear, but the music that accompanies the words, which gives the words subtle and changing shapes. One patient begins each session by asking, "How are you?" which leads us to answer in a reassuring way to help her feel the analyst is in a stable, secure state. Another patient asks this same question and we feel intruded upon. One patient remembering a dream in the middle of a session can lead us to sense a new found capacity for the freedom to associate, while with another patient we may anticipate an interruption of a dangerous thought. At the same time we also strive to be with the patient in their emotional readiness to hear us. We may think we hear an unconscious fantasy in the patient's associations, but there are many questions we have to go through before saying something. These are not obsessively brooded upon, but should be part of our preconscious thinking. Is the patient in a state where she can hear this fantasy elaborated? Can we find the words or metaphor to express our thinking in an empathic manner? Can the patient use a metaphor or is her thinking too concrete? The list goes on.

In our attentive listening we convey to the patient, although not in these words, "If we listen carefully to what is coming to your mind . . ." so that analysis is about noticing what one's mind is doing. When the patient suddenly falls silent, it is the difference between asking the patient, "What are you thinking?" and appreciating that, for some reason it has been threatening for the patient to continue, respecting the threat, while helping the patient understand that something just happened in their mind that interfered with their freedom to think.

In spite of the extraordinary power of the patient's use of the method of free association, I find us too ready to interrupt, or prematurely interpret free associations. I have previously described some factors that account for this (Busch, 1994), but in my own experience and in listening to the work of others, I place high on the list the demands that free association makes on the analyst's psychic functioning. Unconsciously experiencing and trying to contain the patient's projections and projective identifications can give rise to sometimes unbearable tension; this may be experienced by the analyst as an attack on his internal structures, and often leads us to *act* in a desperate attempt to stabilize our psychic equilibrium. We are always dealing with the fact that we are more or less vulnerable, based on our moment-to-moment needs to protect ourselves, and our "capacities to tolerate helplessness, uncertainty, culpability, or affective closeness" (Schwaber, 1990, pp. 31–32). It seems to me that often it is the need to stabilize ourselves that leads us to withdraw from listening, or start asking questions, or interfere with the patient's associations in multiple ways. In all of these ways we attempt to feel more in control again.

71

Interferences in free association

After listening to hundreds of clinical presentations over the years, my impression is that we aren't very good at listening to the patient's associations. We are:

1   Too eager to be active, and thus derail the analysand's associations before she has a chance to begin;
2   Too ready to listen for the story we think the analysand should be telling, and thus miss the story she is telling;
3   Often we listen for the story that isn't told, rather than the one that is.

Below I will present two typical ways of listening and working that *bypass* the patient's use of the method of free association. We have all engaged in one or more of these practices at some point, and it is only to remind us of the potential interferences that I raise them.

The interpersonal approach

Working within the Sullivanian interpersonal model, Levenson (1987, 1988, 1992, 2000) presents a view of psychoanalysis where he is an active interlocutor in the analytic process. At the center of Levenson's method of working is the "directed inquiry," which involves the *analyst's active questioning of the patient in order to deconstruct his story.* At times he sees it as equivalent to free association and at times leading to free association.

The directed inquiry is embedded in Levenson's view that it is the process itself, not the meaning one derives from it, that is the curative process. As he's stated,

> If you think therapeutic effectiveness depends on getting across some sense of understanding, then I think you really are involved with persuasion; you're laying on the patient a particular conceptual set about what matters. I've always said that there's a commonly held praxis of therapy. There's something all therapists do and essentially I think it is to get involved in a *deconstruction of the patient's narrative.* Whenever the patient tells you the story of his or her life, you either expand it by free association or by a detailed inquiry. In the process of working through, I think the patient is getting better, not because your metapsychology works, but because somewhere in that process you're doing a real *deconstructive inquiry.* The detailed inquiry isn't intended to make it all clearer, but to open things up: to unpack the story in such a way that it gets more complicated and more enriched and more interesting, clinically.
>
> (Levenson et al., 2005, p. 598)

In other words it reorganizes their perception of things. It isn't a linear process wherein exclusively or even largely, you and the patient are talking about something and getting it clear, but rather that you're operating to keep unpacking or opening the inquiry in such a way that the patient's formulations are loosened and opened up, and then the patient does something with it, which you have no direct connection to.

(p. 599)

In some ways Levenson's views are similar to my own, in that we both believe *the process of knowing* is a central curative factor. However, I see his fundamental position as an *interference with the method of free association*. Further, Levenson tends to eschew insight while, as mentioned earlier, I see it as essential for the analysis to establish the conditions where insight is possible. Levenson (1992) believes the asking of questions is something all analysts have in common, and views the directed inquiry as a powerful facilitator of free association. He has also described the directed inquiry as a way "to deconstruct the patient's iconic myths, the prepackaged version of his or her life. The stories tend to fall apart as inquiry proceeds. In this sense, inquiry operates much like free association" (Levenson, 2000, p. 119).

Levenson (1988) believes the asking of questions is something all analysts have in common:

It is my contention that the impulse of the analytic process emerges from just this forcing of data; i.e., the deconstruction of the patient's prepared text, the clinical material, rather than the analyst's explanation of the plethora of data which emerges.

(p. 5)

As a prototypical example of his method, Levenson frequently (1987, 1988) uses a session from Silverman (1987), where his female patient has a fantasy that a mad scientist and his nurse tie her down to give her bigger breasts. She wants bigger breasts, but still feels like a slave to the doctor.

Using the Jewish mystical movement, Kabbalism, as a stand-in for his method of deconstruction, Levenson suggests the analyst might ask the following questions:

How mean is the mad scientist if he is giving her what she wants, big breasts? What's so marvelous about big breasts, anyhow? Why breasts, not legs or behind? How will that change her world? Does she believe that men will then be interested in her? Does she want interest, especially on those terms? Does her mother have big breasts? What will the mad scientist actually do? Will it hurt? Just what *is* the fantasy?

(1988, pp. 10–11)

And the questions keep coming.

While it's possible to see the value of the data Levenson may get from his "directed inquiry," and it is theoretically consistent within his general view of the curative process, the main problem I see with is that *it is at the cost of interfering with the patient's narrative as seen in her associations* and bypassing resistances. Rather than analyzing the reasons for a patient talking in a vague, elliptical or halting manner, Levenson presses the patient to clarify the lack of specifics in her thinking, while it just might be this lack of specifics that is the point.

In Levenson's method of working, the resistances that develop in the course of the analysand's associations, and especially the fears that motivate them, do not seem to be analyzed. If an *unconscious* fear is at the basis of a resistance, what does it do to the patient to be directed to talk about what is resisted, except to submit to the analyst's authority? There is by now general agreement that we help to free a mind closed upon itself by fears, via analyzing resistances, *not overcoming them*.

In short, while Levenson sometimes presents the "directed inquiry" as leading to free association (2000), at other times he equates it with free association. Yet, I would see it as the *antithesis of free association*. While the basis of the method of free association is for the patient to allow his mind to roam as freely as possible, the "directed inquiry" is designed to reflect on *the analyst's inquiries*.

Theory driven interpretations

The Kleinians' readiness to interpret the unconscious transference seems to be another way of derailing the process of free association. It appears, at times, as if they more or less scan the patient's associations for particular references to the unconscious transference, interpreting it as if it were preconscious, and ignore the rest of the analysand's associations.

Below is an example of this approach from Bott-Spillius (1994).

Picking up in the middle of a session the week before the analyst's vacation, the patient mentioned being pleased to have found a nice cleaning woman. The analyst said, "The good cleaning woman was perhaps a substitute for the bad analyst, who wasn't going to be cleaning her up during the holiday" (p. 1123). The patient then described redecorating her loo (bathroom), and described in detail her plan to buy a mahogany seat.

The analyst said, "The loo here does not have a mahogany seat. But there is one room here in which there is a lot of mahogany."

"Oh," she said, "You mean here in this room." She looked carefully around the room. "Yes," she said. "This room is full of mahogany."

The analyst then said, "When you stress that your loo seat is to be made of mahogany, it's as if you are shifting the mahogany from the consulting room into the loo."

"Oh," she said.
The analyst reports feeling like

> I was spelling things out to an interested but rather bewildered child. Was she really so unaware of what she was saying, I wondered to myself, or had I confronted her too brusquely? It was one of the few occasions up to this time that I was aware of the "obliviousness" that she said other people sometimes complained of.

> "And so," I went on, "You are putting the consulting room into the loo, flushing me and your analysis away. I'm the much-valued cleaner, but when it's the last week of our sessions, I'm flushed away. It's not a case of my leaving you; it's a case of your flushing me away."

(pp. 1123–1124)

In this example, every utterance of the patient is perused for its symbolic, unconscious transference implication. The main problem is that the analyst then interprets to the patient as if these potential symbols of the transference were the same as conscious references to the treating analyst. There seems to be less attention to the readiness of the patient to hear and understand the analyst's interpretation of the possible symbolic meaning of what she (the patient) may be saying about the treatment, or allowing the patient to elaborate what she may be able to let come to mind. The analyst's ability to read the symbols becomes confused with the patient's ability to understand these readings. This paves the way for the patient to seem like a bewildered child. It is striking that even after the analyst senses that the patient does not understand, she continues to interpret deeply. Instead of waiting for the associations to emerge, or not, the analyst forges ahead based upon the Kleinian theory that the patient's associations are most often attempting to *do something* to the analyst's mind (Blass, 2011). Thus, from this perspective, *the analyst is always looking for what is hidden in the associations according to a particular theory*. It is a different view of free association in that they are used by the Kleinian analyst to search for symbolic references to the transference, *rather than wait for the unwitting connections of the preconscious* that might relate to the transference or not (e.g., intrapsychic conflict). Staying with another aspect of the Kleinian perspective, Betty Joseph's way of working is especially attuned to the use of the patient's associations as actions, but its meaning is again, often narrowed to the transference.

In a remarkable article, Nina Searl (1936), an English analyst who broke away from the Kleinians, and then was hounded by them (Busch, 1995c), succinctly stated what the problem is with many ways of working that focus on giving insight rather than freeing the mind for the development of what Sugarman (2006) called, "insightfulness."

- "that which is important is not the extent to which we may be able to impart to the patient our knowledge of his life and psyche, but it is *the extent to which we can clear the patient's own way to it and give him freedom of access to his own mind*" (Searl, 1936, p. 487, italics added).

- "I believe that only when one abandons the attempt to deal directly with absent content and with truly unconscious material – or at least when one tries to do so – does one become aware of the wider possibilities of analytical work which lie hidden in the conscious and pre-conscious material – the regrouping, the re-arrangement of it, the dissolving of compulsive fusions, the tracing of hidden links, unsuspected connections, etc. This work of putting things in the places to which they belong, making true wholes and separating false ones, can be more effectively carried out, I believe, if the analyst keeps his own work in the place to which the patient allows that it belongs – voluntarily expressed material. It can hardly be necessary to say that one does not abandon one's knowledge of the 'true unconscious' because one makes no attempt to apply it directly. All that is in question is the best way in which the patient himself may reach such knowledge" (Searl, 1936, p. 484).

In fact, if we allow it, patients tell us their stories in their use of the method of free association. We don't have to go search for them. However, in our way of working to *create a psychoanalytic mind* we try to demonstrate that in their words and actions, in their negations, denials, and intellectualizations, in the telling (or not) of their dreams, in the expression (or not) of their intense feelings – in short, in all the multitudinous forms of expression available – patients tell us their stories. In these stories we find the why of our patients' coming to us, and the roads by which they leave us. In between they tell us stories about why they shouldn't tell us stories, and vehemently deny that there are any stories to be told. Sometimes patients are happy to have us hear and understand their stories, but will be uncomfortable owning them. Sometimes they can only tell their stories by this unique form of action, language action. And at some point we become part of their stories.

There is nothing more inhibiting to creating a psychoanalytic mind than for patient and analyst to believe they have discovered *the* patient's story. While psychoanalysis helps identify key stories that have inhibited the patient's life trajectory, the very fact of this identification should enable a deepening understanding and a readiness to understand old stories in newly configured forms, and the freedom to identify new stories.

Patients come to us because they are inhibited from living out their own stories. They live out somebody else's story instead, or they are afraid to see the story they're living out, or they cannot bear the consequences of the story they've constructed. They feel the pain of an unlived life, and they want to know whose life they've been leading and how they can learn to lead their own. The goal of analysis is to help patients discover the stories they've been living, and in this way find the stories they choose to live. Authorship of one's story is a crucial component in the "good-enough" analysis. While other people may play a significant role in the formation and continuation of our patients' stories, analytic progress toward well-being occurs only when authorship is accepted of the stories that emerge in the analytic process, and of their formation, continuation, and results.

Notes

1 As Freud (1914) stated, what the patient cannot say is acted out. For example, the patient tries to: create a more cohesive self; to enact an object relationship; or have the analyst feel split-off feelings.

2 Having a home office, one cannot avoid the occasional electrician or carpenter coming to fix something. Many patients fantasize about what's happening. Milton never mentioned anything. Over time we discovered his intense curiosity about what was going on, but felt he shouldn't look. It was only recently that Milton remembered sleeping in the bedroom next to his parents. At a certain point in his life he was terrified whenever he passed the parental bedroom.

3 This is one of those occasions when, out of awareness, one's preconscious appreciation for something going on is invaluable in understanding. However, it isn't without its countertransference problems when used as an unerring guide to the treatment. This will be discussed later in the chapter on countertransference.

4 Over time we came to realize that, at times, Milton was talking more to have me listen rather than to listen to himself.

8

WHY DO WE ASK QUESTIONS?

(Part b of 'Free association')

It is a daunting task to sit with a patient with a complex symptomatology, and a history of suffering. We want to help. We want to understand. Nothing seems more natural than, with respect and caution, to ask questions. This technique is often called *exploration*, and seems to occupy an increasingly common role in some psychoanalytic cultures. So it may not seem so obvious why it might be useful *to question asking questions*. Further, there was a time when analysts were trained under a doctrine that prohibited asking any questions at all. Having modified these apodictic restrictions we welcome the greater freedom of thinking that appreciates an occasional question. However, as so often happens, the pendulum seems to have swung so far that asking questions seems to have become a standard intervention.[1] So it seems worth wondering what we are doing – and what we are avoiding for that matter – when we ask our patient a question.

The reason I raise this issue here is that questions often work *against the method of free association, and derail the psychoanalytic process in ways that I will show in this chapter*. My basic position is: *There is no such thing as a good or a bad question; there are only questions that further or interfere with the psychoanalytic process*.

In fact, rarely has a method been so widely used, with so little written about it. Over 50 years ago Olinick (1954) observed, "Of the technical interventions available to the psychoanalyst, perhaps none has been more taken for granted and less subjected to careful scrutiny than has questioning" (p. 57). Over the next 35 years this astute observation resulted in little more on the topic. In 1989 Boesky came to the same conclusion as Olinick, noting,

> The questions the psychoanalyst chooses to ask the patient are an important but neglected aspect of the psychoanalytic dialogue. Our failure to date to give an adequate theoretical accounting of these questions represents a discontinuity between daily practice and general theory.
>
> (p. 579)

Now, some 20 years later, questions remain a favored technique with, to this observer's ear, the same discontinuity noted by Boesky. That is, *we ask far too many questions, based upon far too few reasons and we still have no well thought out psychoanalytic theory of asking questions.* Further, embedded in the increasing use of questions are shifts in the psychoanalytic model of the mind, the psychoanalytic method, and the role of the analyst's way of being in the curative process that are deserving of discussion. These include: a shift away from the method of free association; a focus on the analyst ferreting out distortions via reality; an over-emphasis on what may mistakenly be identified as empathic attunement with the patient, and so forth.

This situation seems to be based on a misunderstanding and a decreasing experience of the power of free association. One aspect of this is what Hoffer (2004) noted, i.e., that contemporary critics question the extent to which 'free association' is 'free' rather than subject to the 'demand' of the analyst. Ogden (1996) expresses the concern that free association can be a demand that exhorts the patient to speak, thus promoting a non-analytic process in which the patient is not free to be silent or to have a private reverie. These are valid concerns, but to use free association in this way would certainly be a misunderstanding. In my understanding of the method, silence or reverie is as important to the process as what is spoken. In fact, it is a *question that interrupts silence or reverie, and makes a demand on the patient to speak.* The frequently heard question in the midst of silence, "What are you thinking?" exhorts the analysand to say something. It is my impression that the more free association is viewed as essential to the process, the fewer questions are asked.

Frequent questions

Below I discuss some of the questions we frequently hear analysts ask. Some acceptable conscious reasons for asking these questions seem to be: to stimulate the patient's thinking; because the analyst is curious about something that seems left out; to not be stilted in one's listening; as a sign of the analyst's involvement with the patient; and to help a patient out of a defensive position. In general I find that these *frequent* questions have the effect of interfering with the psychoanalytic process. Thus, while questions usually intend to further the psychoanalytic process they might on the contrary interfere with the development of psychoanalytic thinking. This perspective is pointedly captured by what Balint is alleged to have said: "*The problem with asking questions is that you get answers*" – thus beautifully highlighting the potential pitfalls of asking questions. While the analyst may be trying to stimulate curiosity about the unknown, my experience is that questions most often bring to the fore what is already known.

How did that feel?

Asking our patients how something feels suggests they can find out what they need to know by questioning themselves, rather than seeing what comes to mind. It conveys to a patient that we want her to be interested in *this* question, rather than allowing her the right to be interested or not interested, as they wish, and analyzing this. It bypasses the premise that if the patient isn't interested in pursuing a feeling, the best way to help them is to understand their lack of interest rather than the avoided content. Thus, by asking this question we frequently bypass important resistances, thus not appreciating the patient's need for resistances and the underlying fears that motivate them. We deprive the patient of the liberating quality that analyzing resistances has on the patient's capacity to think and feel. Further, we may wonder why we are so interested in the patient's feelings when he is not. Is this an enactment of some not-understood dynamic?

The question, "How did that feel?" most often comes up when we expect the patient to have a feeling, but they don't say anything about it. For example, a patient begins the session by saying "I went to dinner at my parents home on Sunday. When I arrived my father and the dog greeted me, but my mother stayed in the kitchen." This led the analyst to ask, "How did that feel?"

There are a number of problems with this question at this point. First of all, we don't give the patient the chance to tell us, in the way she needs to, whatever she is going to tell or *not* tell us about this thought. However, if we listen carefully to what is on the patient's mind, or not on her mind, we will probably understand more about "how that felt" at a deeper level than any answer could have told us. If the patient goes no further we may also learn why the patient didn't want to explore her feelings at that moment, a necessary step before further exploration takes place. For example, if the patient goes on to tell a story about a friend ignoring her and how irritated she was, we might point out the association as a reflection of the patient's discomfort in directly feeling angry with her mother. If it was early in the treatment and the patient's associations led to the enjoyable parties she went to over the weekend, we might not say anything, as the need to keep her feelings about her mother split off might be too strong right now. Or the patient might expand on these enjoyable parties by describing how various men were attracted to her, which she responded to by giving them the cold shoulder. Whether we make a connection to her mother's behavior with her and what we might say, depends much on the stage of treatment. By asking a question we ignore the importance of the patient's use of the method of free association in guiding us to how best to understand and help the patient.

How do you understand that?

This question takes various forms, such as, "How do you understand why you thought/felt/did that?" The basis of analysis is that most of what is important to know about is unconscious. By asking this question we give the patient the impression that if he asks the right questions, and thinks really hard about some-thing, he will find the answer to what is troubling him. This question, like many others, merely *turns the mind to what is already known, while in psychoanalysis we are looking to make known what was previously unknown.* In short, such ques-tions often call for an answer already consciously available, rather than leaving an empty space for the patient to search for ways to communicate what is emerging into the preconscious and is *potentially representable*. Questions frequently stimulate concrete, rational thinking, whereas analysis attempts to stimulate associative, playful, creative, even irrational thinking.

In the latter stages of analysis this question may lead to a series of associations, but there are still various problems with it. Such a question suggests the patient has some understanding of the issues at stake, but bypasses the issue of why the patient may not be reflecting on his thoughts. This is an important component of every analysis. We are all familiar with the patient who associates freely, but who is reluctant to reflect upon his associations.

Can you tell me more?

In the middle of a session a patient says, "I'm frustrated," and after a brief silence the analyst asks, "Can you tell me more?", which the patient might do. However, how do we know the silence isn't the most important part of the moment? Does the patient wish to frustrate us as well? Is the patient blaming us for his frustration, or expecting us to do something? Is the patient attempting to suppress the feeling? Is he attempting to stay with the feeling, recognizing the wish to undo it? Is he in a reverie in association to this feeling? Is the silence dark, demanding, brooding or blank? There can be so much in the patient saying, "I'm frustrated," and then falling silent. By asking the question we disrupt the patient's spontaneous reaction to this statement and silence, which is our main way to gain understanding. Further, by rushing in with a question we may convey our own difficulty in tolerating an uncomfortable feeling. Asking the patient to tell us more bypasses what the patient spontaneously does in reaction to this feeling, which is the most meaningful to the understanding of the patient. Further, we also convey our own comfort with uncomfortable feelings if we can sit in silence waiting for the patient to struggle with what is best for him to do at this moment.

Questions like this are sometimes presented *as a way of filling in the gaps* in the patient's narrative (Aron, 1993, p. 303), but often seem to become a form of interrogation, reminiscent of the old police movies where the accused, with a bright light in his face, is asked, "Where were you on the night of . . .?" From my perspective, *gaps are what is happening in the analysis, not something to be filled in*. Gaps can be, amongst many possibilities, an attempt to leave the analyst confused for a variety of reasons; an attack on linking (Bion, 1962); an unconscious mimicking of the analyst's vagueness; a defense against specific content; a sign of a thought disorder. Gaps are interesting as such; they are the openings that leave room for something yet unknown to emerge

Unsaturated questions

There are certain questions that are an invitation to reflect rather than give an answer. I call these questions *unsaturated*, borrowing from Ferro's (2002a)

concept of unsaturated interpretations, which he describes as not directed toward any particular content, dynamic, or part of the mind.[2] Unsaturated questions can be characterized as basically saying, "I noticed something. Can you notice it too?" It is an attempt to bring new connections to the patient's mind, *without suggesting any direction the patient should take*. It may lead to playful musing, diversionary obfuscation, or multiple other responses. Further, the question is phrased in a way that fosters the creation of *a psychoanalytic mind*, rather than searching for answers.

Asking an unsaturated question might occur when a patient is talking, and there is a noticeable change in affect that goes unmentioned. At some point one might say, "I wonder if you noticed that after talking in an interested, upbeat manner, you seemed to become more somber?" In this phrasing I first raise the issue of the patient noticing. If he hasn't noticed I assume that for defensive reasons he couldn't register what was happening, even retrospectively, and therefore there is little point in following this line at this time. If the patient can notice, I leave it up to him which part, if any, he is able to think about. This is the "unsaturated" part. It allows the patient's mind to roam in any direction it chooses, and in this way help us understand what is most preconsciously available for elaboration.

Most of what I call "unsaturated questions" are phrased in the manner above, with variants on "I wonder" such as "I noticed that . . .", or "I think I'm noticing something here . . ." As one can see, I'm not stating something to be true, or validating its correctness. I am wondering with the patient as to whether we can observe the same phenomenon, and allowing the patient to muse on wherever his mind takes him.

Unsaturated questions serve another important purpose in a sometimes-overlooked component of the psychoanalytic method, i.e., *the importance of the readiness of the patient to share in the analyst's observation before interpreting the meaning of the observation. We have not always carefully distinguished between the phenomenon we observe, and the interpretation of the phenomenon.* A not uncommon sequence in a session might go like this. Two weeks before a vacation break, the patient is complaining about a friend who didn't show up for dinner, and other people who disappointed him by not being there for him. The analyst then says, "I think my vacation is on your mind, and how disappointed you are that we won't be meeting." Working in this manner, the patient is supposed to understand the displacement, and make the link between what he's said and the analyst's interpretation. This is a capacity that develops only very gradually over the course of the treatment. On the other hand, if it was so easily made clear to the patient, why wouldn't he just say it? Further, as noted earlier, our patients' thinking is very concrete throughout major parts of the treatment, leading them to not be able to follow a line of thinking as they are talking. Their thoughts are more like discrete entities. Therefore, as a beginning to explore the meaning of an observation, we need shared agreement on what is being explored. This is not necessarily a conscious process, nor does it mean that the patient has to verbally agree to our observation. Mostly we see a shared meaning in the nature of the associations that follow.

A different perspective

Stern (1992) presents a different view of questions. He believes the analyst is *always* searching for the good question, and that several questions are common in most sessions. He sees this as one way the analyst opens up new areas of inquiry for the patient. In this view he is following Levenson's "detailed inquiry." As noted earlier, in this method, which Levenson sees as equivalent to the method of free association, there is a deconstruction of the patient's prepared text in order to get at what is most anxiety provoking and repressed.

In an example presented by Stern, a supervisee reports a session where a patient tells a dream. In the dream the supervisee enters the bathroom and sees what the patient describes as his small penis, leaving the patient feeling embarrassed. The supervisee asks the patient why he feels embarrassed, to which the patient replies it seems obvious, and the supervisee eventually agrees. The inquiry leads nowhere. With this specific question Stern sees a countertransference enactment,[3] while later characterizing the question as "perfectly good" (p. 329). From my perspective I would see the question as interfering with the patient's readiness to explore the dream, or not. We cannot know *a priori* what part of the dream is most available to the patient, both in terms of his own mind and the analyst's interest. If the patient is silent after telling a dream, is the silence a time for reflection, or an invitation for the analyst to intrude, as in the dream? If the patient explores the dream, but leaves out his embarrassment, would we want to inquire about it? The "good enough" question Stern comes up with seems to come from his view of the position of the analyst as deconstructionist of the patient's narrative.

Stern reveals that he knows the bathroom in the clinic where the dream supposedly takes place (a bit of good luck), and that the supervisee couldn't possibly see the patient's penis when entering the bathroom. This leads to some inquiry, which leads to the patient's admission that he was sitting down when the supervisee entered the bathroom. Stern acknowledges that this may have come out in the patient's free association, but suggests that many patients are not "so psychologically minded nor so analytically sophisticated" (p. 329). However, I would say that free associations are not based upon psychological-mindedness or analytic sophistication, but rather *the patient's preconscious readiness to explore and the degree of unconscious defensiveness that exists*. Clearing the way for new possibilities via defense analysis puts the *patient* at the center of the analysis. As far as I can tell, deconstructing the patient's reality puts the *analyst* at the center of the analysis as a kind of psychoanalytic detective. Finally, this method harkens back to Freud's topographic model and first theory of anxiety that postulated it was the uncovering of what was most unconscious that reduced anxiety.

Questions and a shift in psychoanalytic technique in the USA

Embedded in the increased use of questions are various changes in the psycho-analytic method, along with changes in the analyst's way of being in the analysis, from how psychoanalysis was practiced in the United States into the 1980s, and is practiced throughout the international community, most of whom have been influenced by French psychoanalysis and the Kleinians (especially the modern Kleinians). In these perspectives, reliance on the analysand's use of the method of free association is paramount. One rarely hears these analysts ask a question.

While the changes in technique brought about by the self-psychologists, the relational analysts, and object relations theorists, just to name a few, have brought about helpful additions to our work with patients, I will highlight their problematic nature in the asking of questions. I have already mentioned some these issues, for example confusing empathy with niceness.

Shifting the focus

1   Along with the shift away from the method of free association we see a shift in the locus of analysis from the patient's to the *analyst's* mind. That is, rather than seeing what the patient is capable of telling us or not, we direct the inquiry to what *we think is most important*. The patient is directed to think about the analyst's query. In general, I believe we need to try to help the patient to enter a world of his own, not unlike the mental state of daydreaming or what Ogden (2007) called a waking dream. It is difficult to do that if the analyst is too explicitly there. In fact, every time the analyst speaks he potentially brings the patient away from this world.

2   A second shift in focus is the emphasis on "reality" to ferret out contradictions in the patient's narrative. That is, rather than using what the patient is able to say as the data of analysis (and I include here words as action), the analyst searches for absent content by focusing on "reality." This way of working seems to contradict a basic premise of psychoanalysis, that if an analysand is hiding something in his mind, it is out of fears and anxieties, which are not to be taken lightly, and we cannot get to what is unconscious by directed attention.

3   *The fear of appearing authoritarian* – By asking questions we may want to avoid any appearance of knowing something the patient doesn't know, hence being authoritarian. So we ask our patients as if they were the best authority in their own cases. Of course it is well known that certain patients, like those labeled as thin-skinned narcissists by Rosenfeld (1987), are interpretation-phobic. Any interpretation from the analyst is experienced as an assault on a mirror fantasy, or as the analyst's attempt to lord it over the patient with his superior mind. With such patients an interpretation given in the form of a question, rather than an observation, is the only way a new idea might be considered. In this way the analyst's mind fades into the background, while

the patient's sense of agency is given preference. There are times in most treatments where such a method may be necessary. However, this doesn't explain the widespread use of this technique throughout many treatments. A typical example is when an analyst thinks his patient is afraid, embarrassed, or angry over a certain issue x, and rather than saying so asks his patient: "Could it be that you are afraid of (or angry or ashamed about) x?" In discussions about this method, it is my impression that this is seen as a new form of "neutrality," where (as with the narcissistic patient) the analyst doesn't want to appear to impose his point of view on the patient. The question is seen as being less "authoritarian" than an interpretation. The question of the analyst's authority has been a source of lively debate for some time. However, when the analyst is reluctant to use his own voice throughout the treatment, the analyst may well be avoiding showing he has a mind of his own that thinks independently (a sign of otherness, separateness and of being an object available to the patient). He deprives the patient of the experience of grappling with otherness. Kernberg (1996) pointed out that the analyst's excessive concern with the effects of authority on the patient can lead to a masochistic submission on the part of the analyst, and likely will inhibit exploration of the reasons for the patient's vulnerability. Tuch (2001) considers it an abdication of the analyst's responsibility. In short, while questions as interpretations may be a necessary and useful method for periods of time with certain narcissistic patients, as a primary method of interpretation they circumvent conflicts with the analyst as an "other," with his own mind and expertise, and show an excessive concern with the patient's vulnerability.

4   *The countertransference reaction* – We have our conscious reasons for asking questions, such as: the wish to explore; to show interest and empathy; and to give the patient something. At any one time all of these could be useful and necessary. However, we also know that in reaction to a patient's material, unconscious reasons may dominate our asking questions. These are responses to: feeling excluded; fear of the patient's hostile or erotic transference; feeling helpless in the face of not knowing, and the myriad projections we experience in analysis. *Thus the potential question in our mind might, at times, be best thought of as a useful guide to an important unconscious transference–countertransference* understanding. Strachey's (1934) view of questions as an attempt to reduce anxiety still seems apt.

Clinical vignette

In this session we again see Milton (from the last chapter) enacting a primal scene fantasy, leading to my countertransference response of asking a question. Milton had been close to one of his aunts who lived nearby, and served as a substitute mother. In one session he was musing on how his aunt's bedroom had been off-limits to him and his cousins, and how it held this sense of mystery and foreboding. For the first time he mentioned that when he was an adolescent, after his aunt and uncle divorced, his aunt brought home a younger man (Neil) who she met at a conference. Neil stayed the summer (presumably in her bedroom). He didn't like this guy at the time as he thought he was kind of mean to him and his cousins. He reminded me that he met Neil some years later, and palled around with him for a while, and it turned out he was a pretty good guy, although when he got drunk he could be nasty. I then blurted out, "Was this Charlie?" I immediately knew something was up, as "blurting out" questions is not (as the reader may have gathered) my usual style. Let me first give the rational reason for this question. Charlie was another friend from this later era with whom Milton palled around. Charlie was a highly respected writer who graciously helped my patient at various points in his career. Milton, Charlie, and Neil had all gone on a road trip together, and Charlie often interceded on Milton's behalf when this other guy criticized him when he was drunk.

Upon reflection I could see how I was feeling "left out" throughout much of the session. When Milton was talking, references were vague, stories were left in mid-sentence, and I wasn't sure to whom or to what he was referring much of the time. So rather than his being the one who experienced feeling left out of his Aunt's bedroom, I was the one feeling left out in the session. Also, my need to rush into asking a question could be seen as a parallel wish of Milton's fantasy (elaborated at a later time) of rushing into the bedroom to throw out this interloper. Further, I realized that during the session Milton made various references to the mean man who was sleeping in his beloved aunt's bedroom that were similar to how he'd described me. Thus, my rush to identify this man as the "nice guy" who wasn't in his aunt's bedroom seemed a defensive countertransference reaction.

A final thought

We've come a long way from Eissler's (1953) position that

> Deviations from the basic model technique are occasionally lightheartedly suggested by some analysts under the assumption that the effect of any therapeutic measure can be analyzed later. As a general statement this is definitely wrong.

> (p. 111)

While technically unassailable at the time, it seemed to morph into a fiercely held doctrinaire view that had no room for a humane and humble approach to the complexities and genuine needs of working with another individual. However, I sometimes fear we are still reacting against this theory-driven, spare method of working, by turning to an a-theoretical, feel-good approach, which emphasizes the relationship over ways the mind creates itself, as well as the relationship. It sometimes seems we have forgotten about the unconscious, except as a repository for veridical past object relations. It is within this context that questions become a way of showing interest in the patient, and we lose the understanding of the power of careful, respectful listening.

Notes

1 This is especially true in the United States.
2 Ferro (2002b) describes unsaturated interpretations as a "polysemous event that permits opening up of meaning and narrative development" (p. 184). He goes on to say, "New thoughts need unsaturated space and the possibility to oscillate, as there is always the risk, as F. Guignard would say, of advancing 'stopper' interpretations that impede the development of thought" (p. 184).
3 In this Stern seems to confirm Boesky's view of questions as enactments. One could imagine the patient taking the question as, "Why are you embarrassed over having me see your small penis?"

9

WORKING THROUGH AND
RESISTANCE ANALYSIS

In this chapter I will discuss two psychoanalytic terms that have thousands of references in the psychoanalytic literature, but still remain ill defined. Twenty years after my first publication in this area I am as convinced as I was then that *resistance analysis* is rarely mentioned, and what passes for resistance analysis seems more like overcoming resistances (wrestling them down) rather than analyzing them. It is probably not surprising then that one of our basic concepts, *working through*, which Freud based upon resistance analysis, has no agreed upon meaning in the literature, and remains a term individually defined by the theoretical view of the analyst.

Since around the middle of the last century, when there was a flurry of attempts to define working through,[1] there has been little in the literature to clarify divergent views. Often lost in the discussions were references to Freud's initial views on this topic. I would suggest that in ignoring Freud's views we lose valuable insights into a process that is fundamental to achieving lasting and solid change. Surprisingly, Freud referred to working through in only two papers, i.e., "Remembering, Repeating, and Working Through" (Freud, 1914) and "Inhibitions, Symptoms, and Anxiety" (Freud, 1926). In both he clearly tied working through to the newly discovered *unconscious ego resistances*. In 1914 he states,

> The analyst had merely forgotten that giving the resistance a name could not result in its immediate cessation. One must allow the patient time to become more conversant with this resistance with which he has now become acquainted, to *work through* it, to overcome it, by continuing, in defiance of it, the analytic work according to the fundamental rule of analysis.
>
> (p. 155)

And presciently again in 1914,

> This *working through* of the resistances may in practice turn out to be an arduous task for the subject of the analysis and a trial of patience for the analyst. *Nevertheless it is a part of the work which effects the greatest*

changes in the patient and which distinguishes analytic treatment from
any kind of treatment by suggestion.

(p. 155, italics added)

It is my contention that the ego resistances, especially the *unconscious ego resistances*, are still central to working through. We have to remember that *the unconscious ego resistances guard against the most primitive fears and anxieties known to man. It seems to me that these catastrophic dangers to the human psyche must be understood in the process of working through.* Yet we often ignore them. How can we transform the under-represented into something representable, without helping the patient understand the dangers that led them to be discarded or repressed? How can the analysand's freedom of thought become freer when the factors limiting freedom remain vaguely terrifying and not fully represented?

Is there a symptom that doesn't have as part of its basis an unconscious fear? I would maintain that the centrality of unconscious fears as *one major contributor in the formation of neurotic and character symptoms* is inherent in every major theoretical persuasion, although the causative factors may be understood differently. Yet listening to discussions of the clinical process, one is impressed with how little analytic work is focused on an analysand's ability to listen to and understand the multiple factors that drive these fears. In short, knowledge *of* the unconscious is not particularly useful to the patient unless it is accompanied by the patient's capacity to become knowledgeable *about* the unconscious. Thus, the complex issue of how the patient gains access to his or her unconscious via the method of resistance analysis is of great importance for our techniques.

While increasingly analysts have struggled to understand the most severe resistances to analytic work with borderline and psychotic patients, psychoanalytic work with the common, everyday, *subtle resistances that are prevalent in the analyses of neurotic and moderately severe character disorder, has lagged behind.* When clinical data are looked at closely, there are often innumerable times when these more subtle resistances are continuously expressed throughout a session. We see these resistances in a sudden change of affect, a feeling expressed and then undone, the dream told but unremarked upon, the brief pause before a word is chosen, a word chosen and then replaced by a more "correct" one (the list goes on and is endless). Unanalyzed, they serve as an ongoing, secret barrier to working through. What we sometimes forget is that while the neurotic doesn't live with a weakened ego state as does the borderline, *the fears that fuel a reaction in the unconscious ego are malevolent enough to cause severe restrictions in thought and action.* It follows that how we analyze these resistances, brought about by terror, is decisive with regard to the analysand's greater freedom of thought.

Freud on resistances

Freud recognized resistances as early as 1895, and often came back to the topic. It is my contention that differences among clinical techniques of resistance analysis are mainly based on how closely the analyst follows Freud's *view of "the ego as the sole seat of anxiety,"* and in one's understanding of the differences between Freud's first and second theory of anxiety. *"Whereas the old view made it natural to suppose that anxiety arose from the libido belonging to the repressed instinctual impulses, the new one, on the contrary, made the ego the source of anxiety"* (Freud, 1926, p. 161, italics added). It has not been clearly emphasized that it was only with the introduction of the Structural Theory and the second theory of anxiety that a full psychoanalytic meaning of working with resistances was possible. In Freud's first theory of anxiety, the anxiety leading to the resistance was seen as a byproduct of dammed-up libido. Therefore, the primary purpose of the psychoanalytic clinician was to free the libido by bringing the unconscious libidinal wishes into consciousness. The resistances were a barrier to be over-come, although not in the old sense, as in the hypnotic phase when the resistances were bypassed completely. Instead, after they were brought into consciousness, the psychoanalyst was called upon to use various methods (e.g., promising the rewards of health, using the positive transference, suggestion) to help the patient push on in the face of ongoing and continuously rebuilding resistances.

In Freud's second theory of anxiety, however, the ego is seen as the source of anxiety. That is, anxiety is seen as occurring when the ego perceives danger (i.e., when it fears being overwhelmed), which is further seen as a repetition of an earlier traumatic situation. The resistances are viewed as the ego's response to anxiety. With this conceptual understanding of the underlying psychic mechanisms in place, psychoanalysts could grasp the full meaning of the resistances as the result of the perceived danger to the ego. Thus the importance of Freud's second theory of anxiety is:

1 For the first time resistances could be understood in a psychodynamic, functional and structural fashion rather than only in an energic one;
2 A psychoanalytic working through of these resistances could truly be undertaken which would center on an understanding of the danger to the ego underlying the resistance;
3 Resistance analysis could be understood as a valuable part of psychoanalytic treatment in strengthening the ego (i.e., making fears less fearful), and thus allowing greater access to repressed unconscious fantasies.

However, at the same time of Freud's epiphany of the ego as the source of resist-ance he could not see a way of *analyzing* resistances rather than *overcoming* them.

> If the resistance is itself unconscious, as so often happens owing to its connection with the repressed material, we make it conscious. If it is conscious, or, where it has become conscious, we bring forward logical arguments against it; we promise the ego rewards and advantages if it will give up its resistance.
>
> (Freud, 1926, p. 159)

In this we see that even though Freud opened the door to a purely analytic approach to the resistances (i.e., helping the patient understand the sources of anxiety and the danger behind this), he returned to his technical view of using influence or suggestion to entice the ego's cooperation in dealing with these interferences. Freud's struggles with this view remained unresolved throughout the rest of his writing, and influenced those who followed.[2]

A historical myth about American ego psychology

Wallerstein's (1988) depiction of the hegemony of ego psychology in American psychoanalysis was a myth then, and a myth before then. Until the 1980s there was never an American *clinical method* that consistently encompassed analytic ego psychology (Busch, 1999a). While the words of those identified as the major translators of "ego psychology" into clinical practice in the 1960s through the 1980s (e.g., Arlow, Brenner) sounded like ego psychology, it was consistently contradicted in their clinical examples. What frequently was confused in their work was the difference between an *analysis of the fears and dangers that led to and kept the unconscious resistances in place*, and an *analysis of the fantasies and feelings the resistances had to protect*. What Fenichel wrote in 1941 also characterized the next four decades in American psychoanalysis:

> One of the stimuli to the development of so-called "analytic ego psychology" was insight into the fact that resistance in the analysis is a real therapeutic agent in that pursuing the aim of analyzing resistance has as a prerequisite a thorough analytic investigation particularly of chronic attitudes of resistance anchored in an individual's character. Here again, the volume of the literature concerning the newly gained psychological insight is incomparably greater than the number of papers which seek to utilize this insight to contribute to an improvement of psychoanalytic technique.
>
> (Fenichel, 1941, p. 106)

Greenson, a champion of American ego psychology in the 1960s, provides an example where the two levels of resistance analysis become confused. That is, while attempting to get at the *feelings the patient is attempting to protect against, he ignores the dangers that keep the resistances in place.*

> A physician in analysis with me for several years begins to speak medical jargon in the middle of an analytic hour. In stilted tones he reports that his wife developed a "painful protruding hemorrhoid" just prior to a mountain trip they were planning. He said the news caused him "unmixed displeasure" and he wondered whether the hemorrhoid could be "surgically excised" or whether they would have to postpone their holiday. I could sense the latent anger he was withholding and could not refrain

from saying: "I think you really mean that your wife's hemorrhoids are giving you a pain in the ass."

(Greenson, 1967, p. 66)

By confronting the patient with his latent anger (i.e., the supposed painful feeling he is avoiding), Greenson gives up the opportunity to explore his use of "medical terminology" which, at this time, is the most obvious resistance. If resistances guard against catastrophic dangers, we simply cannot bypass them. In Greenson's approach the answer to the question of why this patient is fearful of his anger, except in generic terms, is not answerable. Greenson *is more interested in getting out the strangulated affect than in understanding the reasons for it being kept in.* This is a return to a view of anxiety in Freud's first theory, having little to do with ego psychology.

This is one of many examples when the analyst feels there are clear examples of unexpressed thoughts or feelings left out there by the patient. At these times we are tempted to say, "You are feeling or thinking this." If it was so simple, why wasn't the patient just saying it? As Schafer (1983) notes,

To begin with, it is the hesitation, the obstructing, the resisting that counts. If the analyst bypasses this difficulty with a direct question or confrontation, the analysand is too likely to feel seduced, violated, or otherwise coerced by the analyst who has in fact, even if unwittingly, taken sides unemphatically.

(p. 75)

In this regard the patient's response to Greenson's bypassing of the resistance is telling: "That's right, you son of a bitch, I wish they would cut it out of her." We see the patient's fury at the bypassing of the resistance, which is understandable if we fully grasp their importance as guardians against extreme dangers.

Throughout most of the analytic world ego psychology in America was associated with Hartmann. Internationally his ego psychology was criticized for turning away from the unconscious, which was not accurate. He simply explored what up till that time had been left unexplored – Freud's ego psychology.

In my view it was a mistake to dismiss Hartmann in such a radical fashion.[3] He, along with Rapaport, was one of the first psychoanalysts to focus on what has become a central interest in clinical psychoanalysis, *thinking about* thinking. In one sense Hartmann may have been ahead of his time, in that his work set the stage for a subtle approach to the understanding of those factors in the ego which affect receptivity to thoughts dependent on such things as: changes in ego states (e.g., fragmentation), regressions in levels of thinking (e.g., from formal operations to preoperational thought), and the degree to which communication is dominated by action. All of these ego states are more easily comprehended because of the work of Hartmann. Further, as early as 1939 Hartmann noted the significance of *linking representations*, more so than reconstruction, in moving the analysis forward. He felt the interpretive emphasis on reconstruction, while important, should not take precedence over *"instances in which the causal connections of elements, and the criteria for these connections, are established"* (Hartmann, 1939, p. 63).

In this view Hartmann follows a principle first elucidated by Freud (1895) in the Project, elucidated further by Schmidt-Hellerau (2001), and foreshadows the understanding of how experiences are stored in the recent discoveries in the neurosciences (Westen and Gabbard, 2002). The defenses against these links are crucial in the work of Bion and Green.

The developing technique of resistance analysis

It was in 1982 that Paul Gray published a groundbreaking paper on resistance analysis. Its premise was:

> It has for some time been my conclusion, rightly or wrongly, that the way a considerable proportion of analysts listen to and perceive their data has, in certain significant respects, *not* evolved as I believe it would have if historically important concepts concerned with the defensive functions of the ego had been wholeheartedly allowed their place in the actual application of psychoanalytic technique.
>
> (p. 622)

He goes on to state,

> Freud's phrase, "There is resistance to uncovering resistances" could well refer to an ubiquitous reluctance to consider, perceive, and conceptualize – both to oneself and to one's analysand – the detailed workings of the ego in its defensive measures against specific drive derivatives.
>
> (p. 651)

Below I'll present a brief vignette from a supervisee that highlights some basic components of resistance analysis, taking into account this view of the ego's role in forming resistances. In working this way we attempt to show the moment when anxiety was aroused in the ego, leading to shift in content or affect. We pay special attention to how this is represented by the analyst so that it may be *preconsciously grasped by that part of the patient's ego not immersed in the conflict of the moment*. This involves a first description of the resistance in *concrete* terms, as (noted earlier) this is a patient's way of thinking in the midst of conflict. Our intent is to *try and represent the disturbing affect in the ego* that led to the disruption in the patient's association, which is basic to any understanding of resistances. Clinically, what one finds is that as treatment progresses the analysand will preconsciously note the disruption, and his associations will give depth to our understanding.

Jeff typically showed excessive concern for his wife's feelings, and rarely disagreed with her. In one session he came in reporting how he cleaned out books from his library but had not yet removed them from his home. He told his wife he was going to his weekly golf game, and reported that she said, in what sounded like an order, "You are not going anywhere until you get rid of those books." He responded, "I'm going to play golf, and I'll take care of the books later." Immediately after telling the analyst of this uncharacteristically assertive stance, Jeff began to justify his wife's behavior, saying, "She had every right to make that request of me and my anger was not appropriate."

After telling the analyst of his taking an assertive stance toward his wife, Jeff has to quickly undo it. The resistance at this moment is not to the assertiveness with his wife, but in *telling the incident to the analyst*. It is immediately after this moment that "something happens" that makes him uncomfortable. It is this "something happens" moment, just before Jeff undoes the expression of assertiveness, where we see the resistance set in. This is what we are trying to help the analysand understand. What is it at this moment that leads to the undoing?

I would work with this resistance this way: "I wonder if you noticed that immediately after you told me of your new found assertiveness with your wife, something seemed to happen and you immediately started to justify your wife's behavior. It was as if telling me about your assertiveness with her made you uncomfortable."

In short, I would represent in the transference that it is the moment after Jeff told the analyst of what happened with his wife that he became uncomfortable expressing his anger in the analytic moment with the analyst. I wouldn't be representing anything else but the discomfort, as there is no way the analyst can know what part of this discomfort, if any, the analysand will be able to explore. *It is the discovering of the multiple reasons for the discomfort as they become preconsciously available in the analysis that is the essential component of the working through process. That is, each resistance has multiple parts and over time each one will need to be explored. In exploring the resistance in this unsaturated fashion, we allow the patient the greatest degree of freedom to point us in a direction he is most able to work with at this moment. If the patient cannot capture the resistance in his own mind at this point, there is no point in pursuing what happened at the moment.*

Let me now present a clinical vignette that demonstrates this central issue of resistance analysis, and thus working through, i.e., *the difference between analyzing the fears underlying the resistances rather than directly uncovering the fantasy or feelings behind these fears. It is the difference between helping the patient become aware of the fears of knowing a thought or feeling, rather than getting them to see they have a specific thought or feeling they are afraid of expressing.* This difference is central to working through, and the *analysis of the ego's response to danger.* The central achievement in the session to be reported *is the patient's awareness and capacity to represent her anxiety as a response to desire.*

In addition, this example will demonstrate some basic contemporary principles of resistance analysis:

1   We rely on higher-level ego functioning to explore the more regressive levels of ego functioning.
2   Exploring the dangers of specific resistances is a primary method of opening up pathways to deeper regions of the unconscious. Only by understanding the threats they face will a patient feel safe enough to openly explore these areas. By the time we interpret a patient's polymorphous perverse sexual fantasies, it shouldn't come as a shock to the patient.
3   Our understanding of the ego in the midst of conflict is that it functions at a concrete level, and thus we must work concretely for a while until the conflict can be understood, and the patient is ready for symbolic interpretations.
4   It is easiest for a patient to understand the workings of a resistance when it is identified in the present moment.
5   Resistance analysis begins in an unsaturated fashion. We want to first help the patient see a resistance in action, and wait for which part, if any, he is able to explore via his associations. *The single biggest error made by beginning analysts is to interpret a resistance before the patient is able to see one is taking place.* If resistance analysis has been consistent part of the analysis, it is not unusual for an analysand to show a resistance and then associate to what it's about. This is what happens in this next example, although it is still early in the analysis.

Lydia

In this example we can see the principles of how we help patients grasp that a resistance is taking place via representation in a concrete, unsaturated fashion, and then wait to see where the patient's thoughts lead for a deeper under-standing and freedom of thought. This is an essential part of the working through process.

Lydia is a 27 year-old physician, an attractive woman, who came to analysis with a life-long feeling that she never enjoyed herself. In the second year of her analysis, after cancelling the previous session, Lydia came into the session looking pale and exhausted. As soon as she lay down on the couch she began trying to stem her runny nose with the multiple tissues she brought with her. When Lydia was able to talk she said she felt so "embarrassed." There was then a silence.

Many of us might have guessed at this point that this embarrassment and silence had to do with the missed appointment, and maybe we would say something to this effect. However, this encourages a kind of thinking, i.e., analysis as intuitive speculation, which ultimately is antithetical to the creation of a psychoanalytic mind. While the analyst's empathic intuition is central to his understanding, it needs to be used in a disciplined fashion to best help our patients in the goal of self-analysis.

When Lydia talked again, she apologized profusely for cancelling the previous appointment. She then stopped talking, saying she felt anxious. She told me that she even had to cancel her appointments at the hospital, and then began berating herself for how she was such a "baby" about illness. She "explained" that she got up with this cold yesterday and was ready to go to work, when her coughing and sneezing convinced her this wouldn't be good for her patients. She thought about cancelling her appointment with me since she was so tired and she thought it best that she rest. However, she couldn't rest because she was anxious. It was only when she realized she had a slightly elevated temperature that she called to cancel.

F.B.:   It seems your embarrassed silence over cancelling yesterday's session came from your concern you were being a "baby." Only when you feared you might harm others could you take care of yourself.

Lydia's next thoughts turned to the previous weekend. She wasn't feeling so great, and was on call. She stayed in her apartment most of the weekend, but still hadn't been able to put up any of her pictures or posters, and there was still stuff to be unpacked (Lydia had been in the apartment 2 months.) It depressed her. She thought of getting cable so she could watch some of her favorite TV programs and movies, but she talked herself out of it because she wasn't at the apartment that much. How could she justify the expense?

F.B.:   Your thoughts go to how you find it difficult to take care of yourself in your apartment. It seems like there too you're worried about "babying" yourself.

There are a number of components in this clarification of a transference resistance that are central to working through. First, we try to raise awareness of the existence of the resistance and the uneasiness that leads to it. With Lydia, it is the uneasiness over being a "baby," or taking care of herself. Until the patient can grasp this element there is no point in going further with interpretations. It would be like asking someone to understand a story that was written in a language she didn't understand. We can best help the patient understand the inhibition by first clarifying it, and then allowing the patient to explore what further part of this "babyness" she can allow herself to think about. We had previously explored this in terms of growing up in a puritanical family, where "idle hands were the devil's workshop," but we cannot know at this clinical moment what the fear of "babyness" means.

At times of resistance it is important to repeat the sequence that leads to the clarification, as the patient cannot recapture this when working at a concrete level. At these times the analysand often has no spontaneous capacity to follow a sequence of thoughts. Further, I am pointing out something that happened right before us as a way of helping the patient feel the emotional impact, as well as having the best chance to grasp a heretofore unnoticed central psychological event.

These are the beginning steps necessary to analyze the resistances as part of the working through process. Our purpose is to bring them to awareness so that associations to them might emerge to further clarify their meaning.

Following my intervention, Lydia remembered that Saturday night there was a party given by a neighbor. She didn't feel much like going, but she went anyway. A friend of this neighbor was there, and she liked him. They were talking for a long while, and near the end of the evening he asked her out for dinner the following weekend. She told him she was on call in what seemed afterward like a stern voice, and didn't think at the moment to tell him she would like that or suggest other times. Not surprisingly she didn't see him the rest of the evening.

F.B.:   This memory follows your concern over being a "baby." You were able to see after the incident it was important to convey to this man you were a hard worker, not one of these indulgent type women who enjoy going out to dinner with a man.

Lydia: What's coming to mind is my first boyfriend, Tim. I don't think I ever mentioned how we broke up. We had been going out for about a year, and had fooled around a little bit, mostly above the waist, but also some touching through clothes further down. It was all very exciting to that point, and then we decided to take it one step further. When we first got naked it was still very exciting, and then Tim suggested we should touch ourselves. It disgusted me, and I immediately got dressed. Tim apologized and tried to talk about it, but I wanted nothing to do with him. I still have trouble masturbating.

F.B.:   Idle hands are the Devil's workshop.

Lydia: [Laughs] I never thought of it *that* way . . . or maybe I did.

After representing a resistance to thinking about taking care of herself, and the "baby" feeling it aroused, we see another element emerge, i.e., disgust over touching herself, which potentially has many more meanings. This is the essence of how resistance analysis leads to working through. As different elements of symptoms become represented, more complex representations are built, allowing for a greater freedom to think.

In reading this account, some colleagues might wonder about underlying conflicts over aggression and castration. While there is much merit in these speculations, they get to a major point that is central throughout this book. That is, do we help our analysands best by working with what is preconsciously available in associations, or do we need to bring to the preconscious the unconscious derivatives? My answer is that we can only usefully bring unconscious derivatives to conscious awareness via their expressions in preconscious associations, and working through the resistances that protect against this process.[4]

A final word

In an attempt to highlight the role of the unconscious ego in resistance analysis and the importance of resistance analysis in working through, I have presented a truncated version of both concepts. Of course, there are other ways of approaching resistances that have equal validity. For example, at a later time in treatment, with a thin resistance, I believe one can work as described by Green (2005), "sometimes making use of ellipses or allusions, proceeding by limited touches, stimulating the associative work, counting on the participation of the patient . . ." Further, working through is more than just resistance analysis. Also, there is not only working through of the fears that lead to the resistances, but the unconscious fantasies associated with them. Resistances have multiple functions, and each resistance is layered within many levels of disorganization.

As noted earlier, the author Haruki Murakami takes no credit for his imaginative flights, claiming to be just a vessel for his imagination. While we work with our patients to take responsibility for their thoughts, the freedom and surprise of thought described by Murakami is something we see as essential in a psychoanalytic process. In this chapter I have tried to show the utility of appreciating the fears that stultify thinking that is the basis of resistance analysis, and an important component of working through. Resistance analysis, well done, is essential to working through, and is essential to the analysand's greater freedom of thought. Yet, all the potential advancements in resistance analysis brought about by the changes in Freud's models, have been resisted. This is still another story.

Notes

1 See Kris (1985) for an excellent summary of the literature from that time. It is fascinating to note that of the 1,000-plus references to working through in PEP, 630 of those were written between 1950 and 1965, while in a 15-year time period from 1994 to 2009, there were only 30 articles. Like many basic psychoanalytic concepts, it seems to have been left behind.

2 For a full review of how psychoanalysts continued to struggle with these issues after Freud, see Busch (1992) and Gray (1994). Reich's (1933) work captures Freud's ambivalence perfectly. In the first part of his book on character analysis, Reich shows his understanding of the resistances as the ego's response to danger, and he offers the first technical suggestions based on this premise, which reflect a true psychoanalytic working through of the resistances and not simply overcoming them. Yet later in this same book he returns to a view of resistances as something to be attacked, showing *how easily one may fall into an adversarial view of the resistances.*

3 For an excellent perspective on Hartmann, see Bergmann (2000).

4 *A caveat*: We sometimes think that resistances are there or not. However, this is not the case. It is useful to think of thin and thick resistances. One needs to work differently with each type, depending on a clinical appreciation for the state of the patient's mind rather than what I often hear as a robotic approach by those who are primed to analyze resistances at every turn. Jumping on a resistance whenever one appears can have a chilling effect on the method of free association, as the patient is waiting for that dreaded interruption indicating that they've resisted again. It goes against the whole spirit of resistances as inevitable. Such an approach often stops thinking, rather than the freeing effect that resistance analysis helps create.

10

WORKING WITHIN THE
TRANSFERENCE

Nothing can replace the fact that returning to oneself comes about by
making a detour through the other.

(Green, 2000b, p. 99)

This is a vast topic, and I will not attempt to do justice to the complex layering of
thinking on these matters. For excellent reviews of the literature see Orr (1954),
Cooper (1987), and Smith (2003).[1] I will limit myself to observations on how I've
come to understand *working within the transference* in the context of creating a
psychoanalytic mind, and some of the problems I see analysts struggling with in
their daily work.[2]

While most analysts believe in the centrality of transference in psychoanalytic
treatment, there are many variations in what this means. The differences revolve
around: what it means to interpret the transference; the timing of transference
interpretations; and the goals we have in interpreting the transference. In general
I find analysts *looking for the transference rather than finding it. We tend to be
more eager to bring the transference into the room, rather than letting it be in
the room.* For instance, when the patient is talking about some interaction outside
the consulting room, and the analyst asks, "I wonder if this has to do with you
and me?", the transference may be forced into the neighborhood rather than
allowing it to be there. We seem to believe that unless we are addressing the transference we aren't doing real analytic work. However, it is my impression that
many interpretations of the transference leave patients feeling bewildered, and
thus one of the most powerful tools of the analytic method becomes something
imposed and alienating rather than experienced. We make far too many transference interpretations, too quickly, resulting in an intellectualized appreciation
or outright rejection.

The demands of analytic work are enormous. We need to contain, hold, and
reflect upon primitive mental states, often resonating in our unconscious. We need
to try to maintain our own healthily stable narcissistic state, libidinal investment
in, and concern for the well being of the other, and since this is not always possible,
we inevitably enact something with our patients. In every treatment we become

narcissistically out of balance, and it is at these moments our involvement with the patient's perspective wanes. I see this as an important factor in our tendency to over-interpret the transference, especially with regard to our effect on the patient. Before any break in the treatment it is almost inevitable that one hears the analyst interpreting whatever the patient is talking about in terms of the upcoming separation from the analyst. While likely there is some validity to the idea, it is my impression that most often such interpretations are premature. Who are we interpreting for at these times? As the patient is screaming "go away, leave me alone, I don't need you, but not too far away, but not too close," we tend to interpret the transference need, while ignoring the transference defense, or the wish to have us be the alone one (see 'Amanda' below). To continue our work, with a profound psychic involvement with our patients at multiple levels, we sometimes need to feel we matter. It is my impression that this is one important factor in the profusion of transference interpretations.

Green (1974) captured the complications in interpreting transference in the following:

> This brings us to the question of interpreting the transference, which is undoubtedly the driving force of the analytic process. However, it is important to realize that an analysis conducted solely through interpretations of the transference often puts the patient under unbearable pressure. The analysis takes on an aspect of persecution even if these interpretations are designed to help the patient understand what is happening within him. The respect for the patient's resistance is one condition of the *development* of the analytical process. It is sometimes necessary for the patient to project on to the analyst, i.e. to get inside him in order to see what is happening there; but it is also essential that from time to time both look *together* towards a third object.
>
> (p. 416)

Principles of working within the transference[3]

1   A transference interpretation is only as effective as the analysand's readiness to understand the interpretation in an emotionally meaningful way. Most transference interpretations need to be directed to what is preconsciously available, although the occasional surprise interpretation can be evocative once there is an analytic patient to hear such an interpretation. In my understanding, the preconscious clarification of the transference, *as it is occurring in the session*, is a crucial factor in making the transference feel like something that is happening rather than inferred or hypothesized.

2   We need to *accept* and let the transference into the room before attempting to do anything with it. If a patient is talking in an argumentative manner, it is this way of talking that needs to be allowed and listened to. It is only within the action of the hour that ideas and feelings become alive. As understood by

Freud, we need to treat the patient's illness as an *actual force, active at the moment, and not as an event in his past life.*

3   We need to *clarify*[4] the phenomenon we think of as the transference, as it is happening in the immediacy of the analytic hour, *before we interpret it.* It is this clarification that is the first step in analyzing *within the transference.* The patient needs to have some experience and preconscious awareness of what we're interpreting before we interpret it. As noted earlier, the analysand's thinking in the midst of conflict is concrete. It takes a lot of analytic work before the patient can experience and observe their thoughts and feelings as their own. It is only when we clarify what is happening in the session, that we can learn from the patient what part, if any, the patient can tolerate thinking about. One can see in many of the examples mentioned in earlier chapters how the analyst interprets the meaning of the patient's association in the transference, before the patient has an idea how the analyst came to his conclusion. A patient might rightly feel bewildered when the analyst interprets associations around missing her children as a response to the weekend break from analysis.

4   While the enacted transference is most often about repetitions of fantasies and memories associated with internalized object relations, it doesn't mean that it can or should always be interpreted as such. Yet, it is my impression that many current analytic theories dictate that we mainly interpret transference as a repetition of a past object relationship in the present. Partly this may be due to something I don't think has been noted previously, i.e., from the very beginning, Freud (1912a) had *two views of transference.* The first is the one most commonly used:

> If the "father-imago," to use the apt term introduced by Jung, is the decisive factor in bringing this about, the outcome will tally with the real relations of the subject to his doctor. But the transference is not tied to this particular prototype: it may also come about on the lines of the mother-imago or brother-imago.
>
> (p. 100)

However, in this same paper Freud also suggests a broader definition of transference. This included seeing the analytic relationship representing the stage on which the patient re-enacts his symptoms, memories, dreams, and current experiences, i.e., the transference can be *a state of mind in the analysis, not only a representation of past object relations.*

This duality of the transference as a result of a repetition of past object relations, and *a state of mind in the analysis,* is seen in this famous paragraph from *Remembering, Repeating and Working Through* (Freud, 1914):

> For instance, the patient does not say that he remembers that he used to be defiant and critical towards his parents' authority; instead, he behaves in that way to the doctor [a past object

relationship]. He does not remember how he came to a helpless and hopeless deadlock in his infantile sexual researches; but he produces a mass of confused dreams and associations, complains that he cannot succeed in anything and asserts that he is fated never to carry through what he undertakes. He does not remember having been intensely ashamed of certain sexual activities and afraid of their being found out; but he makes it clear that he is ashamed of the treatment on which he is now embarked and tries to keep it secret from everybody. And so on.

> (p. 150, parenthesis added).

We see in this paragraph how Freud's view of what was expressed in the transference was multi-faceted. He shows us how a *state of mind* (e.g., intrapsychic conflict between id–ego–super-ego) dominates the transference. Within our own time we've come to understand how defending a fragile self-state can lead to an aggressive transference, or how fears of love lead to distance. However, it still seems Freud's view of the transference as a repetition of a past object relationship came to dominate our views of transference. Transference as the result of a *state of mind* seemed to have faded as a causative factor.

5   I agree with Freud's (1913) view that there is no reason to interpret the transference until it becomes a resistance. In this way the transference is like the background on a canvas, ever-present but not necessarily spoken to. The overemphasis on transference interpretations can lead to a repetitious, sterile, intellectualized situation, where the analysand can anticipate the analyst's interpretation. Such interpretations often lead nowhere or arouse antagonism in the patient, which often becomes a confirmation for the analyst. Further there is a lot of analytic work done outside the immediacy of the transference. Moreover, there are ways of interpreting lateral transferences that are closer to what is happening in the session rather than primarily as an external event. This can be seen briefly in the case of Samantha below.

Finally, while Betty Joseph's views of the *total transference* opened up a whole new way of thinking on how to work *within* the transference, we differ on how much the transference is based entirely on past object relationships, and the degree to which transferences are the result of the patient *putting something into the analyst*, as in projective identification. In this I agree with Hanna Segal's view on the topic:

> I can see what Klein was about. A very nice young analyst said his patient had put confusion into him. Mrs. Klein said, "No, dear, she didn't put confusion into you – you were confused." She was afraid of countertransference being made an excuse. And you know if somebody tells me they do this or that because the patient projected it. I say, "Look, countertransference is not an excuse."
>
> (Hunter, 1993)

Working within the transference

Most examples that follow show how and why we need to ease into the transference rather than drive in. In this way, the path is open to working within the transference, rather than talking about the transference

Anna

In this vignette, we see the transference expressed, not atypically, in language action. A major part of our analytic work is accomplished via listening polyphonically to language action and attempting to represent it through clarification. While the content of the session is evocative, it is familiar and seems to be representative of one aspect of what is being enacted. Potentially subtle meanings are inferred through my countertransference (as is typical with language action). However, I am able to contain my thoughts about the countertransference, and *clarify* how the transference is expressed in language action in a way that can be preconsciously recognized. It leads to the memory of a dream in which anger and fear are expressed.

It is a Monday appointment and Anna flies into her analytic session. Before she even lies down on the couch Anna states, "I couldn't wait to tell you about this weekend." In a rush she begins to tell me, at great length, of the various ways her husband mistreated her. It was not told in any great distress, but more in the form of conspiratorial togetherness. It was a story I heard many times from Anna, so her feeling that "she couldn't wait to tell me" struck me as an important indicator *of some way she was viewing the analysis and/or our relationship.* When Anna paused for a breath, I empathized with how distressing this seemed to be, and also wondered about this "couldn't wait to tell me" feeling. She cut me off saying, "Yes, yes, but let me tell you about this other incident that happened." Anna then proceeded to tell me a lengthy story where she visited her parents, and her mother spent a long time on the phone with her sister. There were many other slights as well. I was again impressed with how propelled she was to tell me this story, again familiar, of mistreatment. My previous remarks seemed to hardly register. I felt pushed out of her narrative. Another story of a similar nature quickly followed, presented in this same breathless manner. Listening to this story I sensed an excited quality in her breathlessness. After a brief silence, I said to Anna that again, she seemed in a *rush* to tell me what happened, so much so that it seemed difficult to register what I said. After a brief pause Anna said, "I hate your voice." Puzzled and intrigued I waited. She then said, "I had a sexual dream about you last night. It wasn't you in the dream, but it was a tall guy with a beard. We made love in the most tender and exciting way. When we finished I cried. Obviously I didn't want to tell you. It makes me so sad when I think of being loved instead of fucked. Better to go on feeling angry about being fucked than this overwhelming sadness. It's really scary. But maybe the dream indicates it's not as scary as it was."

This vignette is a prototypical example of how I work *within the transference.* That is, in words, action, and language action the patient tells me of some aspect of how she is viewing the analyst as a threat to her defenses against the wish to be loved. It's more comfortable to feel fucked, as she did in all her associations. Rather than analyzing this from *outside* the immediacy of what is being expressed, for example, addressing the enactment as a past relationship, or the current relationship to the analyst, *the expression of the transference first needs to be empathically captured and clarified by the analyst*. With Anna, it is only when this rush to tell me stories to keep me out is clarified, that the anger and sadness over the exciting and scary things she wants from me can be revealed in her dream, and begin to be mourned as a step toward finding what she desires. Anna is defending and enacting with this rush to tell me. Only by clarification can we see if the defense is thick or thin. If the patient continues to rush by our observation, we know we are dealing with a thick resistance that needs further containment before it can be approached. Clarification of thin resistances in the enacted transference, as is the case with Anna, leads to further associations.

Others may have interpreted Anna's thoughts and actions in another way. For example, some might have seen Anna's rush to tell her stories, combined with the "waiting" story, as a reaction to the weekend, and the long wait to see the analyst. Some analysts may look to the past to understand her masochistic position. Still others may have felt the pull to interrupt Anna's stories more strongly, and thus may have interpreted her push to repeat the masochistic mistreatment. All of these possibilities have validity. The analyst usually hears the meaning of the clinical material within a context of multiplicities. Again, what I'm highlighting is that before interpreting transference content, it is important to clarify the specifics of the dynamic within the way of the patient's relating. It is a way of concretizing the manner in which the transference fantasy is being expressed in the analytic session, and seeing what part, if any, the patient is able to elaborate (respecting defenses).[5]

Working in displacement[6]

From the very first contact patients have transference reactions to the analyst, his office, his way of conducting the work, and so forth. However, this doesn't mean that the patient is ready to own these thoughts and feelings, or that they've reached the level of the preconscious. In this regard, over-emphasis on transference interpretations from the beginning of treatment can be deleterious to the treatment, except of course when they bespeak of important resistances. Blum (1983) captures the problem when he states, "only valuing transference interpretations will tend to become 'all transference' and mold or artificially force all material into the transference, leading to inappropriate, excessive transference interpretations" (p. 597).[7]

Heimann (1956), an early supporter of Klein, who then modified her own views, touches on the issue of the analysand's unawareness of transference feelings and how to deal with them in the following:

> An interesting sideline concerns the patient's unawareness of his analyst, especially for instance when the analyst himself has had some distressing

experience. Such a lack of perception in patients may spring from tact, or insensitivity, or from the need to deny whatever threatens the use of an object as a source of gratification. Such incidents reveal important aspects of the patient's personality in his immediate contact with an object; yet in my view it is not possible to interpret them directly.

(p. 307)

Samantha

It is early in the treatment, and Samantha is thinking of getting married. She is still in the phase where she sees her problems as outside herself, and is expressing some reluctance about the time it takes to come to analysis, while finding the sessions themselves "helpful." Samantha often missed a few sessions a month, and frequently came 5 minutes late to appointments. Due to certain parts of Samantha's history (for example, she reported her mother as being excessively controlling), the analyst felt it was initially necessary to patiently analyze rather than questioning her difficulty in holding the frame.

The problem for analyzing this type of patient is how to deepen the work, while allowing her to feel she is in control of the analysis. It is a central issue for interpreting transference, i.e., while the transference may seem obvious to the analyst, interpreting it too quickly may lead the analysand to need to expel what will likely be experienced as an intrusive other (who is also wanted). In this vignette we see how the analyst, working in displacement, deals with a central defense with important implications for the transference.

The patient comes 10 minutes late.

Samantha: I feel bad. I have no idea why. I can't find the words to explain it. I have mood swings. My calm feeling from last week is gone. I would like to retreat, to be alone. [Silence for five minutes.] Bill was at my place all weekend and he was depressed. Most of the time he complained about how he hasn't been able to see his friends, and he's getting worried about feeling shackled by the marriage. He didn't seem to realize how this would affect me. Finally, I told him how I felt when he said these things, and that he ought to see someone in counseling to deal with these problems. He was surprised at how upset I was. He is so stupid and unaware of what he's doing.

Analyst: You come in feeling badly without knowing why. Your thoughts then go to how upset and mad you were at Bill. For some reason you sever the possible connection.

We see here how, sensing Samantha's skittishness over too much closeness, the analyst doesn't pick up on the transference messages of wanting to be left alone, which is enacted shortly after the session begins (i.e., Samantha says, "I want to be left alone," and then immediately stops talking). What she does speak to in displacement is the split between her feelings towards Bill and her "bad" mood. Dealing with it in displacement is potentially much closer to Samantha's "neighborhood." In this way one tries to begin the analysis of an important defense, that has implications both inside and outside the transference. While crucial with Samantha, it is my experience that this is a necessary way of working early in the treatment. It takes a long time for patients to be able to experience and own their feelings in the transference, and both are necessary for a successful transference interpretation. What I also want to highlight is that while dealing with the transference in displacement, the analyst is describing it as a live event happening in the session. For example, she says, "you come in describing," and also notes the "split feelings" as occurring before us. Thus, rather than just talking about what happened with Bill, she's bringing it closer to what is happening between them.

Samantha: I can see that. I'm wondering why I couldn't see it before. An incident is coming to mind. I was in fourth grade, and my best friend Betsy and I were playing. I had a feeling she was cheating, I can't quite remember why, but I told her to stop it. She got all angry and walked away. Things were never quite the same with us.

Analyst: You wondered why you couldn't connect your angry feelings toward Bill and your bad mood. Your thoughts then go to knowing about your anger and saying something about it, which you connect with driving the person away.

By staying in the displacement Samantha is free to first feel curious, which leads to an important feeling, i.e., the connection between knowing of one's anger and driving the other person away. While Samantha could "know" she was angry with Bill when he was with her, when he was "gone" she couldn't keep the connection because of the fear of abandonment. In staying with the displacement we build a bridge to the transference, but wait until it's closer to the patient's "neighborhood." In general, the analyst must contain her own insights until the patient is ready for her own insights.

Working in displacement and within the transference

Lee

In this vignette the analysand describes an interaction with transference implications, and then enacts some component of it in the transference. It shows a way of working that moves between the two expressions of the transference, and a way of interpreting external interactions that bring them closer to within the transference.

Lee came to analysis due to ongoing feelings of unhappiness, and some depressive symptoms. Although very accomplished in his field, he would downplay his achievements, and dampen down the enthusiasm of those around him. This was evident in our work together. In this session Lee's description of his dampening down excitement was first expressed in displacement. When it briefly appeared within the session I brought it into the transference, and from that point on the lateral transference informed the transference within the session. I see this as typical of how transference becomes elucidated with less severely disturbed patients, and when the work is progressing. Each component of the transference can strengthen the other. The danger is that the analyst turns away from the heat of the transference to something external.

Lee begins the session by talking about going to dinner the other night with Bill, a law clerk in his firm, and how he started to feel badly. It was clear to Lee that Bill was looking up to him and considered him an important mentor. Bill indicated how much he appreciated how Lee had created a stellar career for himself, and Bill wanted to hear more about how he did it. Lee then made a slip and talked about having *lunch* with Bill. He spontaneously wondered if "the idea of dinner with Bill was too exciting." He went on to talk about how he enjoyed hearing how much Bill admired him, and there were all these attractive young women around. Later in the dinner they started to talk about books they were reading, and Bill mentioned various authors he read, Lee started to feel badly that he hadn't read these books. He then told me about various books he had read, and the senior thesis he did in college on Orwell.

F.B.:   After feeling excited with Bill, you start to feel badly about not being as well read as him. Now you seem to be trying to show your literary side.

The feeling of being excited with a man arousing homosexual anxiety, followed by self-denigration, was increasingly part of the analysis. I couldn't tell if what was uppermost in Lee's description of his literary accomplishments was self-reparative, or an attempt to impress me, or make me feel badly. Therefore while noting it, I didn't feel it could be interpreted further. Yet it was clear that something was just enacted within the transference that needed to be noted. Thus, my clarification needed to be unsaturated.

Lee then told me he went to his friends' beach house (Will and Esther) on the weekend. At dinner one night, Will was going on and on about Obama's stand on Israel. Will finally asked Lee what he'd been up to, and Lee mentioned a talk he was going to by this lawyer–physicist–humanitarian. Will immediately said he didn't like this guy, and Lee (uncharacteristically assertive) said it was because this guy wasn't politically correct enough for Will. This stopped the conversation, and in thinking about it later he felt badly for not asking Will more about why he didn't like this guy. Then Esther asked about his kids, and Lee started talking about how great his children were doing. Later on he remembered that Esther had talked about her daughter's marital and alcoholic problem, and he felt badly. He could see that maybe he might have been more sensitive to Esther, and the same with Will's comment. Yet he knew he felt Will had cut him off in a dismissive way, and he was pleased with the retort he came back with. "Esther is generally like a bull in a china shop, offering opinions on everything. If she were my mother I'd become an alcoholic to dull the rage." He felt it was "crazy" to feel badly about what he said about his children.

F.B.:   I wonder if in labeling your behavior as "crazy" you're now beating yourself up with me, like occurred after the evening with Will and Esther.

At this point I saw the feelings he described all weekend, feeling badly about what he said, were now in the room. That is, while seemingly recognizing that his feeling badly was misplaced, he continued to do the same thing with me by labeling his thoughts as "crazy." This word, "crazy," was filled with meaning, as this was how he described his younger sister, who seemed to be borderline, and had been a constant burden on the family.

Something came to Lee's mind. He and his wife had dinner the next night with new friends that he'd enjoyed meeting. He felt it was so great to find new friends later in life. They were really interesting and thoughtful. This couple was doing research on the problems with schools in the inner city, and Lee started to feel badly during the dinner because he was not doing that kind of research any more.

F.B.:   Again, a bad feeling follows your excitement.

While staying with the displacement, I allude to the transference with the word "Again."

Lee: Why can't I figure that out on my own?
F.B.:   Maybe because it would feel too exciting to do that with me.
Lee: It would be very exciting.

Lee then described an interaction with another partner at his law firm. He felt confused when talking to him about a case this fellow was preparing. He finally figured out what was troubling him about the case, and he felt he expressed it simply and articulately. He felt really good about it. Lee then bemoaned how long it took him to figure this out.

F.B.:   After describing your pleasure in articulating the problems with this fellow's case, you put yourself down with me. You seem drawn toward feeling badly so you won't feel too excited with me.
Lee: I'm thinking about how much I hated being on the Law Review in law school, because I feared my opinions would be damaging. [Lee's talked about this fear before, but his opinions seem to be greeted with respect.]
F.B.:   Maybe this is part of why you downplay your excitement. You feel your excitement will be too damaging.
Lee: Well, isn't it? Look what happened to Sylvia! [Sylvia is Lee's cousin, with whom he had some sexual foreplay when they were young teenagers. In

college she developed manic-depressive symptoms, which she continues to struggle with. Lee "knew" she grew up with a very disturbed mother, and alcoholic father. Earlier in treatment he talked about spying on his "crazy" sister when she was getting undressed.]

F.B.:   You see your sexual excitement as a powerful, malignant force.

Lee: Sure [and with a laugh of recognition of the absurdity of what he was about to say], after all I killed my parents. You mean I didn't. [laughs] That's a relief. Or maybe it isn't.

I think this is a good example of how what's occurring within the transference, and in the lateral transference, inform each other, leading to a deeper understanding of the fear of excitement. It is only when the lateral transference is expressed within the transference (i.e., when Lee labels himself as "crazy") that the transference in the room becomes interpretable. When Lee is able to associate after this moment to external events that elaborate the transference, I see him as comfortable enough to broaden understanding of this central transference.

The compulsion to interpret transference

In the "Analyst at Work" series in the *International Journal of Psychoanalysis* we have the chance to see how analysts from different cultures work. I would like to briefly describe the role of transference in a beautifully described analysis from this series where an anonymous empathic analyst sensitively shares his/her struggles to deal with a patient (Amanda) in a way that is a model for how most of us wish we would work (A. Anon, 2005, pp. 233–240). I bring this material because I am admiring of the analyst's work, yet I find a familiar *push* to bring the patient's material into the transference in a way that leaves the impression the process becomes derailed. I am impressed with how even the most skilled analysts are often compelled to make transference interpretations even when doubting their utility. For example, in Michael Feldman's (2007) excellent article on "The Illumination of History" he says the following about making a transference interpretation: "*I found it difficult to resist* making the obvious suggestion that she had felt abandoned by me when I left for a week's holiday" (p. 620). It is this "difficult to resist" quality about transference interpretations that I find all too common.

In the analysis described below the analyst finds him/herself dealing with a familiar situation. It was necessary for the analyst to take a brief, but unexpected break in the treatment. The patient, who is very sensitive to not being attended to, wants a more detailed explanation than the analyst is willing to give. While the patient has no preconscious awareness of feeling like the analyst *did* something to her by suddenly cancelling two sessions, the analyst continues to interpret the patient's feelings of being *painfully hurt*. While at an unconscious level the analyst is no doubt correct, the patient's need to protect against these feelings and instead focus on the reality of a lack of an explanation is bypassed. This attempt to get to the *real* transference reaction rather than the one the patient is expressing bedevils all our work, and leads to an ignoring of the resistance to the transference.

Amanda

From the beginning of the treatment the patient has focused on the absence of tissues by the couch as an indication of the analyst's neglect. Not surprisingly this mirrors Amanda's experience of her mother, captured in an incident where she went grocery shopping with her mother at around age 3, and her mother left the grocery store without her. It was only when an employee of the grocery store called the mother did she realize she had forgotten Amanda. Again, not surprisingly, Amanda has been hyper-alert to what she perceives as any self-interest in the analyst's interpretations, especially transference interpretations, and the analyst has given great thought to this in what he/she says to the patient. In the background of the sessions, the analyst recently had to cancel two sessions because of a medical emergency that needed to be taken care of immediately. Amanda wanted the analyst to tell her the reasons for the cancellations. The analyst attempted to explore this with the patient, but it never got beyond platitudes. Over the next few weeks it came up occasionally, with Amanda feeling humiliated that she received no explanation, and she ended up feeling she should have more assertively pushed for an explanation. The analyst then states, "It was in the context of this ongoing but dead-end conversation that Amanda's mother arrived from her hometown for one of her rare visits."

In the first reported session Amanda tells of how her mother talked of her own depression, an open secret that had never been acknowledged by her before. Amanda felt she had to bolster her mother's self-esteem. The analyst then notes,

> The idea that she has to stifle herself to bolster somebody's fragile abilities as a caretaker is a familiar theme; it represents a major dissatisfaction in her relationship with the men in her life and is also a powerful if subtle theme in the transference. *I am pulled to make an interpretation that would bring her feelings into the transference*, but am afraid that to do so would be heavy-handed and that it would register with Amanda as self-centered.
>
> (italics added)

It is this *pull* to make a transference interpretation that I'd like to highlight, especially since the analyst reports, "Amanda has been enthusiastically wrapped up in the details of her story – something that rarely happens in what is frequently (although, recently, less typically) a somewhat deadened atmosphere in the room."

Throughout the session the analyst beautifully describes how he/she is able to stay close to what Amanda can tolerate, leading to the patient bringing in new historical information about the grocery store incident. However, again we hear the analyst worrying about *the lack of a transference interpretation.*

> Although this incident itself was new to me [i.e., the mother's depression], I was not surprised by it, and Amanda herself seemed neither surprised nor moved. Her description of the event as "horrifying" sounded glib to me; her deeper feelings were bound up in the weekend with her mother and, I thought, even more in what had been going on recently between her and me. But this created a dilemma for me: I know Amanda well enough to know that making a transference interpretation would amount to telling her that she had been talking about the wrong thing throughout the session, and that this would be especially painful because she had been enthusiastically engaged in what she was saying. Yet to avoid the transference interpretation would be to collude with a kind of displacement of what she was feeling with me into the early relationship with her mother. I felt trapped between being critical and, in my own way, neglectful [i.e. like her mother, not wanting to know how she was feeling about what I had inflicted on her].
>
> (parentheses added)

Here we see the analyst feeling neglectful because he/she didn't make a transference interpretation, in spite of the fact that the patient is *enthusiastically* engaged in what she's talking about, and new information has emerged. There seems to be a *push* to interpret the transference, which the analyst feels is most *real* while Amanda would experience it as *unreal*. While the analyst is looking for what is unconscious, what is available preconsciously seems to be viewed as superficial.

Again, if we limit our transference interpretations to what is immediately expressed in the session associatively or in language action, we are in a much better position to help the patient understand what is occurring. Further, as noted earlier Freud (1913) cautioned against making interpretations of the transference unless it was used as a *resistance*, and this still seems a useful guide today. From my perspective, the only potential clarification might have come regarding Amanda's "glib" approach to the grocery incident. However, given that this likely was a necessary protection against potentially overwhelming feelings, I don't believe it would have been wise to follow this route at this time. Some defenses are necessary for the story to go on.

To go back to the material, the analyst does make a first transference interpretation in the middle of the next session.

Amanda: I talked with my girlfriend Leslie after the weekend. Her mother died seven years ago. She still misses her. Her mother is so present for Leslie. With me, it's out of sight, out of mind.

The analyst says, "Like when your mother left you in the grocery store."[8]

"Yeah," Amanda responds, "That's a story." The analyst then notes:

> Her "That's a story," although spoken somewhat sardonically, came across to me as an invitation. I thought she was letting me know that this event, which must have had such a powerful effect on a little girl, had been ground to bits in the mill of family myth-making and self-justification. She couldn't find what she needed to find in that story, which had been so reworked; perhaps she was offering me a chance to do more with it.

So I said, "And like when I cancel at the last minute and don't want to tell you why."

In this sequence the analyst first interprets what seems like Amanda's identification with her mother as the one who forgets people. The analyst understands Amanda's sardonic response as this "ground to bits" memory without much emotional meaning at this point. It is then fascinating that when Amanda is at an emotional distance the analyst interprets the transference in terms of Amanda being the forgotten one. It seemed possible to me that the analyst brings in Amanda's transference when the analyst is feeling shut off from the patient.

> "Mm," Amanda replied. "I was thinking about that. But it's in the past. I'm not going to get anything out of that now; I can't fix it. So what's the point?"

"It's striking," I said, "how quickly something between us becomes part of the past, a part of the past that's preserved in formaldehyde so that it can't be changed or even approached."

It seemed more like the feeling of something going on between analyst and patient was more in the analysts mind.

Amanda responded with "Mm" again, less thoughtful than the first time, and lapsed into a silence that lasted five minutes.

Hoping that something might be gained by pushing forward, I broke the silence: "I guess by bringing it up now, I expose you to the humiliation all over again."

> "Maybe," Amanda replied. "I was getting confused. It's like the past and the present merged." She fell silent again.

I was interested; Amanda isn't usually so psychologically creative. Past and present merging is an intriguing idea; it seems to signal the possibility of collaboration between us. So, after a moment, I asked her to say more. This is something I don't particularly like to do, but I felt all right about it in the moment because I wanted to affirm Amanda's interest in using her mind creatively just as she was starting to slip into the inertia she had earlier described.

"It's neither past nor present," she said. "I'm not sure what to do with it. I do think – what's the point of rehashing something that will ultimately leave me humiliated. There's nothing I can do to change it . . . I'm not sure what else I can say about it. It's like a third dimension; not past, not present, but both at the same time."

Here we see how the transference interpretations, which have been waiting in the wings, led to Amanda shutting down. We sense a certain aggressive side to the interpretations as the analyst "pushes forward," and uncharacteristically asks the patient to say more. From my own experience I've seen that I sometimes prematurely interpret the transference when I'm having a counter-transference reaction, discovered retrospectively, of feeling left out. I find myself wondering if the analyst was reacting to this "out of sight, out of mind" quality in Amanda's way of thinking. It's like the analyst finds it hard to accept that the cancelled appointments are not still on Amanda's mind in any preconscious sense.

Thinking that she was discovering transference, and that perhaps she was ready to work with it, I said, "That can be overwhelming, as there's no place to go to get away from the bad feelings."

"I guess so," Amanda said, with resignation and with a clear implication that my time was up, that I'd outstayed my welcome. "I don't know what to do."

"Perhaps you lapse into silence as a way of deadening yourself, avoiding the pain," I said.

Usually we feel if we outstay our welcome with a patient we keep quiet.

And, then, Amanda fell into the now familiar silence. It was a bit shocking to me at first, and I felt that I must be a noxious presence, perhaps the voice of pain itself.

Here I think the analyst is correct about being a "noxious presence," but more because she is interpreting beyond what Amanda can grasp.

I found myself wondering what she is thinking. Sometimes, in moments like this, I've asked, more because I want her to know I'm there and in the hope that doing so will bring some life to the room than because I believe that my asking will really help her to think. But this time I don't ask, although I do wonder. My hunch is that if I asked she would take her characteristic escape route, which carries her into the details of her day; there are always many details, because her work is complex and she is always balancing one obligation against another. She can get lost in these alleyways, and often does.

113

Again, these details seem to be experienced and are probably meant to have the analyst feel left out. However, the analyst's transference interpretations and actions revolve around the opposite, the patient's feeling left out.

Summary

Used judiciously, transference is a powerfully ally of the curative process in psychoanalysis. In this way, as Freud noted, the patient's problems come into the present in the relationship with the analyst, rather than as only an external event or a relic from the past. However, transference interpretations cannot be rushed, or they will be rejected or become intellectualized. Dealing with the patient's conflicts in displacement is often necessary, and helpful to the patient (i.e., in building representations), until the patient's transference is clearly in the room, most often as a resistance. While Freud's reference to a tiger jumping only once is overstated, it captures an important caution in interpreting transference.

Notes

1 Two articles on transference that deserve attention are by Glover (1924), who was the first to use the term working "within the transference," and Heimann's (1956) attempt to bridge Kleinian thinking with Freud's Structural Model.
2 I will limit myself primarily to those patients where the importance of working within the transference develops gradually, rather than the severe borderline and narcissistic states where the patient experiences the transference as a reality from the moment of the first greeting.
3 There are over one thousand references in PEP to the phrase *within the transference*. It primarily seems to be used as a *general* term indicting that the analyst is focusing exclusively on the transference, in whatever form that takes. It is sometimes used to describe the depth of the patient's absorption in the reality of the transference. Sometimes authors use it to denote the analyst taking a role within the transference, and enacting it.
4 I use the term "clarification" as defined by Bibring (1954). He described how in treatment clarification aims at "those vague and obscure factors (frequently below the level of verbalization) . . ." (p. 775).
5 Of course, any understanding of the transference is dependent on the analyst's capacity to tolerate and contain the feelings expressed, and in this way allow it to flourish.
6 From a supervision.
7 Gill, one of the early supporters of early transference interpretations, later became attuned to this problem and stated "*it is especially important to remember* [*that*] *one's zeal to ferret out the transference itself* [*can*] *become an unrecognized and objectionable actual behavior on the analyst's part, with its own repercussions on the transference*" (Gill, 1979, p. 285, parentheses added).
8 It is interesting here that the analyst changes the patient's active stance to something passive. That is rather than seeing Amanda as the one who forgets others, the analyst portrays her as the forgotten one. While the analyst might be correct that the patient is turning from passive to active as a defense, to turn it around without appreciating the uneasiness that accompanies such a defense, is usually not effective.

11

WORKING WITHIN THE COUNTERTRANSFERENCE

Countertransference is our best servant and worst master.
(Hanna Segal, in Hunter, 1993, p. 14)

The discovery of the importance of countertransference thoughts and feelings as a crucial source of information in the psychoanalytic situation has been one of the most significant contributions over the last 60 years.[1] We've come to realize its value in understanding every patient at *some point* in their analysis, and its benefits in understanding some patients even *right from the moment they walk into our consulting room.* As essential as it is as a tool in our analytic work, it also provides data that are difficult to sort out and translate. We have a rich body of literature on interpretations where the analyst uses his countertransference, and the clinical results are often impressive. However, it isn't always equally clear what processes within the analyst resulted in what kind of intervention. Here are some thoughts that I consider useful when working *within the countertransference.*

We often are tempted to take our countertransference reactions (in particular when they are strong) and use them directly for interpretations in the sense of a Descartian somersault: "*I feel therefore you are.*" By definition countertransference is an unconscious response in the analyst to an unconscious communication of the patient. The analyst's unconscious reaction will become noticeable to him via its preconscious and conscious derivatives. For instance, the analyst might feel something, i.e be unusually concerned, annoyed or anxious or find himself in unbidden surprising or uncomfortable reveries. Since these reactions interfere with his more balanced and neutral stance, the analyst is now vulnerable to enactments, in order to rid himself of these inner disturbances. Yet these very interferences to a balanced (free hovering) analytical stance can be used as a signal: Something is put at work in the analyst's mind that requires attention.

As early as 1934 Sterba developed the concept of the therapeutic split between the *experiencing* and the *observing* part of the ego. The former was elaborated by Freud in his first topographic theory, the latter was added in 1923 with the introduction of the ego in his Structural Theory. It is the *experiencing* part of the ego that engages in the transference, and the *observing* part of the ego that provides the capacity to reflect on these experiences. Hence countertransference reactions within the analyst occur within his *experiencing* ego (that is empathically attuned, makes use of trial identifications and is the recipient of the patient's current transference object) and are noticed with the observing part of the ego. While this is a continuous process of back and forth between both sides of the analyst's ego functions that is usually carried out through free hovering attention below the conscious radar screen, its dynamic is particularly pertinent when the analyst feels an urge to say or do something. To notice this impulse with the observing part of the ego allows for a first step: to analyze the upcoming feeling or fantasy in relation to the patient's material: How is what the analyst feels or is tempted to say or do, related to what the patient seems to be working on? To be able to reflect on these complex processes is what we are now used to calling containment in the sense of an active, metabolizing process. The analyst's task is to *represent* and translate not only his own psychic processes into something that offers new insight into the patient's quests and struggles, but also to proceed to formulating these results of his inner work into a message *digestible for the patient*. Working within the countertransference means that the analyst manages to do this self-analytic and transformative work. In short: Feelings and reveries will come up in the *experiencing* part of his ego; they will then be reflected by his *observing* ego functions with regard to the *process*, that is the patient's *way of working in the analysis*. The analyst will reflect on how the patient is communicating and how that plays a role in his own countertransference. It is my position that in this way we respect the patient's communications as leading us first to our countertransference, then to a better insight into the patient's unconscious and preconscious conflicts, and finally to an intervention that suits the patient's capacity to gain a better understanding of himself, opening his interest in the ongoing process and hence his readiness for the continuation of free association.

Interpreting within the countertransference

Working *within* the countertransference requires *both* an empathic attunement to the patients' anxieties and needs, and the analyst's empathic attunement to what is potentially stirred up within him. Further, and what I will highlight in what follows, is that before attempting to interpret *meaning* to the analysand based on our countertransference responses, *the analyst uses his countertransference to clarify, first for himself, how the patient is communicating and how that plays a role in the countertransference. It is my position that in this way we respect the patient's communications that lead to the analyst's countertransference. The patient's communications are most often unconscious and/or not yet fully thinkable. In order to analyze such a communication we need to start by representing it in a way that might be grasped by the analysand's preconscious at the clinical moment in the analysis.*

In short, in the method I'm suggesting, the analyst's countertransference feelings will lead him to look more closely at *the patient's way of working in the analysis*. For example, in a good-enough treatment that became stalled I began to feel inadequate. I noticed that while thoughts still came to the patient's mind, she claimed to have no understanding, and I found myself somewhat clueless. Wondering about this I realized there were subtle hints that the patient was questioning the value of trying to make anything of her thoughts. Over time I become aware of something familiar within me, i.e., of being late to recognize a pattern of waning interest in me, thinking instead that if I just keep trying, the person's interest will soon return. The interpretation *to the patient* of what was happening in the transference–countertransference began with this subtle shift in *how* she was thinking *in the analysis* (i.e., there's no value in understanding her thoughts). Why is this important? As noted earlier, we have the best opportunity to help build new representations if our interventions are geared to the preconscious. Therefore, we start the work on using our countertransference by seeing if the patient can "hear" what she is *doing* with her words. *It is potentially the most observable part of what is occurring, it is concrete (as is patients' thinking is at these times), and therefore has the greatest chance of becoming noticed.*

As noted earlier, we can rightly assume that if a psychological state is presented in language action, it is buried more deeply in the unconscious than are verbalized associations. We can further assume that what is more deeply unconscious has been strongly repressed, or represented without words or thoughts. For these reasons, trying to speak to what is deeply unconscious is unlikely to prove helpful. It is too fiercely guarded against, or in a form that will not be responsive to verbal interpretations.

Once we recognize a countertransference reaction, and reflect upon it, the patient's attempt to enact something in language action has already begun to be translated, i.e., *represented within the mind of the analyst*. From here the analyst can formulate the language action into words as a necessary step in helping patients find increasing degrees of freedom to think and feel. That is, after reflecting on our countertransference feelings, we try to understand what a patient is doing with[2] us in their words, tone, phrasing of sentences, and ideas expressed. *It is the understanding with the patient of how this doing takes place within the session* that is usually the first important interpretive step in freeing the patients from these repetitions in action by making them representable.

Implications for treatment

Types of countertransference in less disturbed patients

There is a range of the use of language action and resulting countertransference reactions depending on the severity of pathology. With the neurotically organized patient, we expect that *at some point* the analysis will be dominated by language action, but for the most part the analyst's countertransference will take place in the range of the symbolic. With severe narcissistic character disorders and border-line patients, language action is there from the beginning of treatment, and our countertransference reactions are more intense, and disturbing, as we are buffeted by more primitive affects and wishes. We've all had the experience of meeting a new patient, and within the first few minutes we are caught within a maelstrom of confusing emotions, where our usual ways of responding lead to conflict and intense negative or positive reactions.

In the remainder of this section I will describe different types of counter-transferences, and my ways of working within them.

Eliot

I will begin with a typical example of the transference–countertransference dynamic with a patient who used a *combination of language action and represented associations* to express an unconscious transference dynamic. The patient, Eliot, was in his forties, very smart, but a chronic underachiever. He had been under-employed since graduating from a prestigious college. He was married, blamed his wife's clinging behavior for keeping him from opportunities, and was generally angry at the world around him. A violent outburst at his wife scared him and led him to seek treatment

In growing up, Eliot was said to have developed normally until his mother went back to work when he was 2, when it was said he reacted with a severe regres-sion in speech and toilet training. Over time Eliot's mother became increasingly depressed, resulting in several hospitalizations starting when he was in latency. Although he had an older sister and brother, for some time I thought he was an only child, as much of what he shared about his childhood was about being alone. In addition to depression, his mother struggled with alcoholism, resulting in angry, seemingly irrational outbursts. At the beginning of treatment his father, a successful investment advisor, was devalued, although as it turned out he was the more consistent maternal presence in the home.

It was two weeks before I was to have surgery that was going to keep me out of the office for 4–6 weeks. I wasn't in any imminent danger, but the need for the surgery came up suddenly. When I told Eliot about this, in his characteristic manner he said a few formal words of sympathy. Then he immediately began to talk about what happened the previous weekend, which took up most of the session. This was his usual manner of dealing with absences, but I was struck by his non-reaction to what I'd just told him.

I felt deadened and withdrawn from what Eliot was telling me. I wondered about a projective identification or an unconscious attempt to angrily or defen-sively deaden me for abandoning him. However, I also realized I was narcissisti-cally vulnerable at this time, so who was contributing what to my withdrawn and deadened state of mind was unclear. I had already informed a number of patients about the surgery and impending absence by the time I told Eliot. While some had a similar reaction to Eliot's, my feelings about their reactions were not similar to those with Eliot, so I thought there was something more than only my fragile narcissism fueling my reaction. Yet, I had to consider if there were reasons why I had this reaction to Eliot more than other patients. What came to mind was surprising. Earlier in treatment Eliot objected to my practice of charging him for missed appointments, since he "knew" he was wealthier than most patients and therefore he could take more vacations, and thus felt he was being penalized by my policy. There was little room to work with Eliot's grandiose view of himself as an "exception" at the time, and we agreed on a compromise solution for the moment. I wondered if I was still irritated with his "depriving" me of my fee. I was especially vulnerable to feeling "deprived" given that my sense of myself as an active, healthy man was challenged by this surgery. However, what was occurring in Eliot's mind was unclear to me.

As I returned to listening to the words and music of Eliot's narrative, I noticed two things. The first was a cadence to his voice, which was different. Eliot was usually a non-stop talker, and his associations were often lively. It was this libidinal investment in his thoughts and mind that led me, in the beginning, to have hope for a positive analytic outcome, in spite of his life-failures over the past 20 years. In this session I realized there were unusual pauses, and I kept feeling I was losing the connection to where he started and ended a series of thoughts. It was this loss of connection via the cadence of his speech that caught my attention as one possible factor in my countertransference withdrawal. While the obvious content interpretation of my now being the "lost" one, as a projection of Eliot's split off feelings of loss came to mind, *I first pointed to the change in the cadence of Eliot's speech, and the difficulty I was having following his thoughts.* He hadn't noticed it, but could see it once I brought it to his attention. He also realized he was losing his train of thought while he was talking. Eliot's thoughts then turned to a meeting he was at where, throughout, he was highly attuned to what others were thinking of him. His preoccupation revolved around whether others were thinking he was too loud, too brash, or putting himself forward too much. As Eliot elaborated on this story, I found myself thinking of his narcissistic, depressed mother, who he felt he had to care for from childhood through most of his early adult life. When his mother locked herself in her bedroom and threatened suicide after a fight with the father, it was Eliot who was sent by the father to coax her out of her room. Throughout his life he felt he had to be what his mother wanted him to be so that she could be enlivened. For him it was a matter of life and death. He was her self-object. It took me a while to understand that after his mother died Eliot's lament that he couldn't keep his mother alive was a metaphor, and not simply magical thinking. Eliot also felt his mother wanted him to be a "potato," and she would call him "my little potato." For Eliot this represented how his mother wanted him to be "silently growing" out of sight, causing no problems, except when she needed him to entertain her. In this one can also see the symbolic meaning of Eliot's mother seeing him as food or nourishment, where his presence had to feed her.

My countertransference reaction, Eliot's association to the meeting, and my associations, led me to say the following:

F.B.:   After we both notice losing the connections in what you were saying, your thoughts go to a meeting where you're worried that you're drawing too much attention to yourself. I wonder if this is similar to concerns you had when I told you about my surgery?

Eliot: I felt selfish. You were the one having surgery and my thoughts should be more about you. But I got scared. This bad thing was happening and how would I do? Then I told myself you would be fine and I calmed down.

F.B.:   So reassuring yourself that I would be OK blotted out your feelings of being scared, which worried you because you felt you weren't focusing enough on me.

Eliot: [through tears] I just had another thought. When I saw you today you seemed to be holding your arm in an awkward position, as if you were in pain. As I thought that I felt some pains in my chest.

F.B.:   Maybe we can say you were drawn to even feel my pain.

Eliot: I remember, near the end of my mother's life, how I felt sick to my stomach all the time. [His mother died of stomach cancer.] But I felt I had to be chipper and upbeat, pretending like I didn't know the end was near. [Eliot begins sobbing for several minutes.] I don't know why I keep thinking this. [He then tells an elaborate story of a very expensive trip he is planning for his wife's birthday even though it isn't at a good time for him.]

F.B.:   Just like you felt you had to sacrifice your own worries to take care of me, you do the same with Robyn [his wife].

Eliot: When you say that I start to feel anxious. I know Robyn doesn't feel like she needs this kind of extravagant vacation, and it's the worst possible time for me. Yet I still feel like I have to do it.

As we can see, Eliot's unresponsiveness to my informing him of my impending surgery is, in fact, the result of a complex reaction. Eliot's concern for his own welfare immediately arouses anxiety over being "selfish," and his focus shifts to how he should be concerned about me. However, showing concern also seems to be threatening (i.e., as it's associated with losing himself) and the resultant compromise formation is silence, as Eliot reassures himself that I will be OK. Eliot ends up having no concern for himself or me, and the analysis goes on as if nothing has happened. This "nothing happened" is what we frequently interpret as an attack against the analyst (as I felt in my first countertransference reaction), when in this instance we can see it as an attack against the self (i.e., Eliot's worries for himself need to be discarded due to anxiety), and as we shall see a protection of the object.

*   Listening to Eliot's associations we hear that he is afraid others are seeing him as self-centered. When I'm able to connect this concern with his unresponsiveness, Eliot is able to feel the pain he first ignored. However, it is another's pain. It is*

what he imagines as my pain, just as he was only able to feel his mother's pain as she was dying. He cannot easily feel his own pain, as it is frightening and dangerous. "Selfish" is the word he uses to describe being "scared" when I tell him of my operation. He must turn his attention to the object, and pretend like nothing happened, or his tenuous connection to the object will be shattered.

Eliot's thoughts then lead us to see another meaning in his "not noticing," i.e., caring for the object. Thus he needs to "not notice" when his mother is dying, just like he didn't notice when his mother was hospitalized, and like he didn't notice his mother's narcissistic self-involvement or angry tirades, and most importantly, his own reactions to any of this. His associations lead him to how he is driven to care for his wife, even recognizing that it has little to do with her. In Eliot's mind caring for a woman is to literally keep her alive, and thus to feel enlivened himself. This was his job in life – to keep his mother alive. "Not noticing" became one way of doing this, and thus its manifestation in the transference–countertransference when I tell him of my impending surgery.

In working with my countertransference reaction, I first pointed to what Eliot is doing with his speech (i.e., losing connections), rather than interpreting the meaning or content of projecting his feeling of loss (e.g., "Your way of talking leaves me feeling a loss of connection. I wonder if in this way I'm the one who feels the loss rather than you."). Instead I point to what is potentially most observable within the transference–countertransference dynamic. This leaves it up to Eliot to see which part, if any, he is able to deal with during this complicated time in the treatment. As happens with more neurotically organized patients, an association comes to mind that allows for greater understanding of one aspect of Eliot's reaction to my surgery and lengthy absence.

Follow up[3]

Eliot returned to analysis 4 weeks later. He seemed glad to see me, and after a few words of sympathy for my having to go through an operation, he said he was pleased I was back. His thoughts immediately turned to different situations where he felt, if he said what was on his mind, others would be critical of him or retaliate against him. For example, because of his productivity at work he was in line for a significant salary hike. However, he was sure that if he went to his section head to mention this, this woman would put him down. *So once again Eliot's fear was that expressing his own needs or wishes will lead others to turn away from or retaliate against him.*

After a while Eliot wondered if he was avoiding thinking about what it was like to be back in analysis. His first thoughts were about how busy he was during the last month, and he was glad to have the time. Eliot then described a meeting he arranged for his colleagues to alert them to new legislation that would affect their way of doing business. He was angry with the people who weren't there, and those who left in the middle of the meeting. Eliot then remarked again that he was glad I was back, as so many things had gone on. He had been thinking about the fact that I lost a month's income, and thought he would pay me for the month anyway. *In this I feel Eliot is saying he had no needs toward me while I was gone (i.e., he was so busy), but he was angry with these other people who weren't there. This feeling triggers unconscious anxiety, as it is probably too close to how he feels about my absence, and Eliot once again imagines he has to take care of me by paying for the time I missed.* I then say to him:

F.B.: After describing situations at work where you imagine being cut down for wanting something (a salary raise), and feeling angry at the people who don't show up for you, your thoughts go to taking care of me by paying me. I'm wondering if your telling us that if you felt angry at my not being here for you, it makes you uneasy, and then you feel you must *take care of me.*

Eliot's thoughts turned to the previous weekend where he made the plans for Saturday evening with another couple. Although everyone seemed to be having a good time, he worried that he "dragged" everyone into what he wanted to do. He couldn't concentrate on what people were saying.

F.B.: So meeting your needs makes you worry what you're doing to someone.
Eliot: I was just having trouble following you. The same thing happened when you mentioned my feeling angry. Like Saturday night, I lost my concentration.

In Eliot's return to analysis we see a repetition of his relating to me as if I was his "dead mother." He fears his own needs will lead to disapproval or retaliation so he becomes a "potato," and can only say what it's like to be back but not what it was like for me to be gone. In fact what he can only be aware of was how convenient it was that I was gone. When he gets close to feelings of anger over being abandoned, he becomes anxious and immediately needs to care for me by thinking about paying me for the time I was away. Thus any need to take care of himself or wish to be cared for must be obliterated, replaced by the need to care for the other.

Clarifying and interpreting

While I've focused on the need to *clarify the transference action* playing a part in the analyst's countertransference, before interpreting its meanings, of course there are times when we interpret the content of transference actions. *It is when the transference action is closer to the unconscious–preconscious border* that a more direct interpretation is more likely to be understood by the patient. Here is an example.

Larry, in the termination phase, and still dealing with the difficulty in knowing of his competitive feelings (while still being very competitive), remembered a movie. In this World War II movie, one American soldier was leading another through Japanese-held territory to the American base camp. The soldier who was leading them had to carry the other soldier much of the way as he was injured. The final step in getting back to their base camp meant running through an open field with high grass. They assumed there were unseen Japanese soldiers guarding this dividing line between the two armies. The soldier leading the way decided they would have to split up, so at least one of them might get back. They did so, and given the transference, the movie had the leader as the one who was shot, while the other guy made it back to safety. It was an allegory for the dangers of seeing oneself as a leader. It was also an example of how one could win by seeming to lose. In the movie it was the damaged guy who lived. It was another piece of a familiar pattern in the Larry's life, which I interpreted. A few days later in listening to the patient, I found myself feeling this analysis would never end (an analytic failure). In catching this, and listening more closely, Larry was talking in a desultory fashion that lent a depressive tone to his words. I said,

F.B.:   Your desultory tone suggests today you may be trying to win by losing, like in the movie.

Thus, with only a nod to the "doing" part of the session, I interpreted what Larry was unaware of, but felt was potentially closer to awareness.

Larry suddenly remembered that he left out the ending of the movie. He was amazed he forgot it, but could then see its importance. The rest of the movie was that the Japanese soldiers retreated later in the day, and the next day they found the supposedly dead leader soldier, hurt but alive in the tall grass. In short, what Larry "forgot" to mention was that the leader was still alive. In this way, his imagined victory via defeat was not complete. The leader (analyst) was only hurt, not dead.

In this example, rather than pointing to what the patient was doing with his words, I interpreted the unconscious fantasy captured in his theme and tone, i.e., it was best and safest to win by losing. Larry readily recognized my interpretation, and his remembering the real end of the movie, where the leader was alive, confirmed and deepened the interpretation. Again, I think this type of interpretation can only be made later in an analysis, where we have already begun to represent unconscious fantasies that bring them closer to the border of the preconscious.

Countertransference in defense enactments

Baranger et al. (1983) wisely noted, "Not all phenomena of transference and countertransference correspond to the same model or to the same mechanism; nor should they be treated in this way" (p. 3). In this section I will try to define a defense (i.e., *defense enactment*) that leads to a roll-responsive countertransference, and differentiate it from *inhibiting defenses* and *projective identification*.

A defense enactment differs in a number of ways from the inhibiting defenses described by Gray (1994). *Primary among these differences is that in defense enactments the analyst first grasps that a defense is occurring via awareness of a countertransference response.* In contrast to inhibiting defenses, which may or may not be specifically related in the clinical moment to the transference (e.g., a lifelong inhibition of sexual thoughts), a defense enactment is created within the transference/countertransference. As an example of the distinction I am trying to make, let us look at the defense of intellectualization. We often observe a patient expressing a previously defended thought or feeling, and then quickly using intellectualization as a defense. Frequently we can observe such a defense and, in a comfortable manner, help the patient observe what has just happened. However, once we start to feel intensely about the patient's use of intellectualization (e.g., to become bored or irritated), I believe we have moved into experiencing a defense enactment. *At a descriptive level it may be useful to think of the inhibiting defenses as arising from an unconscious intrapsychic process, whereas defense enactments are an unconscious interpersonal transference–countertransference process.*

While the analyst's experience of the countertransference, at the moment it occurs, may seem similar to experiences of defenses with severe narcissistic and borderline character disorders, and with other countertransference reactions, the countertransference in defense enactments stems from a different source, and the feelings of the analyst will be dissimilar. Sandler's description of the *analyst's role-responsiveness* (1976, p. 44) comes close to capturing the analyst's experience with defense enactments. Sandler described the analyst's role-responsiveness thus: "Within the limits set by the analytical situation he will, unless he becomes aware of it, tend to comply with the role demanded of him, to integrate it into his mode of responding and relating to the patient" (p. 46). Sandler viewed this as due primarily to the patient's resistance to awareness of an attempt to gratify an infantile relationship that is an intrapsychic representation of an earlier object relationship he or she may unconsciously be attempting to impose on the analyst. The analyst responds with a corresponding role-responsive countertransference. However, *in defensive enactments the analyst unconsciously takes a role to help protect the patient from a dangerous thought or feeling.* The role-responsiveness is to the patient's defensive position. *The analyst's countertransference is to help keep a defense in place, not gratify an infantile wish.* It is an unconscious response to the patient's feeling of danger. However, our role responsiveness to particular defense enactments likely has to do with our personal history and conflicts. One's ability to step back and analyze what's going on is a determinant of whether these issues help or hinder our understanding.

In severe character disorders derivatives of unconsciously driven transferences become dangerously close to awareness from the beginning of treatment, and the primitive defenses against them begin immediately, leading to countertransference reactions in the analyst almost from the moment treatment begins. *In contrast, with the patients I am describing, the patient's awareness of unconsciously driven transferences, and the defenses against them, develop only over the course of an analysis.*

As I understand it, the underlying mechanism in projective identification is different. Bell (2001) suggests that many see projective identification as synonymous with the capacity to evoke feelings in the analyst. However, the Kleinians view projective identification as both a defensive maneuver and an *unconscious fantasy*. It is the unconscious fantasy of what has been projected into the object that defines projective identification for most Kleinians. The defense is projection, and the unconscious fantasy is that the self can be forced into other objects, to enter and affect those objects from within, altering them and controlling them. It is an omnipotent fantasy that leads the patient to react to the analyst as if the defended-against feelings were really in the analyst. When the analyst reacts in a way that contradicts the patient's fantasy, the patient feels in great danger and reacts accordingly. Hinshelwood (1989) points out the "intensity and numbingness" (p. 184) of the analyst's subjective experience when patients use projective identification.

The experience of the countertransference in the midst of a projective identification appears to me to have a distinct quality that should enable the analyst to differentiate the occasion when he is the object of a projective identification, and when there is a defense enactment occurring. With a projective identification the analyst unconsciously senses there is a demand upon him to play a role in his patient's fantasy. We usually have a strong countertransference reaction of wanting to reject the projective identification, and a belief that these feelings are justified by the objective experience. It is at these times we tend to defensively argue against the projection, or criticize the patient for having it. A typical patient's reaction to the analyst's acting in a way that is counter to a projective identification is stunned rage. A dangerous stranger is what a patient experiences when the analyst doesn't act in accordance with a projective identification. *An unwelcome acquaintance is what a patient may experience when the analyst points out a defense enactment.* Further, in a defense enactment one usually doesn't have the feeling of being so completely controlled as one does with a projective identification, or that the countertransference feelings are justified by the objective experience. Rather than feeling caught in the totality of one's countertransference response, there is a greater likelihood that the analyst can observe himself reacting in ways that don't fit with one's usual manner of working. Finally, *although I have made clear distinctions between the analyst's reaction to defense enactments and other defenses, the reality is there are degrees of each that shade into each other.*

Working with severe character disorders

The main difficulty in working with more severe character disorders is that while there is an intense pressure to make something happen in the transference–countertransference dynamic, the defense these patients have against recognizing what they are trying to do is equally strong. Thus the analyst is bombarded by primitive unconscious messages to *do something or be a particular way*, while the analysand is defending against knowing this. The forms in which these messages are conveyed might, at first, seem like free associations. Meanwhile the analyst feels propelled to *do* something, which is difficult to represent or contain, let alone employ this countertransference reaction for a useable intervention. Partly this is due to the primitive unconscious messages the analyst is registering, *stimulating primitive elements in his own unconscious*, and partly due to the language action method by which the message is conveyed.

Michael

From the first moment I met Michael I rather disliked him. I have never had this reaction to a patient before or since. It was quite puzzling at the time and, although I can point to certain physical characteristics I immediately noticed, this was only part of the picture. His mismatched t-shirt, short shorts, and dirty flip- flops, were overly casual and slovenly even for the college student he was. Over time I learned that Michael was like one of those 10-year-old boys who one would go up to and, with a friendly pat on the back, affix a sign that said, "Hit me." Much of the analysis revolved around my attempt to understand this frequent countertrans-ference reaction I had to Michael.

Unsurprisingly, Michael came for treatment because of his social isolation and poor grades. He had no friends I heard about, and the reasons for this were externalized. This worked at an earlier time, when he felt he was disliked because of envy, i.e., he was smarter than other guys. This didn't hold up when he came to a prestigious college. He put off women, and he rationalized this by saying it was more important to concentrate on his studies. An uncle had a successful analysis, and idealized the analyst. It was my impression Michael came wanting *to have* an analysis but not wanting *to be analyzed*.

Michael was an only child raised by his physician father and artist mother, who divorced when he was 12. While they cared for him their interest in him was intermittent. There were frequent fights throughout the marriage. He would be terrified and run to his room when these fights started, but then he would excitedly listen to hear if his father would hit his mother, which was rare but did happen. He was never hit, but was psychically smacked around by cruel denigrations casually administered. Classmates bullied him throughout his schooling.

In my work with Michael I first tried to listen to what he was conveying in the content of his associations. Interestingly this proved frustrating rather than interesting to me. I found myself thinking about saying, and sometimes saying, things that weren't useful. I would ask him questions, or wonder why he wasn't free-associating in the *regular* way. It took me some time to understand this as repeating part of his history whereby I was psychoanalytically smacking him around.

Again, this is one of those times when the patient's transference actions stimulate something in the analyst's unconscious that is not being contained and reflected upon at the moment. While it intuitively makes sense that this is more difficult to do when the analyst is faced with severe pathology, it may also be true that we think of certain patients this way because they stimulate a part of our unconscious we haven't fully worked through.

Oftentimes Michael would talk for an entire session, and I would find myself thinking of the last line from Phillip Roth's novel, *Portnoy's Complaint*, where it becomes clear he's talking through the whole book to his analyst, who says his only words in the last page: "Now vee may perhaps to begin. Yes?" Over 200 pages, and the analyst finally speaks. As I understood my association, it captured the perverse nature of Michael's enacted beating fantasy. Michael's language action was unconsciously designed to have me beat him with denigrating words or disapproving silence, and it touched something within me that I continually had to work on.

Here is a brief example of the type of session during this time. Even when I'm not enacting my projected role in the beating fantasy, it becomes for Michael part of a beating fantasy.

Michael: [As is often the case, Michael fills the session with declarative statements. That is, his words are statements of how things *are*, which lead neither to questions, reverie, or surprise.] I'm thinking about my difficulty with paying attention to things. It would be a good time to try one of these drugs for a better attention span. I have this friend who tried it, and he said it worked wonders. I know it also has to do with my mother's lack of attention [a very old formulation repeated many times], but I think there is a chemical component involved.

All of the above was spoken in a defensive manner, as if he was in a fight with me, believing I would argue against his trying medication, and tell him psychoanalysis was all he needed, and this is what I spoke to.

F.B.: I sense your anticipating I would argue against your taking medication.
Michael: Well yes. I know you haven't in the past, but this is different. We've talked about the psychological reasons for my poor attention, but there hasn't been much change. There was this study reported in the paper, how there were likely thousands of adults with ADD that hadn't been treated as children. I didn't have problems with attention as a child, but I think there is a lot they don't know about it yet.
F.B.: It still seems like you're still arguing with me on something I haven't argued against.
Michael: So are you saying I'm not doing this right. You know I just can't do anything right in your view. You tell me to say what's coming to mind, and when I do you say that's the wrong thing.

At this point I felt my irritation growing, and I wanted to argue in a way that would antagonize him further, leading him to excitedly engage in further provocations. I felt myself ready to withdraw into silence, as I couldn't think of a way to find some part of Michael's observing ego to think about what was occurring.

Michael:	[continued] so now you're not saying anything. I guess I didn't get it right again. You are such a jerk!
F.B.:	This seems familiar. Whatever I say or don't say, leads you to feel like I'm beating you up, and the more it happens the more excited and lively you become.
Michael:	If you say so.
	[The session continued in this way until the end.]

I see this example as typifying the difficulty of using one's countertransference in work with the more severe character disorders. For much of the time, representing and containing countertransference reactions can help prevent the analyst from enacting a role the patient has assigned him (e.g., in Michael's case it was trying to not engage in a verbal beating). In this session I was able to *try* and find an observing part of Michael's ego that could give him some space for reflection. However, it seemed like the excited push for feeling beaten was too strong at this point. Over time we were able to find more space for both of us, but Michael's urge to be beaten remained a constant, albeit at a lower level.

Problems in interpreting countertransference

In general I think we need to approach our countertransference reactions cautiously so that we may reflect on them and their multiple possible meanings, before using them to interpret something to the patient. However, the wish to extrude feelings we sense are put into us is often very strong, so that we are all prone to push them back on the patient. Further, in our never ending attempt to simplify complex processes, we frequently are drawn to view our counter-transference reactions as an *unerring guide to something going on in the patient's mind*. We rarely hear of an analyst reporting that he had this or that feeling, interpreted on the basis of this feeling, *and it turned out to be inaccurate*. Further, there are some theories of the mind that lead to countertransference reactions being interpreted in a singular direction, while other possibilities tend to be neglected.

Love, hate, care

Understandably, split off and projected aggression is frequently seen as what stirs our countertransference reactions. However, I think it is necessary to take heed of what Schmidt-Hellerau (2001, 2002, 2005) pointed out, which is that there are a number of unfortunate consequences in Freud's (1920) move to the drive theory of libido and aggression. Primary amongst these is that the concept of *self-preservation* as a drive was lost, and aggression was put in the position of a primal drive rather than a force in obtaining gratification. Schmidt-Hellerau (2001, 2005) has made an impressive case for the retention of a preservative drive, striving not only at the preservation of the self, but also at the preservation of the object. Without such a notion analysts have been primed to see any turning away from the analyst or analysis as an aggressive act, rather than the possibility of it being a self-preservative one. If focused on exclusively, it can lead to blind spots in understanding the analysand's attempts to preserve himself and/or the object. For many years it led to a view of resistances as an attack on the analysis rather than an attempt at self-preservation. Below is a brief vignette where conflicts over libidinal strivings, object preservation and self-preservation are acted out, and get reduced to aggression against the analyst.

A college student with fears of the damage her accomplishments would cause, came to a session with her female analyst exultant over recent successes. After describing a successful social weekend, she reported that in the writing class she was taking, where there was a big lecture that then broke up into small groups, the instructor and assistant instructor fought over her. Each wanted her in the group they were leading. The patient then went on,

> I don't want to be *big headed* about it, but it feels good. I was writing today and almost finished the chapter. Today was a good day. I'm worried though, because when I get so exuberant I say stupid, hurtful things. It makes people angry 'cause I don't watch what I'm saying. It's like being drunk. Things just pop out. It happens when I'm feeling really happy. We once had a babysitter my mother didn't like, and I heard her tell my father she was "fat and stupid." So one time when she misplaced my homework I blurted out that she was "fat and stupid." I was so embarrassed, I felt afraid of her, her anger. She was so mad at me. I am such a fuck up. When I feel good I feel that I can say anything, and I don't realize it. I might say something *big headed*, like telling someone I'm so much better looking than you. I need something to self-regulate, to bring me down a notch.

Suddenly she said, "Oh, is my hair flat? What can I do to fluff my hair? What do you think?"

The patient then went to the bathroom and stayed for 5 minutes. While the patient was gone the analyst felt irritated with the patient (i.e., feeling like she was treating the session as unimportant, which the analyst felt was an extension of her frequently coming late), and wondered to herself whether she had just become the "fat and stupid" babysitter. When the patient returned and said nothing about what happened, the analyst felt like questioning her in a confrontational manner. When the analyst reflected on this she felt she had become the angry person who was dealing with this incompetent analysand, who misplaced the session (like the babysitter with the homework), and interpreted this to the patient, who was bewildered.

In this vignette, we see the analyst's countertransference reaction of irritation while the patient went to the bathroom, leading to her noticing of her wish to be confrontational. This then leads to an interpretation of the patient's split off anger being projected into the analyst.

An equally plausible explanation is that the patient is expressing one aspect of her conflict over being *big headed*. On the one hand she expresses the fear that if she becomes too big headed she will become cruel. Then suddenly, when she is expressing this fear, she expresses a concern she is *flat headed* (i.e., not big headed enough). When the patient returns the analyst feels irritated with her more *big headed* state (i.e., as if the patient's prime purpose in going to the bathroom was a message to the analyst: you are like the babysitter). While this may have been the case, our inclination to view aggression as primary sometimes can keep us from alternative explanations, and justify countertransference reactions. Another way to approach this issue might have been to help the patient see that with her action and associations she presents her dilemma (i.e., how to fulfill her ambitious side, while protecting the object). This could be brought to her attention by saying, "I think you've just shown us the dilemma you're in. If you feel good about yourself, big headed, you feel you get cruel. Yet feeling not so good about yourself, feeling flat-headed, is unacceptable."

In summary I agree with Segal's view of countertransference as "the best servant and worst master." It can allow us a window into the unconscious like nothing else in psychoanalysis, while at the same time it is a delicate tool that needs to be used cautiously, with appropriate safeguards. Further, ways of interpreting using our countertransference have not always fit with the principles of working with what is preconscious. This is especially difficult to do with severe character disorders where, from the very beginning of treatment, *a way of being is enacted to protect from crippling anxieties*, enact a traumatic past with others, and heal damaged self-states, that touch off parts of the analyst's unconscious that are difficult to contain. Ways of working described by the Kleinians, Kernberg, Ogden, Kohut, Green, and many others suggest we are still struggling with how to work with these patients.

Notes

1 See Jacobs (1999) on the history of countertransfernce.
2 I say *with* us, rather than *to* us, as the primary motivation may be self-protective.
3 I was looking forward to returning to work after my convalescence, but wondered if I was in enough narcissistic balance to hear my patients. In this session with Eliot I felt that I was working well enough.

12

INTRODUCTION TO A CONVERSATION
Helping patients begin psychoanalysis

A recent book by the social essayist, Stephen Miller, is titled *Conversation: A History of a Declining Art*. As we know from personal experience, good conversation is rare, but exhilarating when it occurs. Since the eighteenth century philosophers and scholars have talked about the importance of good conversation, and the impediments to it. For me, in its simplest terms, *a good conversation is about creating further conversation*. It's about engaging others in furthering along thinking by careful listening, reflection, and considering one's inner life. This is also a pretty good approximation of what we hope occurs in the analytic conversation. For the patient, we hope to create an atmosphere where an inner conversation that has been disrupted can be resumed with the help of the analyst.

We all know what it's like to be with someone who *wants* to be in a conversation. Some are good listeners and reflect on the conversation. It can stimulate us to think more about what we've said. On the other hand there are those who can't wait to interject their own thoughts. As analysts we struggle with these issues, and it can be a central issue in whether we help a patient into or out of psychoanalysis.

As indicated earlier, it is helpful to think of two types of conversation patients bring to treatment. The first is the ability to use associations to tell a story that is not conscious, but preconscious. A second conversation we hear in treatment occurs in language action, where the words are meant to *do something*. Then there are times when it seems a conversation has come to a halt, or the patient looks to the analyst to lead the conversation. In all these conversations the analyst is trying to understand what leads the patient to this particular type of conversation taking place. In this I'm focusing not only on the content, but also on the form of the conversation. As if things aren't complicated enough, we also need to pay attention to the underlying affect in a conversation. The greeting, "Hello," can be said jovially, in a friendly way, seductively, hissed, spit out, whispered or yelled. Thus we need to listen to the music as well as the words in our patients' conversation.

However, we soon come upon an important question: Why do we want to help further the patient's conversation? – especially with regard to its sub-text. I would answer that a basic tenet of psychoanalytic thinking is that what leads people to our offices revolves around their inability to feel or think something, or else being stuck in repetitive thoughts and feelings. *That is, our patients suffer from interrupted or unproductive conversations with themselves.* This was Freud's monumental discovery.

The increasing capacity of patients to know of and *own* their inner conversations is central to their developing a *psychoanalytic mind.* It is the basis of an exhilarating freedom of the mind. In contrast, it is the inhibited, restricted, interior conversations, which leaves them feeling depleted, confused, and unappreciated. We have to help them understand the fears that led to them falling internally silent, so they can pick up again the thread of these conversations. In short, I find the metaphor of interior conversations useful, as it captures a way of thinking about the therapeutic process, especially the analyst's role in aiding or interfering with the patient's conversations.

A supervisee recently told me of the following clinical moment.

P: I was angry when I left here yesterday . . . it's hard to remember what happened.

A: Something makes it difficult to remember *that* you were angry at me. Do you have a sense of discomfort and want to move away from your angry feelings?

P: No . . . I'll get back to it . . . other things are on my mind.

Here we have the patient barely getting started in her conversation, a conversation about why it might be hard to have a conversation, when the analyst steers the conversation to what she's interested in (the transference). It is also striking that in steering the conversation the analyst changes the nature of the patient's conversation. That is, the patient says, "*I was angry.* It's hard to remember what happened." The analyst says, " Something makes it difficult to remember that *you were angry.*"

As analysts we have always struggled with sifting the patient's conversation from our own. I believe it is important to highlight this struggle, because the analyst's intrusion into the patient's conversation, as well-intentioned as it may be, is a problem across the theoretical spectrum.

In fact, if we allow it, patients will converse with us in words and actions, their negations, denials, and intellectualizations, in their telling of dreams, or not, in their expression of intense feelings, or not, and the multitudinous forms of communication available. In these conversations we will find the why of our patients coming to us, and the road to their leaving. In between they will tell us why they shouldn't have conversations with us, and vehemently deny there is any conversation going on in their mind. At other points patients will be happy to have a conversation with us, but will be uncomfortable with owning their side of the conversation.

The first interview

There are multiple goals in any first interview. We all have to make some type of evaluation of the person's readiness for psychoanalysis, and whether psychoanalysis will be useful to the prospective patient. In the vast majority of people I see in consultation, I haven't felt the need to make a diagnosis, and thus feel freer to convey to my patients that *I can best help them through understanding their own mind*. I don't say anything about this, but hope they experience this in the way I work. For those patients who are capable of becoming intrigued by this way of working, it can be an eye opening and emotional experience. Below is a vignette where it worked out well.

A vignette from a first interview

Sarah came to her first interview because of feeling unhappy and unfulfilled. In a plaintive voice she launched into multiple complaints about her husband, who she felt was selfish and not giving.

In my musings I wondered how she thought I could help her, but recognized in her voice the cry of someone who feels she has no power to change anything.

Sarah continued in this same vein for quite a while, including now her adolescent children in the mix. She then said, "You probably want to know about my growing up," and launched into a story about her mother, and how controlling she was of everyone. Her mother cowed her father, who Sarah saw as a kind and gentle man. Her older brother lived across the street from her parents, and never married. Sarah felt that sometimes she thinks she got married to get away from her mother's influence.

F.B.:   After connecting your unhappiness to your husband's selfishness, your thoughts turn to how no one in your family seemed able to stand up to your mother. I wonder if one reason you're seeking treatment is *to find your own voice so you can speak up for yourself.*

In this I am integrating her associations to her early history with the plaintive tone in her voice indicating, to me, she felt she had no voice. While her husband may, indeed, have been selfish, I saw finding her own voice as a way of helping her understand more about the dynamic between the two of them.

Sarah: I know my father secretly agreed with my complaints about my mother, but he always took her side. I'll always remember the one time he stood up for me. I wanted to go to the movies with my friends, and my mother started saying nasty things to me, making suggestions I was up to no good. My father finally told her to "stop," and amazingly she did. I felt so good after that, but that was it. He probably got hell from her after I left [tears come to her eyes].

Sarah returned a few days later. After a brief period of therapy she entered analysis.

In what I say to Sarah, I am trying to convey that treatment is about listening carefully to what comes to her mind, and in what way. By listening in this way, and communicating how I listen, I convey that her voice is worth listening to. Being able to listen to *her own voice* becomes a central part of the treatment. I saw her tears and association to the experience with her father as an indication of her capacity to work in this way. She appreciated the analyst–father standing up for her, but was appropriately cautious in hoping it might happen more than once.

Betty

In another example from an interview by an experienced psychoanalyst, the conversation deepens through the analyst's interventions, and it also results in this patient entering analysis. The analyst learned later that the patient immediately felt comfortable with her, sensing the analyst was attempting to understand her in a complex way, and this allowed her to open up in ways that surprised her. I will look at the analyst's interventions only from the perspective *of how to invite a patient into an analytic conversation.*

The patient, Betty, is a woman who is about 45, and the psychoanalyst is also a woman. The patient begins the session by talking briefly about being nervous, and looks at the analyst in an inquiring way.

This is a pattern that continues throughout the interview, and it becomes clear later on that it has particular dynamic significance.

The analyst encourages Betty to continue, and Betty comes right to the point. She and her husband no longer have sex, and she is both afraid the relationship will end and she feels the urge to run away. Again Betty stops and looks inquiringly at the analyst who asks the patient if she can say more. The patient says it has always been like this. When she had a sexual relationship it would be good at first and then she would withdraw.

So far we are hearing a number of conversations. There is the conversation of the patient telling the analyst what brings her for help (i.e., her confusion, the sexual problems in her relationship with her husband). The second, underlying conversation, is Betty demonstrating, in action, exactly what she's talking about, i.e., she tells us that in sexual relationships things start out well and then she withdraws. This is what happens every time she starts to talk to the analyst. She begins strongly, and suddenly pulls back. In this sense the interrupted conversation becomes what this conversation is about. The analyst senses this and tries to encourage the patient to continue the conversation. I think this is what most of us would do in this situation. It is much to early to help Betty see the repetition that's occurring, especially since she's relating it to sexual relationships at this point. To do so would likely make her more anxious. So we listen.

The analyst then asks Betty if she has any idea how this came about.

I see this as the analyst's attempt to see what Betty's private theory might be about what happened, which of course is a crucial issue. However, as noted earlier in the chapter on asking questions, it can also give the patient the impression that if she asks the right questions, and thinks real hard about something, she will find the answer to what is troubling her. This question, like many others, merely turns the mind to what is already known. In short, such questions often call for an answer already consciously available, rather than leaving an empty space for the patient to search for ways to communicate what is emerging into the preconscious via free association.

Betty responds to the analyst's question by telling of a party where everyone was pretty drunk, and her husband flirted with, and started kissing another woman at the party. He then fell asleep with the woman curled in his arms. It didn't go beyond that, but Betty couldn't get over it. She saw that her husband wanted to talk about it, but she didn't want to and realized she was withdrawing from him more and more.

At this point the analyst suggested there might have been something before this that led to this difficulty.

Here the analyst tries to broaden the conversation to the history of Betty's relationship with her husband. Again, something we might all do. However, I think Betty may be attempting to convey something deeper, i.e., what happened at the event seemed to be traumatic for her, and she hasn't been able to recover. "Somehow I couldn't get over it," she says. With her "somehow" Betty is conveying the possibility that it is this "not being able to get over it," not just the experience itself, that is part of the problem. She's also saying it isn't the history with her husband that's so important here, but her own feelings. This can be defensive, masochistic, or wanting to help the analyst see she recognizes something in herself that's a problem.

Betty associates to how sometimes she feels constricted by her marriage, and that she has wanted to go out with colleagues so she can feel closer to them. However, she notes again that she has problems in relationships. The more she likes people the more she withdraws from them. Betty *then withdraws into silence.*

Here I might say something about what's being expressed in the withdrawals, as it is now about colleagues and liking someone, and not sex. I might say something like, "I wonder if you've noticed in talking with me you often start out talking in a strong voice, and then suddenly stop . . . like a withdrawal. I wonder if you can go back in your mind's eye and try and capture what your feeling or thinking was at the moment you withdrew." What I would be attempting to demonstrate is that what happens in our conversation will mirror and help us understand the problems the patient is bringing. This can be a very powerful demonstration of the usefulness of the talking (and not talking) cure. Further, by bringing Betty back to the moment before the withdrawal we are conveying that if we look very closely at what happens in our conversation, we can tell a lot about the problems that brought her to the analyst. It is an emphasis on analysis as a special kind of conversation where we can learn about the nature of the patient's problems. It's not about the analyst's special powers of insight or empathy, which can often skew an analysis from the very beginning. Rather it's an attempt to help the patient by indicating in our way of working – I can help you by listening to your conversation with me. By emphasizing it is about the patient's conversation we convey our interest in her. For Betty, who didn't feel there was anyone around who treated her as special (as we will see later on), this in itself could have a powerful effect.

In thinking about withdrawing from colleagues, Betty was surprised to realize she feels she isn't interesting enough, and that she's felt this way since she was young. She then started talking about her childhood, saying at first, there was always a parent home. However, as she continued talking it turned out that her mother was a teacher who devoted long hours to her work, and the children in her classes. Most days Betty went to her mother's school after her classes were finished, but she portrayed her mother as so busy that she hardly noticed her. Betty then said, "Now I sometimes wonder . . ." and then interrupted this wondering.

There are many issues one could pick up on in this increasingly rich conversation. What I would pick up on is when Betty starts an internal conversation, and then has to stop it. That is when she starts to wonder about this after-school arrangement, and then interrupts herself. At this moment we see a conflict in action about a thought or feeling that stops the conversation. It is at this moment we have the best chance to help the patient see that, in their mind, they suddenly turned away from an idea because there was something disturbing about it. It is a window into many issues the patient has raised. She seems to be on the verge of asking some question about why her mother took a greater interest in these other children, and how this relates to her never feeling interesting, but then stops herself. It raises questions as to whether the traumatic nature of what her husband did with this other woman was a repetition of the cumulative trauma from childhood of not being found interesting enough. All of these considerations seem plausible, but we find a window into these issues primarily via her interrupted chain of thoughts. That is, until we can help the patient understand the interruption of wondering, wondering isn't possible.

The secondary, but equally important issue of technique, is that via the method I'm describing the focus is on the patient's mind. We are conveying our interest in what is happening for the patient in the interrupted conversation, i.e., the moment when Betty began to wonder and then had to withdraw. In this way we don't repeat the trauma of primarily talking about what we find interesting in what Betty tells us. If we were to suggest to Betty that "maybe her mother's interest in teaching these other children made her feel less interesting," we would ignore something very basic to Betty, her tendency to withdraw what she's interested in . . . a primary symptom.

While recounting her story, Betty began to cry. She noted again how surprised she was by all this coming out, and then dismissed her concerns as "stupid."

Again we see her defending against the possibility that her story may not be interesting to the analyst.

The analyst then suggests that maybe Betty wondered if she wasn't interesting enough for her mother to be with her.

This raises an interesting question about empathy. Often we feel we are being empathic when we help our patients understand how certain parenting caused them to feel a particular way. Many times this is true. However, we rarely consider that appreciating and exploring the patient's wishes to not know is being empathic. However, I would say it is exactly the opposite. Helping a patient understand why she feels a particular way when she's still debating whether she wants to know about it might not be experienced as empathic.

I have tried to highlight in this vignette a method of introducing patients to the psychoanalytic method by exploring the *interruptions of the conversations* that go on in in Betty's mind. It is exactly where these interior conversations are interrupted that we see a defense against something threatening, that inevitably leads a patient to repeated acting out. My method is a particular way of working where I hope to intrigue a prospective patient with what is going on in her mind, rather than giving answers to question, or feel I have to be a particular way.

I once used the metaphor of "telling stories" to capture the analytic work. I suggested that the capacity of patients to tell and own their stories is central to their developing a sense of well being from analysis. I think patients come to us because they are inhibited from living out their own stories. They live out somebody else's story instead, or they are afraid to see the story they're living, or they cannot bear the consequences of the story they've constructed. They feel the pain of an unlived life, and they want to know whose life they've been leading and how they can learn to lead their own. It is the fostering of this view that I hope to further with my method.

Of course, not every prospective analytic patient is like Betty, ready for a conversation. Some are so overwhelmed by external circumstances they can't talk about anything else. Some can't talk about anything. With each type of patient we might sometimes need to ask lots of questions or keep silent. Figuring out what type of conversation each of these different types of patient can tolerate is difficult, but necessary. In fact it is important to remember that Betty told the analyst a lot in this first interview, much of which was surprising to her, and that indeed she became an analytic patient.

As I noted earlier, we have sometimes tended to focus on *the analyst's way of being to create safety, sometimes to the exclusion of the analyst's ways of analyzing.* In this chapter I've tried to bring forth some methods of working analytically that I think are useful in helping patients into an analytic treatment. I don't mean to suggest it is the only part of an invitation, but I think a part worth highlighting.

13

THE MIDDLE PHASE

Reaching the *middle phase* of analysis is often a criterion for advancement through American psychoanalytic institutes, and an important part of the certification process in the American Psychoanalytic Association.[1] *Yet, what is the middle phase?* Surprisingly, although there are hundreds of articles in the literature that mention the patient reaching the middle phase (starting with Freud, 1919), we have no clear definition of the middle phase. It has remained a descriptive phrase that we use to vaguely designate where the patient is in treatment, but without any clarity on what it means. This is typical of what one finds in the literature: "During the *middle phase*, which lasted about two years, a major trend was the see-sawing back and forth between heterosexual and homosexual material" (Anon, 1988). Here the middle phase is used to describe what the writer assumes is something we are all familiar with, and thus there is no need to elaborate on it. This is one of hundreds of similar statements in the literature, along with equally vague descriptions of the late-middle, and late-late-middle phase. My impression is that when psychoanalytic authors use these phrases they clearly have in mind a changed state in the analysis, but it remains undefined.

In 1913 Freud likened psychoanalysis to chess, where only the beginning and ending moves are open to a definite plan, while believing that the middle defied any such delineation. In agreement with Freud one could say the middle phase *is the analysis*, apart from the beginning and ending. However, there may be a way to think of a discrete middle phase with patients in the range of the neurotic to less severe character disorders, which reflect the concept of analysis as *creating a psychoanalytic mind*. Thus, I would like to suggest a definition of the middle phase based upon *the state of the patient's mind in relation to his own thought processes*.

During an analysis there are certain shifts in how an analysand is able to notice, reflect upon, and process his inner world. Each shift reflects *a new phase in the analysis that, while subject to multiple and shifting regressions and defenses, becomes a central component of a psychoanalytic mind*. In fact, these shifts have to occur for the patient to progress in his treatment. In their description of the middle phase Novick and Novick (1998, 2001) come closest to what

I'm describing. "The patient's mind becomes an object of inquiry, and we begin to track fluctuations in the patient's willingness to engage in the work . . ." (1998, p. 831). Here is how I define three significant shifts in the middle phase.[2]

The first shift that defines the beginning of the middle phase is *self-observation. It begins with the patient's capacity to consider a thought as a mental event and the patient's beginning appreciation for the significance of what is coming to his mind via the method of free association.* The patient starts to see he has a mind that thinks things and does things that play a significant role in his life. It is the start of an understanding of one's mind that is central to the curative process, and is linked with the patient's beginning validation of the method of free association. This is not a stable process that progressively continues, but it is the *beginning of something new in the analysis.*

The second shift one sees in the middle phase coincides with the analysand's capacity to reflect upon his associations as an entry into further thoughts. It is the start of the thinking about one's thinking. The term I favor to describe this phase is *self- reflection.* Self-reflection requires the ability to both associate *and* mentally hold on to these associations, in order to look at them at a later time. It is another developmental step in analysis in that it is not only the recognition of thoughts as mental events (i.e., self-observation), but the capacity to see a string of associations as related mental events, and to keep them in mind long enough to reflect upon them.

The third shift of the middle phase occurs when the analysand moves toward what I call *self-inquiry.* What is self-inquiry? Self-inquiry is a term introduced by Gardner (1983) who resists defining it while insisting on playing with it. He is one of the few analytic writers offering an experience of his definition in the playfulness of his writing. It is a particular space in the mind where the capacity to play with ideas as a basis for self-expression and understanding exists. It is a space where created ideas can be freely explored, a place for curious musings without a particular destination.

The analysand begins to discover curiosity and pleasure in his own thought processes, greater freedom in his free associations, and the capacity to not only reflect upon his thoughts, but a growing capacity to interpret them as well. While this sounds like what one hopes will occur at the end of an analysis, the termination phase brings its own set of issues, which have an effect on the stability of the capacity for self-analysis. Further, it is the greater stability of self-inquiry which heralds the beginning of the termination phase.

The first shift: self-observation

There are two primary ways patients beginning psychoanalysis express their thoughts. The first is a description of what the patient experiences as "real" events or feelings. A male patient saying he was "screwed again by his boss" is, in his mind, simply describing his mistreatment by an older male. For him, it is a real event that happened. A second primary way is when patients enact their thoughts.

As mentioned earlier, this is when thoughts are designed as actions more than communications. During these times the statement "I really messed up today" could be an invitation to be helped or rejected, an invitation to look together at a problem or an offer to be criticized.

In the initial phase of analysis our methods of working are geared toward helping patients consider thoughts that come to mind during an analytic hour as *mental events*. It is a capacity that results from the psychoanalytic process. Thus, I consider the analysand's words "I noticed," along with its many variants and elaborations (e.g., "I found myself thinking," "I wonder") as heralding a move into the middle phase. It can indicate, if only for a moment, a profound change in the analysand's relationship to his own thoughts and feelings (i.e., the patient is not only experiencing his thoughts and feelings, but also reflecting upon them). Two major changes are heralded by this development of the capacity for self-observation. At this instant, the patient is no longer the passive recipient of experiences (internal and external), but the active observer, potentially capable of making choices. Pally and Olds (1998) have likened this change to the difference in a video recorder with and without a tape in it. Without a tape, the individual is left with only fleeting images as they occur. With a tape, the individual can study, review, and go back to the beginning of a sequence of any one response. In psychoanalytic treatment, we see this difference in an analysand's relationship to his own thoughts when entering and ending a successful treatment. In the beginning of treatment, most patients experience their thoughts and feelings as momentary real events (e.g., "I was sad yesterday": saying it reimmerses the patient in the totality of this feeling). At a later time in treatment, the patient can experience such a statement as an experience that can be viewed through various lenses. It can be thought about, talked about, and played with in a variety of ways to understand what this feeling is about, why it came to mind at that moment, what it might be connected to, and what telling it to the analyst might mean. Via the development of a self-observational capacity, an immutable feeling potentially becomes the entry point into multiple possibilities, and its freeing effects that are a crucial ingredient in psychoanalysis. This shift in the analysand's way of thinking is what I would consider the beginning of the middle phase where the goal is to help the patient create a psychoanalytic mind.

In the following example, one can see the waxing and waning of this capacity, *which is typical of the middle phase.*

Steve

> I had an odd experience. For the first time ever, as I was coming in from outside, I noticed that I started to reach for the glove in my pocket. It was like I was going to put it on to protect myself from any germs that might be on the door. Well, of course, this being wintertime and so many people having colds, it's a good idea to be careful where you touch. But I've never done that before. I was even careful when I went into the waiting

room not to touch the doorknob. Of course you may be glad that I don't touch the doorknob because of all the women I've been screwing around with recently. So I guess I'm just concerned about a disease.

In this example, we first see the Steve noticing his "odd experience." He then makes an observation of a potential action (reaching for his gloves), and the thought that accompanied it (avoiding germs on the door). In this, we see how a potential action was transformed into a mental event. There is then a defensive retreat from this being his thought to it being the result of realistic thinking (wintertime and colds). However, Steve returns to the idea this was not simply a "realistic" thought, but an idea in his mind at that moment and also when entering the waiting room. As the sexual nature of the thought emerges it is defended against by becoming my thought ("you may be glad"), and then a generic "disease."

In short, we see Steve moving towards and away from the idea that what he's thinking is a mental event from his own mind. It takes considerable analytic work before the patient can, for the most part, consistently view his thoughts as mental events. This is the work of the middle phase.

The second shift: self-reflection

The patient's entry into the second shift of the middle phase is ushered in by another change in the patient's relationship to his own mind, *the capacity for self-reflection*. Freud first mentioned self-reflection in 1900. He saw it as the development of the capacity to reflect on a series of associations. It is a process whereby the analysand steps back from his experience of the analysis (i.e., his thoughts and feelings), and reflects upon it.

> Looked at in isolation, a thought may seem very trivial or very fantastic; but it may be made important by another thought that comes after it, and, in conjunction with thoughts that may seem equally absurd, it may turn out to form a most effective link. Reason cannot form any opinion upon all this unless it retains the thought long enough to look at it in connection with the others. On the other hand, where there is a creative mind, reason – so it seems to me – relaxes its watch upon the gates, and the ideas rush in pell-mell, and only then does it look them through and examine them in a mass.
>
> (Freud, 1900, p. 103)

In this description Freud differentiates free association from self-reflection in that self-reflection requires the *ability to both associate and mentally hold on to these associations, in order to look at them at a later time*. It is another developmental step in analysis in that it is not only the recognition of thoughts as mental events (i.e., self-observation), but the capacity to see a string of associations

141

as related mental events, and to keep them in mind long enough to reflect upon them.

In his usual pithy manner, Friedman summed up this way of thinking

> as a variant of the normal, characteristically human capacity of reflection, the sort of thing a Piagetian might describe as operating upon one's operations, or a philosopher might refer to as abstracting from one's abstractions, or a man in the street might say amounts to looking hard at oneself.
>
> (1992, p. 3)

Steve (3 years later)

In this vignette we can see how Steve begins this session immersed in the feelings of a dream. However, as he tells a second dream, he begins to reflect on his thoughts as mental events, and is able to associate to them in a manner that leads to potential explanations for why these ideas are on his mind. He's still not able to play with all of these ideas so that he might interpret the dreams, and his experience of them together, but this will come over time and will then usher in the third shift in the middle phase.

Steve starts out by talking about two dreams he had the previous evening. The theme in the dream, and his associations, have a familiar quality of his feeling used, pushed aside, and/or deprived.

In the first dream there was a party going on at his house, but somebody else was giving it. His association began with how he was planning to go on a long weekend with some friends at a house they rented. One friend, Ralph, wanted to go a few days earlier before Steve was able to go. He felt Ralph was always a lot of fun to be with, but he always tried to get a little more in every situation. He'd told Ralph when they rented the house that the owner didn't want anybody at the house until the agreed upon rental date. Steve then talked about bringing lots of supplies the last time this group rented a house together. Everything was used up, but nobody thought of helping with the expensees. He anticipated something similar happening this time.

At this point Steve seems immersed in the feelings stimulated by the dream, while giving the day residue for the dream.

He then goes back to the dream where there was a special beer that was being served at a low cost because someone at the party had a connection with a hotel. Steve thought he was probably the guy providing the low cost beer, as anticipated for the upcoming weekend. He says ironically, "Yeah, low cost for everyone except me."

Steve still seems immersed in the feelings of the dream.

His thoughts then move to going to Germany in a few weeks on business. He asked the human resources people at work if they had a special arrangement with Lufthansa, but they said they didn't.

As one can see in this first part of the session, Steve is caught up in the feelings of the dream . . . i.e., feelng deprived.

Steve then remembers a second dream. In this dream he was at the zoo, and he was making a documentary. He was filming a particular cage where there was a variety of wild animals. Someone then put a dog into the cage. He then imagined himself as being like the dog in this cage. *Referring, I thought, to the way he experiences himself with his rapacious family.* Steve then talks about how, in the documentary, the dog went running over towards the lion in the cage, "chomped" on its neck, and didn't let go. He then explains that the dog wasn't actually biting into the lion's neck, but just holding on. It was more, as if, the dog was giving a sign to the lion that he was there, and would be one of his followers. He was just a dog, and the lion was the king of the jungle. As he describes the neck of the lion, the thought of a penis comes to his mind. He wonders if this has to do with giving a guy a blowjob. With a laugh of recognition he realizes he'd been very careful in describing that the dog hadn't tried to hurt the lion's neck, and wonders now if he was saying, "I'm not trying to bite off this neck-penis."

In this sequence we can see how Steve is not only able to see his thoughts as mental events, but he is also able to think about their possible meaning – an example of self-reflection. He can see the defense against seeing himself as the castrator, allowing his mind to move more freely towards its acceptance, and an interpretaion of the dream. Steve is able to appreciate the idea that the dog isn't just a passive, homosexual follower, but a castrator.

Steve's thoughts then turn to familiar terriotory of how his sister is a bitch, and she is also a depriver.

This return to immersion in the feeling of being deprived (i.e., castrated) seems to be a reaction (guilt? defense?) to his awareness of his castrating thoughts. It also seems central to his symptoms. As the resistent seem "thin", I began to connect them in the following interpretation.

F.B.:　After you can think of yourself as the castrator of the king in your dream, your thoughts return to you as the deprived/castrated one as in the first dream. Here we can see how feeling that you are being taken advantage of is a response to wanting to castrate the king. Others are greedy, but not you.

Steve then remembers how he felt about the previous evening, when he went to dinner with some colleagues, and how off he can be. Throughout the evening he felt one of the women who is quite biting was being really castrating. He then laughed in recognition of the connection between biting and castration. When he mentioned this to his wife, who was there, she was surpised in that she felt that this woman had been especially sweet. He felt it showed him how much his perceptions may be colored by these particular issues. At this point the lion comes to mind, and he remembers that when he began analysis, and my hair was longer, he used to think of me as a lion. He remembered feeling easily criticized at that time.

In this vignette we can see how, after immersion in the feeling of being the deprived/castrated one, Steve's *capacity to reflect returns*, leading him to thoughts that connect how his preoccupation with being a victim represented, in part, his wishes to castrate the analyst/king. It is the establishment of this capacity to freely associate and reflect upon the associations, subject to regressions and resistances, which characterize the second shift of the middle phase.

One might ask what happened that allowed Steve to go from the regressive response to the first dream (i.e., immersion in the feeling) to the reflective stance in the second. I can only guess that it might have been a transference message that I should feel sorry for him, before the aggression in the second dream came to the fore. However, these regressions from and progressions to *self-reflection* are also what characterize this phase.

The third shift: self-inquiry

The third shift of the middle phase can be observed in the analysand's greater freedom to engage in *self-inquiry*, and the enjoyment therein. The analysand now feels free to think about almost anything, and can play, muse, reflect and interpret her own associations. There is a curiosity about her ideas, and a readiness to be surprised by what comes to mind. It reflects a strengthened, more flexible ego, a heightened elasticity between the preconscious and unconscious, and a greater differentiation between inner and outer reality, while also recognizing their mutual influence as something to be thought about with a *psychoanalytic mind*. Hence it is an exhilarating time for the analysand, and the analyst, as one can see the accomplishment of a freer, psychoanalytic mind. What more is there to do, one might ask? Hasn't everything analysis can do been accomplished? A good question, but then there is termination. Termination is another phase in the analysis, with its own set of issues for each patient. I will elaborate on this in the next chapter, especially the regressions that occur on the road toward *self-analysis*.

Louise

Louise, a 45-year-old woman in a related mental health field was in the fifth year of analysis. It was the first day after a long holiday weekend which is generally seen as the end of summer. We were working in the analysis the previous 3 weeks.

Louise began the session by saying how restless she was during the night. She had a difficult time going to sleep, and was up every hour checking to see what time it was. She knew she was anxious about something, but quickly went back to sleep each time. About 5 a.m. she was wide-awake, realizing she was still anxious, and had the following thoughts.

At first she thought about the end of summer, and how it always meant going back to school. She loved going back to school when the summer seemed to drag on too long. Louise wondered if this had to do with getting back to see me after the long weekend, as she had so much to talk about. Over the weekend she'd had some thoughts about a psychology program for high-school students, and she was very excited about it.

Louise then talked about the wonderful day she had yesterday. She felt freer than she had in a long time, and didn't feel she had to work all the time. She lingered over the newspaper, and then made love with her husband. She said, "I didn't feel I had to be so in control of Don (her husband), and it was really freeing." Louise then said that she blew off the rest of the day, as she and Don went to a movie and dinner. She laughed at using the phrase "blow off," and recounted how uncharacteristically she gave Don a "blow job" the day before. What came to mind immediately was the time when she was taking a long time in the bathroom because of having difficulty with a bowel movement, and how humiliated she felt when she came out of the bathroom and her mother accused her of masturbating. Louise then thought of what we talked about last week, something she could never admit to herself before, that she always felt like a bother to her mother, and that she thought her mother wished she hadn't been born. "How sad that makes me feel," she said. She remembered that even when she was in nursery school she always worried that her mother would forget to pick her up.

Suddenly she remembered, and was amazed she had forgotten this, that her mother had called the previous day, and told her she had fallen down and bruised herself badly. Louise then laughed as a song came to mind that explained why she might have "forgotten" the phone call. The song that came to mind was from *The Wizard of Oz*, "Ding dong the witch is dead, the wicked witch is dead . . ." This led her to remember that before coming into see me today, she kept bumping into things and bruising herself. She guessed it was for her "evil" thoughts toward her mother.

Louise then stopped and wondered what all this had to do with her restless night. She realized that before she went to sleep she asked Don to set the alarm early so she could get some work done before she went to her office. This was the one way she could get her mother's approval: with good grades and achievement. She then mused on the possibility that all this freedom she felt yesterday must have made her feel anxious, ready to be accused of doing something "evil," "which of course I was doing," she said with a laugh. Louise then said she thought she was waking up so much because she was afraid of *not* getting up on time. Again Louise was surprised, and realized this must express her ambivalence at having to be such an achiever, and the wish she could just relax and do these "evil" things, like yesterday.

"Well what has this to do with you and me?" Louise wondered. "Am I trying to show you how much I've *achieved* with all of my thoughts, and resentful that it's all talk and no sex? Well that would fit," she said. She then told me she often thought of how tall I was, and wondered how we would fit together in sex. She figured, "Adjustments can be made." She then imagined me saying, "Enough of this, we only can have a professional relationship."

No more "evil" thoughts, huh? As she was getting up from the couch she said, "I think I'll spend the rest of the day just lounging in bed." Before she got to the door she said, "Just kidding . . . mother."

This is a good example of self-observation, self-reflection and self-inquiry, and the pleasure the patient derives from it – all working within a session. First, Louise's ideas range over many thoughts that earlier in the analysis would have never been able to come to consciousness. In her mind these are mental events that she can play with and reflect upon. They give a depth of understanding to multiple factors in her anxiety filled sleep that helped her return to her normal sleep pattern. It is also a piece of self-analysis. As she leaves Louise retreats from me as the exciting sexual partner to my being the critical mother, which she reflected on the following day. It is a sign the analysand is ready for the termination phase, and so are we. It is to this phase I will turn to in the next chapter.

To briefly summarize, in this chapter I've attempted to characterize a middle phase of analysis based on the concept of the analysand's relationship to his own mind. If one agrees that the basic psychoanalytic treatment goal is the patient's changed relationship to his own mind, then we can follow this development via the shifts I've outlined here. It is a rough guide focused entirely on the goal of *creating a psychoanalytic mind.*

Notes

1 In fact, the use of the term *middle phase* seems particular to American psychoanalysis. I have questioned colleagues from Europe and South America, and they are unfamiliar with this designation.
2 I find it helpful to clarify distinctions before turning black and white into gray. Therefore, I am presenting these phases as distinct, although in clinical practice there are regressions and progressions within each phase, and between each phase, and this continues well into termination.

14

TERMINATION

> In spite of the large literature on termination no paradigm of termination
> has been made part of the professional equipment of the psychoanalytic
> practitioner.
>
> (Martin Bergmann, 1997, p. 172)

"How do I know when I'm finished with analysis?" a patient asks early in
treatment. If we asked ten analysts the same question, we'd probably get at least
ten different answers. In part, this seems to reflect the complexity of an anlytic
termination, and our difficulty so far in grasping all that goes into this phase.
Further, an analytic termination is a rare experience in one's training. Novick
(1982) discovered there are a high percentage of training cases that end in "premature terminations," and more recently there has been a decreasing emphasis
on cases in a termination phase as a requirement for graduation, in part because of
the lengthening of analyses.

In this chapter I will focus on a particular area that I've found of central
importance in termination, the *analysis of regressive solutions to conflicts around
self-analysis that develop in this phase.* As I've noted previously, much of the
literature on self-analysis describes it as a result of an identification with the
analyst's functioning. While self-analysis may be a by-product of good analytic
work, I think it is also a result of the way the analyst analyzes. Schacter (1992),
amongst many others, has suggested the importance of the capacity for self-
analysis in the termination phase. However, he, like many, sees self-analysis
as developing *via identifying with the analyst's analyzing function.* In contrast
I believe that *by analyzing in a particular fashion we create the conditions for
the patient's relationship to his own mind that allows self-analysis to take place.*
Further, I have found *the analysis of this capacity or the retreat from it, once the
analysand has reached the ability for self-inquiry, is a necessary step in stabilizing
this achievement for creating a psychoanalytic mind.*

It is a curious phenomenon that it frequently happens that, as soon as termination is in the air, an analysand who has reached a place where we can say she has
developed a self-analytic capacity, retreats from this analytic accomplishment.

147

It is probably not surprising that this happens, as the movement from analyzing with the analyst in mind to analyzing within one's own mind, raises so many issues. Here I would hold that many important themes that have been identified in the literature as crucial in the termination phase (e.g., mourning, separation issues, competition, etc.) could be approached productively within the specifics of the *regression from a self-analytic stance.*

In general, with an increase in sustained *self-inquiry*, the patient can take the final steps toward *self-analysis* and the termination of analysis. As mentioned earlier, *it is a view of termination based on the analysand's relationship to his own mind, rather than the necissity to deal with certain content, solve symptoms, or reach a place of supposed normalcy in their life.* As mentioned earlier, self-analysis necessitates all of of the psychological states that develop throughout the phases of psychoanalysis. Understanding and working through the regressions from and resistance to self-analysis, along with the other states of mind, thus becomes an important part of the termination process. It is the analysis of these processes that allow termination to proceed, as it raises numerous issues regarding the patient taking over the analyzing function for himself, and leaving the analysis and the analyst. I haven't found a particular theme that dominates termination, once a patient has been able to move towards a position of self-analysis. Rather, it is the *fluctuating capacity to maintain a self-analytic stance*, and the conflicts this arouses that dominate the final stages of the termination phase.[1] These conflicts are usally a revisiting of what has been an essential part of the analysis, but with added depth.

I will now present four sessions from a patient working through the termination phase. It was ushered in by a period where the patient, Stan, seemed increasingly capable of the stages leading to self-analysis. Shortly after he brought up termination there was a partial regression in his capacity to reflect on his thoughts or play with them. His previous appreciation for his thoughts as mental events became more sporadic. The retreat from a self-analytic stance, and my countertransference reaction to it, became the focus of the analysis. It led to greater insight into a characterological manner of reacting, while also expressing a heretofore unexpressed fear of deadness that the patient anticipated upon termination. By focusing on the regression from an analytic mind, we see in a follow-up session at 5 months, where the patient has once again found his mind.

Stan

Stan is a 51-year-old English professor and fiction writer at a prestigious university, in the termination phase of a four times per week 7-year analysis. He came to treatment depressed and anxious after having several pieces he wrote for literary magazines turned down, and his departmental chair talked with him about his lack of productivity, and his refusal to be on departmental committees. Stan's treatment has been successful in turning around his academic career, and reaching other life goals such as better relations with his wife and children. In the clinical material I will focus primarily on his temporary regression from making use of his *psychoanalytic mind*.

Stan had brought up termination a few months previously, and had returned to it periodically, but no termination date was set at this point.

First session

Stan began the session by mentioning he came early today, and while he was in the waiting room he did something that he rarely does, which was to check the emails on his phone. Usually he tries to see where his thoughts go as he's sitting there.

It was my impression Stan was saying that while he's usually a good patient in the waiting room, today he was bad.

Stan's thoughts went to some stories he'd been trying to publish in prestigious literary magazines.

I'd already heard a lot about these stories and Stan's attempt to publish them. I was surprised he was talking about them as if they hadn't come up before. I found myself wanting to ask him about this, but this in itself was interesting to me so I waited to see what developed.

The theme surrounding publishing these stories was the same, i.e., it would be a really big deal for him to publish in these magazines. He then wondered about a particular article, which he submitted some time ago but hadn't heard anything back from the editor. Stan contacted the editor recently and felt like he was being a real man (a theme throughout the analysis) in going after it. Stan then realized he'd told me about these issues previously, and wondered why he was telling me this again.

Here we see the first indication of self-reflection in this session.

What came to Stan's mind next was visiting his brother the previous weekend. The brother's teenage daughter was there with her friends. One of her friends was especially beautiful, and he couldn't stop looking at her. At dinner one night, this beautiful young woman was sitting next to him, and asked him a lot about his work. At a certain time (after hearing about all he'd done) she asked him how old he was. When he told her he was 51, she couldn't believe it and said "No way you're 51." It was clear that he was pleased with this, and told me about it with an anxious laugh. Immediately he began to chastise himself for being so kid-like, listing activities like the basketball and baseball leagues he plays in, his marathon running and sailing as examples. He liked this young woman's interest in him, but he still likes to do so many kid things. Stan then wondered about this self-critical feeling developing, and realized it followed his pleasure at this young, beautiful woman's interest in him.

Stan's ability to bring up a series of thoughts without overt concerns for where they may go, and then stand aside and think about their meaning is part of the process of self-analysis. As we'd analyzed Stan's conflicted feelings over the pleasure of feeling manly throughout the analysis, Stan's realization of his retreat from feeling pleased with the interest he was receiving from this young woman was a piece of self-analysis. Embedded within the criticism was that these kid-like things would also bring him closer in age to this young woman.

His thoughts then went to the various situations where he felt conflict over being competitive. He mentioned a faculty meeting where he felt this guy was putting him down. Instead of his usual stance of feeling he did something wrong, he took the initiative and stood up for himself. However, he felt badly afterwards for standing up to this guy. Stan didn't comment on this.

Here we see the absence of self-reflective functioning. I was surprised to find myself irritated with his guilty reaction even though he knew this dynamic well and had just spoken to it. I wondered if there was an unconscious message being conveyed to me in language action. Later I realized that even if a message was being conveyed, I was also dealing with my fantasy of a successful termination, which in spite of everything I thought I knew for a moment didn't include regressions or resistances.

F.B.:   You mentioned feeling badly after you stood up for yourself, a dynamic you know well, yet you didn't comment on it.

While on the one hand I was bringing to light a retreat from self-reflection, I thought I could hear a critical tone in my remark.

Stan's thoughts then went back to his visit with his brother. The brother's older daughter brought her boyfriend to dinner. Stan wasn't that impressed with him, and wondered if he was good enough for her. He also mentioned how good-looking this young man was, and how the teenage girls were flirting with him. His brother was concerned this guy would eventually hurt his daughter. Stan then said in a dismissive tone, "Ah, typical father worries."

After my comment (with an edge) on Stan's retreat from reflective functioning, his thoughts go to a guy who he doesn't think much of (Guess who I thought!), but could be hurtful, which he then dismisses as "father worries." Thus, I thought he likely picked up on the edge in my voice, and returned to a state of mind that had led to my edgy tone. Was he inviting me to do the same thing again, or hoping I wouldn't? I wasn't clear what was happening so I listened.

He remembered a time when he was at college when a woman who he grew up with came to visit, and they had sex. A number of years later he was at a party, and this woman was there with her husband. He felt she said something that could have been interpreted as they slept together. After this remark her husband became aggressive with Stan. He remembered saying something at the time that indicated if he didn't do what she wanted, she would have beaten him up. Knowing his wife, her husband laughed and the tension dissipated somewhat. As they were leaving the party this guy had what Stan called "a fancy, expensive sports car," while he was driving his practical, gas saving, vanilla car. The other guy got in his car, and with tires screeching, zoomed out of the parking lot. The implication was this guy was a "real" man.

I heard this association as a guy getting angry once he has the sense Stan cuckolded him. I also knew Stan was disparaging of guys who needed a "fancy, expensive sports car." I wondered if this was his fantasy of the edge in my voice, the response of the disparaged cuckold.

F.B.: I'm wondering about this angry guy who comes to mind, which led you to put yourself down. I heard an edge in my voice when I talked earlier, and I wondered if you heard it too.

This is what seemed closer to potential awareness, rather than his disparaging thoughts.

Stan: I did, but I pushed it away, maybe not so successfully given where my thoughts went. I'm surprised by my next thought. It's something I mentioned much earlier in the analysis. I remember talking with my mother about something that worried me, and she suddenly started yelling at me for not having self-confidence.

There were now a number of transference figures in the room, i.e., the cuckolded husband/father/analyst, and the narcissistic, phallic mother. Did I trigger these transferences or not? Was his absence of self-reflection an unconscious (coming closer to preconscious) invitation for me to enact by becoming aggressive, or yelling at him? Were these times where there was a lack of self-reflection an invitation to tell him that he wasn't having the "analytic confidence" he had earlier in treatment? Did he interpret my irritation with his regression as my saying something like, "C'mon man, we're in the termination phase, get with it," not dissimilar to his mother? Earlier in the analysis Stan had also told me of various situations where he would present himself in downtrodden ways to female colleagues, who would eventually get irritated with his not recognizing his many accomplishments. While thinking about this I was surprised when I then thought of this "attack" from his mother as getting her "going." But what was this "going"? On the one hand she was depressed much of the time. We had analyzed how her getting angry was one way she seemed more alive to him. On the other hand, much of the session revolved around retreats from erotic excitement. I thought it was important to capture the meaning of this memory, and with both possibilities in mind I interpreted the following:

F.B.: When you showed a lack of self-confidence your mother became angry and riled[2] up. I wonder if this became one way you saw your mother becoming *alive* again, even *excited*, and this is what is being expressed with me, a retreat from analytic self-confidence when you dismiss your thoughts in anticipation that it would make me more alive and excited.

Upon reflection, I wondered if I moved too quickly from the erotic connection with a man getting angry, to the mother? Stan's wish/fear to be penetrated by me to make him a man had been prominent earlier in the analysis, while this possible erotic connection with a woman getting mad was new. This new connection opened up a whole new dimension to his relations with women, where he most often prostrated himself before them. This doesn't answer my question, but may have also played a role.

Stan: [Pause] Hmm! I think that's right. I realize that, in the background, whenever I show a lack of confidence I expect you to get annoyed with me. He then said with a laugh of recognition, "You mostly disappoint me, but I can still hope."

This was potentially an insight into a dynamic that hadn't come to the fore so clearly. The push to have me criticize him had come up before in two ways: as an external super-ego to keep him contained and slow down so he wouldn't do anything "crazy"; and as a repetition of his relationship with his mother, but without the clarity of any purpose.

As one can see the focus on the patient's regression (or enactment) regarding his capacity to think about his thoughts, led to many fruitful avenues, some of which hadn't emerged so clearly. My countertransference reaction also seemed to play an important role in the session, and at this point it wasn't clear to me if my irritation was a response to his unconscious and/or mine.

Session 2: the next day

Stan started out by saying that just before he came into the waiting room he was thinking of the time when he stopped teaching undergraduates. He didn't follow up on this thought.

While on the one hand this thought about stopping something seemed a reference to termination, I also wondered about this not following up as a repetition of the unconscious invitation to ask him about it as a variant on riling me up and/or excite me.

Stan's thoughts then went back to one of the stories he was hoping would get accepted, and wondered why he didn't take the suggestion of the editor (a woman) about the ending. (The editor of the magazine had been encouraging and suggested a slight change to the end of the story.) He wondered if he set himself up to fail. He then had the idea that when he didn't take the editor's suggestion, a small thing actually, he was trying to get this woman irritated. It reminded him of his attempts to get his mother's *attention*.

I had a complicated reaction to this statement. On the one hand I felt it was a good example of self-analysis. I also noted his use of the word "attention" instead of riled up, or excited. Was this a "correction" of my interpretation, a defensive retreat, and/or was it unconsciously motivated to get me riled up and excited? It wasn't clear at this point, but it clearly got my "attention."

Stan's thoughts then went to a meeting he was at today where he said something that confused people (as I was feeling at this moment). Frank (a colleague) angrily confronted him, and said Stan was being confusing. He then said, "Frank is a real man."

This seemed to be a highly saturated communication, as Frank was a homosexual who Stan described as combustible. I found myself wanting to say something about the ambiguity of his statement about Frank. Here he was describing another example of getting someone riled up, and what seemed like an invitation for me to react similarly. Was this an invitation for a homosexual attack, or getting a woman excited, and was this a phallic woman? It wasn't clear.

His thoughts then went to an incident from the fourth grade, which had come up a few times in the analysis. At a parent–teacher conference the teacher mentioned to his mother that she was having trouble deciphering his handwriting. When his mother came back home she started screaming at him. He then said that he thought this was a way of getting his mother and teacher's *attention*.

F.B.:   The issue of your mother getting riled up came up yesterday and again today, yet when you talk about it you think of it as getting *attention*. I wonder if this is a way you're inviting me say something critical about your use of this word "attention"? That I would get riled up about it.

Stan: [Surprised] I forgot all about that. I was thinking about it after yesterday's session, but then it completely slipped my mind.

Stan's thoughts then turned toward what he started the session with, i.e., thinking about stopping teaching undergraduates. He remembered that as time went on, there were more and more requirements for what he had to do with his students. What ended up getting him pissed off was that he had to give these mini-quizzes to the classes. He wasn't sure how to construct these questions, but felt annoyed when these kids would ask him to clarify them. He wanted to yell at them that what was important were the ideas not the questions.

F.B.:   So after I wonder if you're trying to get me riled up, your thoughts go to these students who got you riled up when they didn't get the big picture. I wonder if, outside of awareness, there was a part of you that expected I would get riled up when you didn't get the big picture.

This issue of getting the "big picture" was something we had spent much time on in the analysis, but not in this way (i.e., with an unconscious fantasy that I was getting riled up). Stan found it difficult to keep in mind the themes from previous sessions. This will come up in a later session.

Stan: Mm! Interesting. Remember how much difficulty I had with these attractive young students in the class who idealized me. I generally got high ratings in teaching, but there were always a few students who seemed angry with me. At first I thought it must be the guys, but maybe that was defensive and I thought it was the women.

Was this a defense against the homoerotic that I may have contributed to, or an insight?

After a brief pause Stan thought of this high-powered conference he was going to this weekend. All the important writers, literary critics, and important professors from universities would be there for this invitation-only meeting. Whenever he goes to these things he feels like he doesn't belong. Other people seem to see him as this respected writer and literature professor, but he feels like a nothing.

F.B.:   It sounds like you're inviting me to shout at you too – for not having enough self-confidence.

Stan: Remember my graduate student Lisa from when I first started here. I felt intimidated by her and I ended up thinking I had to give her more. She used to yell at me that I needed more self-confidence. Now that I think about it, there were different situations during the day when I thought I had gotten some woman pissed off.

As Stan becomes self-reflective he gives weight to the idea of the absence of a self-analytic capacities as an enactment in the transference, centered on getting a woman riled up. It helped explain so much about his relations with women, but didn't rule out the homoerotic.

The following Monday

Stan: I know I *should* talk about the conference, but there's something that happened today that really bothered me.

One can see in his opening statement that he's already imagining doing something that might lead me to criticize him, i.e., not talking what he fantasizes I thought he "should" – the conference.

Stan: I don't know if it's a distraction. I had set up this telephone meeting with my advisor from graduate school. We thought about doing a project together. We had a somewhat rocky relationship, but I can't remember why. Anyway, I was meeting with one of my graduate students when the telephone rang, and I completely forgot it was the time we were supposed to talk. This was the second time it happened.

Stan then puzzled why he might have forgotten the call, and essentially dismissed this guy. Is this what he was doing? Was it related to the two of us? The guy is very volatile, and easily loses his temper.

154

F.B.:   Maybe that was the point.

Stan: Hmm! You mean like we talked about last week. I can see that, but I wasn't aware of it.

This last phrase was interesting, as Stan seemed to be questioning the concept of an unconscious part of his mind, which had been a staple of his thinking for some time. This seemed to be another possible unconscious provocation.

Stan: Throughout the conference I found it much easier to listen to the papers presented. But each time my mind drifted I wondered if I was dismissing the speaker. I realize now that I "got" what we talked about last week, but it remains more a feeling rather than remembering the words.

I thought this was a crucial observation in that Stan was one of these patients who, at times, would get the "gist" of what we talked about throughout analysis, but he would have difficulties remembering specifics. He noticed this previously, but would bring it up in a self-berating fashion, with an implicit invitation for me to join in. His current thought about it seemed to be something he was more interested in than berating himself for.

F.B.:   Again maybe that's the point. In this way you may be dismissing me, and imagining you'll get me all riled up in an excited way.

Stan: So interesting that I remember that as a feeling, but I couldn't say or remember the words. This other incident is coming to mind. Before I left for the conference Thursday evening, Jim [the dean of the college] told me to handle a situation with two faculty members who wanted some funds for a project. I ended up calling Jim back twice to clarify the reasons for doing it the way he suggested. I kept expecting him to get pissed off.

F.B.:   So like with me, you get the gist, but don't fully understand the meaning in words, and have to keep asking, anticipating you will piss him off.

Stan: Again, I knew it, but couldn't put it into words. This other thing happened this weekend. Maybe it's a diversion. [laughs] Maybe I hope it is.

I was thinking that the laugh was about recognizing I might be critical of him for this supposed "diversion."

Stan then told the story of how his wife made plans for Sunday to have dinner with a friend. There was another couple there. Stan was pissed off that his wife arranged this without considering he was just gone Friday and Saturday, and that he didn't have a chance to unwind before going back to work on Monday. He kept saying they sort of had a nice time, laughing, realizing that he was half-heartedly endorsing the weekend as fun. He then began to say that this other couple was odd. However, he stopped himself in mid-word and it came out that this couple was "o – ." He continued as if nothing had happened.

155

F.B.: I thought you noticed that you were about to say the word "odd," but were unable to complete it. Was this an invitation for me to ask about it?

Stan: I noticed it too, and it was more odd I didn't say anything about it. We were talking about a number of things over the weekend. Our friend was talking about how narcissistic her mother was, and I mentioned that my mother was severely depressed. Later in the day we were talking about psychotherapy and psychoanalysis, and this guy said, "Does anybody ever do that four times a week on the couch stuff anymore?" I said, "I do," and he asked, "Is that because your mother was so depressed?" It really pissed me off. Earlier this guy was talking about his interest in religious paintings. Someone wondered if it had to do with his Catholic upbringing, and this guy brushed it off. I thought, "What's the point in talking with this guy?"

I found myself thinking about the similarities between his response of brushing off the guy's question, like he brushes off my words, and then writing this guy off for doing the same thing. Realizing that Stan could only take this critically, I could see how I was being invited to criticize him. As it was near the end of the session, I didn't say anything.

Stan finished the session talking of how his wife could see he was not happy all weekend, and was very critical of him for it. He ended the session saying, "So maybe that was the point," *using the same words I had earlier.*

Five months later

During the previous 5 months, the unconscious fantasies feeding the transference in the regression from a developing self-analytic capacity became clearer.

- The image of the angry analyst as the phallic mother returned. In his infantile fantasies he saw his mother's depressed and angry state as a result of not having a penis. This was captured in Stan remembering his favorite limerick from when he was an adolescent.

    > Balls said the queen
    > If I had two I'd be king.
    > The king laughed, not because he wanted to,
    > But because he had two.

- Frank, the combustible homosexual, returned as a displaced transference for a conflict over the wish that his "weakened" analyst/father would get a dick, penetrate him, and give him strength. In this there was also the implicit wish to castrate the analyst/father by seeing him as so weakened.
- The fear of feeling in a deadened state after analysis ended. Part of Stan's fear of termination was the anticipation of an imagined emptiness and loneliness, like he often felt in childhood. Part of Stan's regression from self-analysis

was the enactment of the wish to make the analyst/mother come alive, while also a plea to not let him go.

In the following session you will see how Stan has returned to a fully engaged psychoanalytic mind. Stan, using the full range of his analytic capacities, now understands a number of issues that first appeared when he considered termination.

A session from 5 months later

Stan: You know how we've been talking about this thing. There it is again, where I use this vague term "thing," when I have something more specific in mind. I'll try again. I noticed that when I was in the waiting room I imagined telling you about something that happened today that would make me look like I didn't have confidence. I imagined you saying, "C'mon Stan, we've been over this before." Sounds familiar, this getting someone annoyed. Then I realized that the way I planned to tell you about what happened was a distortion of what actually happened. Remember the graduate student Anne, who constantly asks for more things, like money for someone to do library research, which she should do herself; well she did it again today. You know in the past I've had a lot of difficulty saying "no" to her, which has been especially weird since she's not gifted. So I sat her down today, and was straightforward with her about why I couldn't give her the money she requested, and reviewed with her the difficulties she's having in the program. She was upset at first, but I think I said what I needed to say in a way that helped her see the problems she was facing. She got teary while we were talking, but in contrast to other times when she stormed out of my office if I even hinted at saying "no" to a request, she thanked me at the end of our meeting.

   I just thought of something else. You know how people see me as never ruffled by anything, rarely upset – well I was thinking about that today after getting irritated with an administrator (Ellie) who seems to be a prime example of the "Peter Principle."[3] I wondered if, given how I think about these things, if I'm afraid of showing I'm sexually excited. Remember how I use to wonder how these guys could be so animated when giving talks at a meeting. I also allowed myself to think something today I've been pushing away for a long time. This administrator has a great body. Now that I think about it, maybe my getting irritated with her was some version of feeling sexually excited, while thinking I might excite her. Pretty exciting to think about, but also sad how long this has gone on. Did I just retreat from excitement or was it a certain truth, or maybe both? It's funny, or maybe not so funny, more predictable, that this woman administrator felt continually frustrated with me because she felt I was confusing. I thought she was dumb, but in retrospect I probably was trying to get her riled up. After thinking about all this I went back to speak to her about something else this afternoon, and we had a good talk, and then I felt she became flirtatious with me. I just enjoyed it for a while. Life can be so much more interesting, and yes exciting, when I have my own mind.

So where does this leave us? I guess, well not guess, although maybe I wish it was only a guess – it's time to think about finishing analysis. I have so many mixed feelings. [Looks at his watch, and realizes it's the end of the session] To be continued.

A summary

Shortly after Stan showed the capacities for self-analysis leading to thoughts of termination, this capacity diminished. What was then enacted in the transference was an aspect of his relationship with his mother where he unconsciously made her angry in order to enliven and excite her. Over time we could also understand it as a reaction to Stan's fear of the deadness *he* might feel when he was no longer talking to me. It was also a regressive plea to stay in analysis, and multiple other reasons. Further analysis revealed the fear of how much he loved me, and how much he wanted to destroy me.

What I'm suggesting in this chapter is that termination is an important time for the analysis of the regression from self-analysis for those patients capable of reaching this stage. As one can see in the sessions with Stan, *it isn't something apart from significant dynamic and characterological factors*. Rather, in the analysis of the meanings of a retreat from the factors that led us to think about termination, we uncover deeper meanings of previously understood issues. This is as it should be. The termination of an analysis raises strong reactions in both patient and analyst, and the capacity for self-analysis is, in some ways, the last step. In a "good enough" analysis it is a difficult step for both parties. I have focused on the *analytic goals* for the patient. As analysts we need to retain our own self-analytic capacities in order not to enact a too hasty or too lengthy termination.

Notes

1 Novick and Novick (2006) describe a shift in the patient's thinking from a closed to an open system that has elements of what I see with the development of self-inquiry.
2 This choice of phrase, "riled up," was spontaneous. It suggests anger, but is more about being peeved or irritated. In retrospect, it might have been partly the getting something "up" that led me to this phrase.
3 An organizational principle that states that individuals will rise to their highest level of *incompetence*.

15

REFLECTIONS AND RESOLUTION

In marveling how long it takes to know oneself Ludwig Wittgenstein once noted, at age 62, that he finally realized he hated bread when it is heavily toasted. Without realizing it, and quite unconsciously, he experienced great joy or despair in his relationship with toasted bread.

In the introduction to this book I said that I write about psychoanalysis in order to understand what seems unclear to me in our methods and theories. Throughout the book I've shared with the reader what I've learned over the last decade, and how it might add to our thinking about psychoanalytic technique today. I never had a final chapter in mind for the book, but assumed it would emerge over time, and during its preparation. Then, coming close to the end of this book I realized that, in fact, a final chapter was brewing. However, just as I was preparing myself for this last chapter, a clinical hour presented by a supervisee helped me find a way to bring together what seemed like irreconcilable positions.

I believe the personal and historical reflections that follow had a huge impact on *how* and *why* psychoanalysts analyze the way they do. In spite of over one hundred years of discussions, we have never been able to resolve the most significant differences amongst us. Here, I will only attempt to resolve one issue that differentiates us, first by returning to a question that's been implicit through what I've written previously in this book: *Why has the psychoanalytic method evolved in a way that favors the Topographic rather than the Structural Model?*[1] That is, most interpretive methods still seek contact with regions of the unconscious via direct interpretations, whether in the form of unconscious defenses or unconscious drive expressions. As Paniagua (2001) noted,

> One of the reasons for this is the erroneous idea that the technique derived from the topographical theory is the one that deals with the "real unconscious." This reveals an extant prejudice: that drives are the true unconscious stuff, and unconscious ego activities are *not* authentically unconscious.
>
> (p. 672)

159

In the remainder of this chapter I will explore various reasons why I think this is the case, and then suggest how the two models may be integrated.

Paniagua (2008), in wondering what drives the analyst towards the Topographic Model, suggests it is a certain feeling of power the analyst gets in interpreting in this manner.

> Let us note, first, that the prestructural technique more directly gratifies the analyst's wishes for *omniscience* and *omnipotence*. Supposedly, an appropriate attunement to the analysand's underlying fantasies enables the analyst to elude uncertainty, reaching the depths of the human soul.
>
> (p. 245, italics added)

Paniagua (2001) captures this omniscient, omnipotent stance in a quote from Reik (1948):

> the analyst should trust unhesitatingly the manifestations of his/her unconscious intuitions, for secondary-process reasoning always interfered with trustworthy psychological understanding. Commenting on an intervention he made in a session, rightly guessing an event omitted by the patient, Reik stated: "I did not give a damn about . . . what I had learned in the books. I did not think of any psychoanalytic theory. I just said what had spoken in me despite and against all logic, and I was correct."
>
> (p. 57)

Fenichel (1941) gave a pithy summation of the problem when he archly noted, "the temptation to be a magician is no less than the temptation to have oneself cured by a magician" (1941, p. 12). I have suggested something similar when I remarked:

> While scientists and philosophers may spend lifetimes searching for a small piece of the answer to the great human mysteries, we often feel we come up with our answers daily, if not several times in one day, if we are really cooking.
>
> (Busch, 1995a, p. 118)

From personal experience, something important I've learned over the years is that it's not always easy to follow the model I write about. While my views on the psychoanalytic method have become part of my analytic DNA, I am well aware, within myself, of how tempting it is to practice in all the ways I've questioned. This is especially true of the urge to interpret unconscious content the analysand is unaware of. There is an almost visceral pull to make these types of interpretations at times. This is especially true when analysands are using *language action*. When there is less action in the language, I generally don't feel this same pull. I talked earlier about how language action touches the analyst's own unconscious. However, what remained unclear to me was why this might lead to a pull towards deeper interpretations of unconscious derivatives than the analysand seemed ready to hear. What I would suggest is that in the great majority of instances, when the patient is enacting in language, the *analyst feels forced into what seems like an alien position.* We are well aware of how, over time, we realize we are being pushed to feel like or be: a lover, torturer, parent, child, self-object, super-ego . . . the list is endless. However, what drives us to push back and *force the patient to accept his own unconscious,* are primarily our uncontained countertransferences. It is a way of the analyst getting rid of something uncomfortable stirred in his own unconscious. It has led me to wonder if this is the reason for an observation I've made in the literature on countertransference, which is the absence of reports where the analyst had a countertransference reaction, and then realized it *was not a reaction to the analysand's transference.* That is, we seem to treat our countertransference reactions as *unerring guides to the patient's behavior.* As countertransference reactions are often the result of unconscious messages from the patient first picked up by our own unconscious, it seems more likely there are times when our countertransference reactions are quite idiosyncratic. Pushing these reactions back on the patient frees us from these uncomfortable feelings.

As noted earlier, the Kleinian's view of projective identification includes the patient's unconscious fantasy that the self can be forced into other objects, to enter and affect those objects from within, altering them and controlling them. It is my impression that many forms of enactments in language action include this fantasy in various degrees. However, *the degree to which we feel controlled depends on the unmetabolized parts of our unconscious, and determines the amount of force with which we aggressively interpret the patient's unconscious.* At these times, due to our inability to contain what is unconsciously stirred, we become threatened and do what we all do in such situations, i.e., *lash out at the perceived perpetrator of these unacceptable thoughts and feelings.* Now it is the patient who feels attacked, not us, and our feeling of threat dissipates.

Hopelessness is another feeling that leads to aggressively interpreting the patient's unconscious. In severe character disorders the desperate attempts to protect oneself lead to a perceptual rigidity of self and other. For long periods of time two steps back quickly follow any step forward. Many have written about the numbing affect on the analyst when there is little room for analytic understanding, and the tendency of the analyst is to withdraw into silence. Then, in order to bring us out of our analytic lethargy, we are prone towards analytic *shock therapy.* We have our theoretical reasons for doing so, but there is often a dollop of hostility in such statements as we react to the increasing fear of our own analytic deadness.

Ehrenberg (1995) has raised many important issues regarding the analyst sharing her countertransference with the analysand. I have used this method sparingly, but sometimes with good affect. However, at times one has the impression that Ehrenberg shares a countertransference to ward off another countertransference, and place the patient on the defensive. As noted above, this is what I've seen in my own work, and how it leads us away from helping the patient explore her own mind. Here is an example from Ehrenberg:

> Following a session I had canceled, Michael entered my office with a strange look in his eye. He insisted that he had seen my breast exposed as I opened the door to let him in. When I questioned him about this, he made it clear that he was not open to any exploration of his experience. He seemed completely estranged, even menacing.
>
> I was taken aback and told him that I did not understand what was going on. I also told him that I felt very uncomfortable in the presence of what now felt to me to be a stranger I did not know and could not reach. In fact it was frightening. I added that it felt almost as though I had been abandoned by the person with whom I thought I had a relationship.
>
> Michael's response was dramatic. The wild look in his eye disappeared and he began to report with much emotion that he suddenly understood his reaction as a way of abandoning me to get back at me for having abandoned him. He stated that now he realized how angry he was that I had canceled the prior session.
>
> (Ehrenberg, 1995, p. 219)

As an example, let me present another way of looking at this vignette. It is clear Ehrenberg had a strong reaction to Michael's observation, and "the wild look in his eyes." *However, it isn't clear what caused this reaction.* It's as if we are expected to believe everyone would have such a reaction. Yet, Ehrenberg seems unable to contain her reaction, and forces the causes for her reaction back on Michael. Ehrenberg doesn't suggest in her article that Michael didn't see her breast. She seems unable to consider the effect on the patient of seeing her breast, and that his "wild look" might be the result of any number of reactions Michael might have, or that she may be prone to interpret his look based on something stirred unconsciously. I have found that when we tend to jump in immediately to interpret something the patient did, that we're often fending off something within ourselves. Why not just wait to see where Michael's association leads him to see if we can understand our reaction to his statement? She pushes her breast back into the session in the form of *her feelings*, proclaiming it a good breast not a bad one, a helping breast not a provocative one.

The end result of Ehrenberg's reaction leads to the patient owning up to feelings about a cancelled appointment, with no accompanying associations as to how he came to that conclusion. My guess is that it was safer. That is, when a patient suddenly comes to an interpretation before any accompanying associations, it is often an attempt to stop thinking rather than allowing it to happen. Meanwhile, the most significant question of this session, "What did it mean to the patient to see the analyst's breast?" seems not to have been approached. It becomes lost in the analyst's attempt to rid herself of her feelings of surprise, alienation and threat.

In summary, it seems to me there is something about the experience of the analyst in the analysis that pulls towards greater involvement in the relationship, or towards closer contact with the patient's unconscious, *that makes the containment necessary for an ego-psychological approach unbearable.* Amongst the reasons I would put high on my list is the essential solitude of the analyst in the face of ongoing unconscious transferences, and the countertransferences they arouse. In the United States in earlier times we dealt with these feelings by withdrawal into silence, and now we tend to deal with this by *moving into action.*

What is mutative: two papers that defined
our clinical methods

From a historical perspective, the theoretical seeds for the tendency to work closer to the patient's *experience* of the unconscious can be traced back to Freud's ambivalence over the move from the *first* to the *second* theory of anxiety (Busch, 1993). As noted earlier, Freud never seemed comfortable with the ego as the seat of anxiety, and continued to return to the idea of direct interpretations of the unconscious as freeing (i.e., his first theory of anxiety). This difference in how the analyst works with the extreme dangers that keep defenses in place was highlighted in two 1934 papers, which appeared consecutively in the *International Journal of Psychoanalysis.* The first was by Sterba on "The Fate of the Ego in Analytic Therapy," and the second was by Strachey, "The Nature of the Therapeutic Action of Psycho-Analysis." In the Sterba paper we see the influence of Freud's Stuctural Model, and Anna Freud's (1936) *The Ego and Mechanisms of Defense,* which was soon to appear. In Strachey's paper one can see the influence of Melanie Klein's thinking.

The basic differences between the two papers can be characterized in the following manner:

* Sterba saw the ego as central to the change process in psychoanalysis. He believed that change came about because of the development of a therapeutic split in the ego between the *experiencing* and *observing* ego. That is, the transference neurosis is worked through via the patient's increasing capacity to view his experience of the transference through what he calls the *dissociation in the ego* (i.e., where the patient's ego gradually develops the capacity for contemplation of his feelings and experience). According to Sterba, this allows the patient

  > to recognize intellectually and render conscious the claims and the content of his unconsciousness and the affects associated with these, whilst when that has been achieved, the synthetic function of the ego enables him to incorporate them and to secure their discharge.
  >
  > (p. 123)

- The major difference between Sterba and Strachey can be seen in Strachey's view of the *mutative experience,* which he saw as coming about with the patient's *experience* of the unconscious *in the transference.*

> Every mutative interpretation must be emotionally "immediate"; the patient must experience it as something actual. This requirement, that the interpretation must be "immediate," may be expressed in another way by saying that interpretations must always be directed to the "point of urgency." At any given moment some particular id-impulse will be in activity; *this* is the impulse that is susceptible of mutative interpretation at that time, and no other one.
>
> (p. 150)

> The analyst as a more beneficent auxiliary super-ego, in contrast to the patient's severe super-ego, allows the patient to become aware that "id-energy is directed toward an archaic phantasy object and not towards the real object" (p. 143).

Although Freud (1923a) shifted to the Structural Model, in part, because of *discovering unconscious resistances,* and depicted an unconscious ego in his 1923 and 1933 drawings of the Structural Model, Strachey, inexplicably, views *the ego as primarily conscious.* He states, "for the forces that are keeping up the repression, although they are to some extent unconscious, do not belong to the unconscious in the systematic sense; they are a part of the patient's ego, which is co-operating with us, and are thus more accessible" (p. 130).

To summarize:

1 Sterba believes that basic to the mutative process is a change in the ego that allows the unconscious impulses to be *experienced and observed.*
2 Strachey believes the cooperation of the ego is a given, and that the mutative process occurs via the patient's *experience* of the unconscious, acceptable primarily because of the analyst as an auxiliary super-ego.
3 Sterba follows the Structural Model and Freud's second theory of anxiety, while Strachey's position is closer to Freud's Topographic Model and his first theory of anxiety.

The different routes towards the change process espoused in these papers had a profound effect on psychoanalytic methods of interpretation. They are at the heart of differences between the *early* Kleinians and American ego psychologists, with the French somewhere between the two. The major difference between these views with regard to the psychoanalytic method *still revolves around the role of the ego in the change process.* The manner of analyzing *resistances* remains as central difference between the different schools of thought. To briefly characterize the methods: (1) the American ego psychologists have a specific manner of analyzing inhibitions; (2) the French attempt to overcome inhibitions;

and (3) the Kleinians seem to analyze inhibitions mainly within the context of their unconscious derivatives.

The basic theoretical difference in approach between the French and the contemporary ego psychologists is that the Americans focus more on what they see as *the underlying process that allows for accessibility of unconscious derivatives to preconscious thinking*, while the French focus on *stimulating what is already preconscious to uncover unconscious derivatives*. To put it another way, the Americans focus on working through the unconscious ego defenses, while the French attempt to overcome the defenses by strategic stimulation of the preconscious. The American approach was put succinctly by Gray (1982):

> It has for some time been my conclusion, rightly or wrongly, that the way a considerable proportion of analysts listen to and perceive their data has, in certain significant respects, *not* evolved as I believe it would have if historically important concepts concerned with the defensive functions of the ego had been wholeheartedly allowed their place in the actual application of psychoanalytic technique.
>
> (p. 624)

As stated by Green (2005), "it is customary in French psychoanalytic circles to interpret as close as possible to the ego, sometimes making use of ellipses or allusions, proceeding by limited touches, stimulating the associative work, counting on the participation of the patient . . ." In general, French analysts do not interpret resistances.[2]

However there have been changes in each perspective over time that brought them closer together. For example, the focus of interpretation in the work of Betty Joseph, André Green and my own view, is the patient's *experience* of the unconscious that can be: *assessed via the preconscious; in the here and now; and leans more towards transformations rather than reconstructions*. I have given various examples of this throughout this work. For example, it is my impression that in his work André Green incorporated the Structural Model, yet it is in a particular way that attempts to get *closer to drive derivatives*, rather than through expansion of the ego as one might think would be dictated by the Structural model. As I understand it, Green sees the road to a freer mind via finding the unconscious derivatives most acceptable and *experience*-near to the ego.

While the Kleinians emphasize the importance of the patient's experience of an interpretation, there are differences in how closely they follow Strachey in seeing the desirability of the patient's experiences of his unconscious motivations. As noted by Segal (1989), "These differences concern the technical problem of how and when to interpret explicitly the unconscious phantasy and infantile experience which is being enacted in this interplay between patient and analyst" (p. ix). In contrasting the work of Joseph and Segal, Blass (2011) demonstrates (but doesn't emphasize) how Segal's interpretations confront the patient with deep unconscious truths. Joseph, on the other hand, is more focused on the patient's experience of what is occurring in the immediacy of the transference in the room, content to work with derivatives of the unconscious, and what is more knowable by the patient. In this sense I would say she's attempting to work closer to what is preconsciously available.

In general, the Kleinians have not sufficiently dealt with the fact that *it is difficult to help patients think and reflect because what is most crucial for patients to know is what they are desperately afraid to know*. Implicitly, they still seem to follow Strachey's view of change taking place because of the analyst as an auxiliary super-ego. As Schafer (1997) pointed out, they are still working with insufficient differentiation between the concepts of an ego and the self. I would add that they also have not appreciated the function of an ego distinct from its being a depository for abandoned object cathexis. It is my impression that, at times, current Kleinians are struggling with their heritage from Klein, who had the view that in order to establish and sustain the analytic situation, the analyst must give deep interpretations that locate the level of anxiety (Hinshelwood, 1989).

As the reader has no doubt surmised, my own view is closer to Sterba's. Modifications in methods over the last 30 years have allowed for greater sophistication by which expansion of the ego takes place. At the time both Sterba and Strachey depended on the *analyst's way of being* as a crucial factor in resolving conflicts as expressed in the transference. In some ways we are still stuck in this position. Throughout this book I've offered an alternative perspective based on *how we analyze* to create a psychoanalytic mind. Further, as we've learned over time, the analyst deriving his influence as the result of a positive transference can no longer be fully supported, as we've come to understand the defensive components of such a stance.

A modification

As I prepared this chapter there was something nagging at me, which I kept trying to push away. In my mind the distinct views expressed in Sterba and Strachey explained a great deal about the history of the psychoanalytic method. I still think this is the case. However, the following vignette presented by a supervisee and the discussion that followed, led me to crystallize what was nagging at me, and to think about a way of blending the two perspectives.

A patient who has projected his rage on to the analyst, leading him to fear the analyst's judgments, while at the same time diminishing the analyst's analyzing capacity, begins a session talking of how he can see his *fears* of his aggression lead him to be wary of the analyst. His next thoughts went to someone he and his wife met the previous evening to discuss an alarm system for their home. This guy was playing on their *fears* by exaggerating all the *fearful* things that could occur if they didn't buy the most expensive system. He told the guy he didn't buy this line of thinking.

While the patient overtly accepts the analyst's interpretation of his fears, and feels he needs protection (by buying an alarm system), his associations to a guy who's exaggerating the fears indicate he thinks the analyst is trying to get him to buy into the analyst's system, and he's not buying. However, the patient seems unaware of these contradictory feelings in his association. One could say there was a strong resistance to the awareness that he wasn't buying the analyst's interpretation of his fears, and its affect on the transference. However, there is another piece of this we have to take into account. That is, the patient was able to produce this association rather than defending against it by not allowing it into awareness, falling silent or diverting to another topic. Further, his dismissive attitude toward the analysis had come up more frequently in recent sessions. This suggests the possibility that the dismissive part of the association to the "alarm" salesman was close to the preconscious–unconscious border. The patient "knows," but doesn't "know" what he's saying. I would suggest that it is at these times that a Strachey-like interpretation of the patient's dismissiveness of the analyst's interpretation of his transferential fears (while not ignoring his conscious acceptance) could be important to bring to the fore. It would help the patient see how something partially unconscious is alive in the here and now of the transference. It would likely *surprise* him, but not *stun* him like premature interpretations of the unconscious can. The key to whether it will be in the patient's *neighborhood* is the assumption of the patient's preconscious participation in the association. This doesn't mean that anything the patient brings into the session is a sign of its preconscious availability. The understanding of what is preconscious is contextual. In the vignette just discussed it is what was occurring in previous sessions that led to the consideration of the associations' preconscious participation. Thus, combining Sterba and Strachey we can say that due to the patient's increasing observing capacity (therapeutic split), he can *experience* a feeling close to the preconscious–unconscious border that is interpretable within the transference. I think this is what Green (2005) described when he portrayed working close to the preconscious by "sometimes making use of ellipses or allusions, proceeding by limited touches, stimulating the associative work, counting on the participation of the patient . . ." It is still another piece of analyzing in a way to *create a psychoanalytic mind.*

Final thoughts

In the writing of this book I see a consistency between where I've been, and how I've moved forward. I've expanded on earlier ideas, and broadened my views on others. In some of the more recently written chapters, I was surprised by what was on my mind. This is the gift in writing, along with the need to think through ideas with honesty and courage. For me at least, it is easy to have ideas floating around in my mind, but it is only when I try to put them down on paper that I see the contradictions and gaps in my thinking. If the idea is worthwhile, the end result is a sense of a solid foundational base upon which to engage my clinical work and teach candidates, while keeping in mind the psychoanalytic enigmas one is constantly faced with as a practicing psychoanalyst. It is to these piled up enigmas

I've been harvesting while writing this book that I will now turn my attention, and hopefully share in the not too distant future.

Notes

1 Paniagua (2001, 2008) has written extensively about this. I will be only be adding to his well-documented papers.
2 In reading Birksted-Breen et al. (2010) on French psychoanalysis, one only hears about overcoming resistances, never interpreting them.

REFERENCES

Note: *S.E.* = *Standard Edition of the Complete Psychological Works of Sigmund Freud*, trans. J. Strachey, London: Hogarth Press and the Institute of Psychoanalysis.

Aisenstein, M. and Smadja, C. (2010). Introduction to the Paper by Pierre Marty: The Narcissistic Difficulties Presented to the Observer by the Psychosomatic Problem. *International Journal of Psychoanalysis*, 91(2): 343–346.

Anon. (1988). Case Presentation. *Psychoanalytic Inquiry*, 8: 513–523.

Anon., A. (2005). Two Hours at Work, with Amanda. *International Journal of Psychoanalysis*, 86: 233–240.

Aron, L. (1993). Working Toward Operational Thought:– Piagetian Theory and Psychoanalytic Method. *Contemporary Psychoanalysis*, 29: 289–313.

Baranger, M. (1993). The Mind of the Analyst: From Listening to Interpretation. *International Journal of Psychoanalysis*, 74: 15–24.

Baranger, M., Baranger, W. and Mom, J. (1983). Process and Non-Process in Analytic Work. *International Journal of Psychoanalysis*, 64: 1–15.

Basch, M. F. (1981). Psychoanalytic Interpretation and Cognitive Transformation. *International Journal of Psychoanalysis*, 62: 151–175.

Bass, A. (1997). The Problem of Concreteness. *Psychoanalytic Quarterly*, 66: 642–682.

Bell, D. (2001). Projective Identification. In C. Bronstein (ed.), *Kleinian Theory: A Contemporary Perspective*. London: Whurr Publishers.

Bergmann, M. S. (1997). Termination. *Psychoanalytic Psychology*, 14: 163–174.

—— (2000). *The Hartmann Era*. New York: Other Press.

—— (2001). Life Goals and Psychoanalytic Goals from Historical Perspective. *Psychoanalytic Quarterly*, 70: 15–34

Bibring, E. (1954). Psychoanalysis and the Dynamic Psychotherapies. *Journal of the American Psychoanalytic Association*, 2: 745–770.

Bion, W. R. (1962). *Learning from Experience*. London: Tavistock.

—— (1970). *Second Thoughts: Selected Papers on Psycho-Analysis*. London: Heinemann.

Birksted-Breen, D., Flanders, S. and Gibeault, A. (2010). *Reading French Psychoanalysis*. Hove: Brunner/Routledge.

Blass, R. (2011). On the Immediacy of Unconscious Truth. *International Journal of Psychoanalysis*, 92: 1137–1157.

Blum, H. P. (1983). The Position and Value of Extratransference Interpretation. *Journal of the American Psychoanalytic Association*, 31: 587–617.

—— (2005). Psychoanalytic Reconstruction and Reintegration. *Psychoanalytic Study of the Child*, 60: 295–311.

Boesky, D. (1989). The Questions and Curiosity of the Psychoanalyst. *Journal of the American Psychoanalytic Association*, 37: 579–603.

Bolognini, S. (2010). *Secret Passages*. London: Routledge.

Bott Spillius, E. (1994). On Formulating Clinical Fact to a Patient. *International Journal of Psychoanalysis*, 75: 1121–1132.

Brenner, C. (1976). *Psychoanalytic Technique and Psychic Conflict*. Madison, CT: International Universities Press.

Brown, L. J. (2009). Bion's Ego Psychology: Implications for an Intersubjective View of Psychic Structure. *Psychoanalytic Quarterly*, 78: 27–55.

Busch, F. (1970). Basals Are Not for Reading. *Teachers College Record*, 72: 23–30.

—— (1989). The Compulsion to Repeat in Action. *International Journal of Psychoanalysis*, 70: 535–544.

—— (1992). Recurring Thoughts on the Unconscious Ego Resistances. *Journal of the American Psychoanalytic Association*, 40: 1089–1115.

—— (1993). In the Neighborhood: Aspects of a Good Interpretation and a "Developmental Lag" in Ego Psychology. *Journal of the American Psychoanalytic Association*, 41: 151–176.

—— (1994). Some Ambiguities in the Method of Free Association and Their Implications for Technique. *Journal of the American Psychoanalytic Association*, 42: 363–384.

—— (1995a). *The Ego at the Center of Clinical Technique*. Northvale, NJ: Jason Aronson Press.

—— (1995b). Do Actions Speak Louder than Words? A Query into an Enigma in Psychoanalytic Theory and Technique. *Journal of the American Psychoanalytic Association*, 43: 61–82.

—— (1995c). An Unknown Classic: N.M. Searls's (1936) "Some Queries on Principles of Technique." *Psychoanalytic Quarterly*, 64: 326–344.

—— (1999). *Rethinking Clinical Technique*. Northvale, NJ: Jason Aronson Press.

—— (2005). Conflict Theory/Trauma Theory. *Psychoanalytic Quarterly*, 74: 27–46.

—— (2006a). A Shadow Concept. *International Journal of Psychoanalysis*, 87(6): 1471–1485.

—— (2009). Can You Push a Camel Through the Eye of a Needle? Reflections on how the Unconscious Speaks to Us and Its Clinical Implications. *International Journal of Psychoanalysis*, 90: 53–68.

—— (2011). The Suprising Common Ground. Presentation to the PINE Psychoanalytic Center. Cambridge, MA. January 2011.

Chomsky, W. (1957). *Hebrew: the Eternal Language*. Philadelphia, PA: Jewish Publication Society, p. 3.

Cooper, A. (1987). Transference and Character. *Contemporary Psychoanalysis*, 23: 502–512.

Donnet, J. (2001). From the Fundamental Rule to the Analysing Situation. *International Journal of Psychoanalysis*, 82(1): 129–140.

Ehrenberg, D. B. (1995). Self-disclosure: Therapeutic Tool or Indulgence?: Countertransference Disclosure. *Contemporary Psychoanalysis*, 31: 213.

Eissler, K. R. (1953). The Effect of the Structure of the Ego on Psychoanalytic Technique. *Journal of the American Psychoanalytic Association*, 1: 104–143.

Erikson, E. (1950). *Childhood and Society*. New York: W. W. Norton [1993].

Faimberg, H. (1996). 'Listening To Listening'. *International Journal of Psychoanalysis*, 77: 667–677.

Feldman, M. (2007). The Illumination of History. *International Journal of Psychoanalysis*, 88: 609–625.

Fenichel, O. (1941). *Problems of Psychoanalytic Technique*. New York: Psychoanalytic Quarterly.

Ferro, A. (1996). *In The Analyst's Consulting Room*. London/New York: Psychology Press.

—— (2003). Marcella. *Psychoanalytic Quarterly*, 72: 183–200.

—— (2006). *Psychoanalysis as Therapy and Storytelling*. London: Routledge.

Flavell, J. H. (1963). *The Developmental Psychology of Jean Piaget*. Princeton, NJ: Van Nostrand.

Fonagy, P., Moran, G. S., Edgcumbe, R., Kennedy, H. and Target, M. (1993). The Roles of Mental Representations and Mental Processes in Therapeutic Action. *Psychoanalytic Study of the Child*, 48: 9–48.

Fonagy, P. and Target, M. (1996). Playing With Reality: I. Theory of Mind and the Normal Development of Psychic Reality. *International Journal of Psychoanalysis*, 77: 217–233.

—— (2000). Playing With Reality. *International Journal of Psychoanalysis*, 81: 853–873.

Freud, A. (1936). *The Ego and Mechanisms of Defense*. New York: International Universities Press.

Freud, S. (1895). Project for a Scientific Psychology. *S.E.* I.

—— (1900). The Interpretation of Dreams. *S.E.* IV: 1–627.

—— (1910). "Wild" Psycho-analysis. *S.E.* XI.

—— (1912a). The Dynamics of Transference. *S.E.* XII: 97–108.

—— (1912b). Recommendation to Physicians Practicing Psychoanalysis. *S.E.* XII: 111–120.

—— (1913). On Beginning the Treatment (Further Recommendations on the Technique of Psycho-Analysis I). *S.E.* XII: 121–144.

—— (1914). Remembering, Repeating and Working Through. *S.E.* XII: 145–156.

—— (1915). The Unconscious. *S.E.* XIV: 159–215.

—— (1919). "A Child Is Being Beaten" A Contribution to the Study of the Origin of Sexual Perversions. *S.E.* XVII: 175–204

—— (1920). Beyond the Pleasure Principle. *S.E.* XVIII: 1–64.

—— (1923a). The Ego and the Id. *S.E.* XIX: 1–66.7

—— (1926). Inhibitions, Symptoms and Anxiety. *S.E.* XX.

—— (1933). New Introductory Lectures on Psycho-analysis. *S.E.* XXII: 1–182.

—— (1937a). *Analysis terminable and interminable. S.E.* 23.

—— (1937b). Constructions in Analysis. *S.E.* XIII: 255–270.

—— (1940). An Outline of Psycho-Analysis. *International Journal of Psychoanalysis*, 21: 27–84.

Friedman, L. (1992). How and Why Do Patients Become More Objective? Sterba Compared with Strachey. *Psychoanalytic Quarterly*, 61: 1–17.

Frosch, A. (1995). The Preconceptual Organization of Emotion. *Journal of the American Psychoanalytic Association*, 43: 423–447.

—— (2012). *Absolute Truth and Unbearable Psychic Pain*. London: Karnac.

Gardner, R. (1983). *Self-reflection*. Boston, MA: Little, Brown.

Gill, M. M. (1979). The Analysis of the Transference. *Journal of the American Psychoanalytic Association*, 27: 263–288.

Glover, E. (1924). "Active Therapy" and Psycho-Analysis: A Critical Review. *International Journal of Psychoanalysis*, 5: 269–311.

—— (1955). *The Technique of Psycho-Analysis*. Madison, CT: International Universities Press.

Gray, P. (1982). "Developmental Lag" in the Evolution of Technique for Psychoanalysis of Neurotic Conflict. *Journal of the American Psychoanalytic Association*, 30: 621–655.

—— (1987). On the Technique of Analysis of the Superego: An Introduction. *Psychoanalytic Quarterly*, 56: 130–154.

—— (1990). The Nature of Therapeutic Action in Psychoanalysis. *Journal of the American Psychoanalytic Association*, 38: 1083–1096.

—— (1994). *The Ego and Mechanisms of Defense*. Northridge, NJ: Jason Aronson.

Green, A. (1974). Surface Analysis, Deep Analysis (The Role of the Preconscious in Psychoanalytical Technique). *International Review of Psychoanalysis*, 1: 415–423.

—— (1975). The Analyst, Symbolization and Absence in the Analytic Setting (On Changes in Analytic Practice and Analytic Experience): In Memory of D. W. Winnicott. *International Journal of Psychoanalysis*, 56: 1–22.

—— (1998). The Primordial Mind and the Work of the Negative. *International Journal of Psychoanalysis*, 79: 649–665.

—— (2000a). The Central Phobic Position: A New Formulation of the Free Association Method. *International Journal of Psychoanalysis*, 81(3): 429–451.

—— (2000b). The Intrapsychic and Intersubjective in Psychoanalysis. *Psychoanalytic Quarterly*, 69: 1–39.

—— (2005). Issues of Interpretation. Presented at the meetings of the European Psychoanalytic Federation, Vilamoor, Portugal, March.

Greenberg, J. (1996). Psychoanalytic Words and Psychoanalytic Acts: A Brief History. *Contemporary Psychoanalysis*, 32: 195–213.

Greenson, R. R. (1967). *The Technique and Practice of Psychoanalysis*. Vol. 1. New York: International Universities Press.

Hartmann, H. (1939). *The Ego and the Problem of Adaptation*. New York: International Universities Press.

Heimann, P. (1956). Dynamics of Transference Interpretations. *International Journal of Psychoanalysis*, 37: 303–310.

Heinicke, C. M., Busch, F., Click, P. and Kramer, E. (1973a). A Methodology for the Intensive Observation of the Preschool Child. In J. C. Westman (ed.), *Individual Differences in Children*. New York: John Wiley and Sons.

—— (1973b). Parent–child Relationships, Adaptation to Nursery School, and the Child's Task Orientation: A Contrast in the Development of Two Girls. In J. C. Westman (ed.), *Individual Differences in Children*. New York: John Wiley and Sons.

Herrmann, F. (2001). The Training Analysis at a Time when Theory is in Short Supply. *International Journal of Psychoanalysis*, 82: 57–69.

Hinshelwood, R. (1989). *A Dictionary of Kleinian Thought*. London: Free Association Books.

Hoffer, A. (2004). Is Free Association Still at the Core of Psychoanalysis? *International Journal of Psychoanalysis*, 85(6): 1489–1492.

Holmes, P. (1870). *The Writings of Tertullian*. Edinburgh: T. and T. Clark.

Hunter, V. (1993). An Interview with Hanna Segal. *Psychoanalytic Review*, 80(1): 1–28.

Jacobs, T. J. (1999). Countertransference Past and Present: A Review of the Concept. *International Journal of Psychoanalysis*, 80(3): 575–594.

Joseph, B. (1985). Transference: The Total Situation. *International Journal of Psychoanalysis*, 66: 447–454.

Katz, G. A. (1998). Where the Action Is: The Enacted Dimension of Analytic Process. *Journal of the American Psychoanalytic Association*, 46(4): 1129–1167.

Kernberg, O. (1996). The Analyst's Authority in the Psychoanalytic Situation. *Psychoanalytic Quarterly*, 65: 137–157.

Kris, A. O. (1982). *Free Association: Method and Process.* New Haven, CT: Yale University Press.

—— (1985). Resistance in Convergent and in Divergent Conflicts. *Psychoanalytic Quarterly*, 54: 537–568.

Laplanche, J. and Pontalis, J-B. (1973). *The Language of Psychoanalysis.* New York: Norton.

Lecours, S. (2007). Supportive Interventions and Nonsymbolic Mental Functioning. *International Journal of Psychoanalysis*, 88(4): 895–915.

Levenson, E. A. (1987). The Purloined Self. *The American Academy of Psychoanalysis and Dynamic Psychiatry*, 15: 481–490.

—— (1988). The Pursuit of the Particular: On the Psychoanalytic Inquiry. *Contemporary Psychoanalysis*, 24: 1–16.

—— (1992). Mistakes, Errors, and Oversights. *Contemporary Psychoanalysis*, 28: 555–571.

—— (2000). An Interpersonal Perspective on Dreams: Commentary on Paper by Hazel Ipp. *Psychoanalytic Dialogues*, 10: 119–125.

Levenson, E., Hirsch, I. and Iannuzzi, V. (2005). Interview with Edgar A. Levenson. *Contemporary Psychoanalysis*, 41: 593–644.

Litowitz, B. E. (1975). Language: Waking and Sleeping. *Psychoanalysis and Contemporary Science*, 4(1): 291–330.

Loewald, H. W. (1971). Some Considerations on Repetition and Repetition Compulsion. *International Journal of Psychoanalysis*, 52: 59–66.

—— (1975). Psychoanalysis as an Art and the Fantasy Character of the Psychoanalytic Situation. *Journal of the American Psychoanalytic Association*, 23: 277–299.

McDougall, J. (1978). Primitive Communication and the Use of Countertransference Reflections on Early Psychic Trauma and Its Transference Effects. *Contemporary Psychoanalysis*, 14: 173–209.

McLaughlin, J. T. (1991). Clinical and Theoretical Aspects of Enactment. *Journal of the American Psychoanalytic Association*, 39: 595–614.

Novick, J. (1982). Termination: Themes and Issues. *Psychoanalytic Inquiry*, 2: 329–365.

Novick, J. and Novick, K. K. (2001). Two Systems of Self-Regulation. *Psychoanalytic Social Work*, 8: 95–122.

—— (2006). *Good Goodbyes.* Lanham, MD: Jason Aronson/Rowman & Littlefield.

Novick, K. K. and Novick, J. (1998). An Application of the Concept of the Therapeutic Alliance to Sadomasochistic Pathology. *Journal of the American Psychoanalytic Association*, 46: 813–846.

Ogden, T. H. (1996). Reconsidering Three Aspects of Psychoanalytic Technique. *International Journal of Psychoanalysis*, 77: 883–899.

—— (2007). On Talking-as-Dreaming. *International Journal of Psychoanalysis*, 88(3): 575–589.

Olinick, S. L. (1954). Some Considerations of the Use of Questioning as a Psychoanalytic Technique. *Journal of the American Psychoanalytic Association*, 2: 56–66.

Orr, D. W. (1954). Transference and Countertransference: A Historical Survey. *Journal of the American Psychoanalytic Association*, 2: 621–670.

Pally R. (2007). The Predicting Brain. *International Journal of Psychoanalysis*, 88: 861–888.

Pally, R. and Olds, D. (1998). Consciousness: A Neuroscience Perspective. *International Journal of Psychoanalysis*, 79: 971–989.

Paniagua, C. (1991). Patient's Surface, Clinical Surface, and Workable Surface. *Journal of the American Psychoanalytic Association*, 39: 669–685.

—— (2001). The Attraction of Topographical Technique. *International Journal of Psychoanalysis*, 82(4): 671–684.

—— (2008). Id Analysis and Technical Approaches. *Psychoanalytic Quarterly*, 77(1): 219–250.

Piaget, J. (1930). *The Child's Conception of Physical Causality*. London: Kegan Paul.

Piaget, J. and Inhelder, B. (1959). *The Psychology of the Child*. New York: Basic Books.

Pinker, S. (1989). *Learnability and Cognition*. Cambridge, MA: MIT Press.

Reich, W. [1933]. *Character Analysis*. New York: Farrar, Straus and Cudahy, 1949.

Reik, T. [1948]. The Surprised Analyst. In B. Wolstein (ed.), *Essential Papers on Counter-transference*. New York: New York University Press. 1988, pp. 51–63.

Rizzuto, A. (2002). Speech Events, Language Development and the Clinical Situation. *International Journal of Psychoanalysis*, 83(6): 1325–1343.

—— (2003). Psychoanalysis: The Transformation of the Subject by the Spoken Word. *Psychoanalytic Quarterly*, 72(2): 287–323.

—— (2004). Paradoxical Words and Hope in Psychoanalysis. *Psychoanalytic Psychology*, 21(2): 203–213.

Rosenfeld, H. (1987). *Impasse and Interpretation*. London: Tavistock.

Sandler, J. (1976). Countertransference and Role-Responsiveness. *International Review of Psychoanalysis*, 3: 43–47.

Sandler, J. and Freud, A. (1982). *The Analysis of Defense: The Ego and the Mechanisms of Defense Revisited*. New York: International Universities Press.

Schacter, J. (1992). Concepts of Termination and Post-Termination Patient–Analyst Contact. *International Journal of Psychoanalysis*, 73: 137–154.

Schafer, R. (1968). On the Theoretical and Technical Conceptualization of Activity and Passivity. *Psychoanalytic Quarterly*, 37, 173–198.

—— (1983). *The Analytic Attitude*. New York: Basic Books.

—— (1997). *The Contemporary Kleinians of London*. New York: International Universities Press.

Schmidt-Hellerau, C. (2001). *Life Drive and Death Drive*. New York: Other Press.

—— (2002). Why Aggression? Metapsychological, Clinical and Technical Considerations. *International Journal of Psychoanalysis*, 83(6): 1269–1289.

—— (2005). The Other Side of Oedipus. *Psychoanalytic Quarterly*, 74(1): 187–217.

—— (2006). Surviving in Absence: On the Preservative and Death Drives and Their Clinical Utility. *Psychoanalytic Quarterly*, 75: 1057–1095.

Schwaber, E. A. (1990). The Pyschoanalyst's Methodological Stance: Some Comments Based on a Response to Max Hernandez. *International Journal of Psychoanalysis*, 71: 31–36.

—— (1992). Countertransference: The Analyst's Retreat from the Patient's Vantage Point. *International Journal of Psychoanalysis*, 73: 349–361.

Searl, M. N. (1936). Some Queries on Principles of Technique. *International Journal of Psychoanalysis*, 17: 471–493.

Segal, H. (1989). Foreword to *Psychic Equilibrium and Psychic Change: Selected Papers of Betty Joseph*, ed. Michael Feldman and Elizabeth Bott Spillius. New Library of Psychoanalysis, 9. London and New York: Tavistock/Routledge.

Segel, N. P. (1961). The Psychoanalytic Theory of the Symbolic Process. *Journal of the American Psychoanalytic Association*, 9: 146–157.

Shapiro, T. (1988). Language Structure and Psychoanalysis. *Journal of the American Psychoanalytic Association*, 36: 339–358.

—— (2004). Use Your Words! *Journal of the American Psychoanalytic Association*, 52(2): 331–353.

Silverman, M. A. (1987). Clinical Material. *Psychoanalytic Inquiry*, 7: 147–165.

Smith, H. F. (2003). Analysis of Transference: A North American Perspective. *International Journal of Psychoanalysis*, 84(4): 1017–1041.

Steiner, J. (1994). Patient-Centered and Analyst-Centered Interpretations: Some Implications of Containment and Countertransference. *Psychoanalytic Inquiry*, 14: 406–422.

Sterba, R. (1934). The Fate of the Ego in Analytic Therapy. *International Journal of Psychoanalysis*, 15: 117–126.

Stern, D. B. (1983). Unformulated Experience. *Contemporary Psychoanalysis*, 19: 71–99.

—— (1992). What Makes a Good Question? *Contemporary Psychoanalysis*, 28: 326–336.

—— (2002). Words and Wordlessness in the Psychoanalytic Situation. *Journal of the American Psychoanalytic Association*, 50(1): 221–247.

Strachey, J. (1934). The Nature of the Therapeutic Action of Psycho-Analysis, 1. *International Journal of Psychoanalysis*, 15: 127–159.

Sugarman, A. (2003). A New Model for Conceptualizing Insightfulness in the Psychoanalysis of Young Children. *Psychoanalytic Quarterly*, 72: 325–355.

—— (2006). Mentalization, Insightfulness, and Therapeutic Action. *International Journal of Psychoanalysis*, 87: 965–987.

Target, M. and Fonagy, P. (1996). Playing With Reality: II. The Development of Psychic Reality from a Theoretical Perspective. *International Journal of Psychoanalysis*, 77: 459–479.

Tuch, R. H. (2001). Questioning the Psychoanalyst's Authority. *Journal of the American Psychoanalytic Association*, 49: 491–513.

Viereck, G. S. (1930). *Glimpse of the great*. New York: Macauley.

Vivona, J. M. (2003). Embracing Figures of Speech: The Transformative Potential of Spoken Language. *Psychoanalytic Psychology*, 20(1): 52–66.

Wallerstein, R. S. (1988). One Psychoanalysis or Many? *International Journal of Psychoanalysis*, 69: 5–21.

—— (1998c). *Lay Analysis: Life Inside the Controversy*. Hillsdale, NJ: Analytic Press.

Westen, D. and Gabbard, G. O. (2002). Developments in Cognitive Neuroscience: I. Conflict, Compromise, and Connectionism. *Journal of the American Psychoanalytic Association*, 50(1): 53–98.

Widlocher, D. (1986). *Metapsychologie du sens*. Paris: Presses Universitaires de France.

INDEX